PRAISE FOR THE CLUSTER GROUPING HANDBOOK

"Dedicated teachers work tirelessly to differentiate effectively for the increasingly diverse groups of students in their general education classrooms, but they often lack the expertise and the support it takes to meet the needs of gifted students. In this revised edition of *The Cluster Grouping Handbook*, Brulles and Winebrenner provide both! Compelling, research-based rationale for the Schoolwide Cluster Grouping Model (SCGM); specific, practical advice for implementing and maintaining high-quality cluster grouping services in a variety of settings; professional learning strategies, including a complete plan for creating a SCGM PLC; model communications with parents and other stakeholders; and much, much more—it's all here! I consider *The Cluster Grouping Handbook* to be an indispensable guide for all teachers and leaders who care about meeting the needs of gifted learners in the regular classroom, the setting where most gifted students spend the majority of their time and where educators have the greatest opportunity to improve learning for all!"

—**Sally Krisel,** Director of Innovative and Advanced Programs, Hall County School, Gainesville, Georgia, and Past President, National Association for Gifted Children

"*The Cluster Grouping Handbook* is a must-read for anyone working with gifted education! This updated resource provides the necessary tips and tools for any school or district to engage in successful implementation of the Schoolwide Cluster Grouping Model. The authors define SCGM across multiple settings and scenarios, providing step-by-step guidance for both new and experienced coordinators responsible for identification and services for advanced learners. In addition to the many sample forms and reproducibles, this handbook offers language for communication and support with parents and teachers, as well as realistic teaching strategies for differentiation and personalized learning opportunities so all students are challenged."

—**Michelle Swain, M.Ed.**, Director of Gifted and Advanced Academic Services, Round Rock Independent School District, Round Rock, Texas

"This book is AWESOME! Brulles and Winebrenner hit another home run with their revised and updated *Cluster Grouping Handbook*. The structure of the book is well thought out, the content is reader friendly, and the reproducible pages cover all the bases for program implementation. It is a practitioner's best friend, a guide for administrators, and a parent's hope for services that make a difference. The inclusive tone of the book also champions equity, excellence, and a commitment to do what's in the best interest of students. This resource is a professional development treasure for the field of gifted education."

—**Dr. Jaime A. Castellano**, Professor, Florida Atlantic University, Boca Raton, Florida

THE CLUSTER GROUPING HANDBOOK

>>>Revised & Updated Edition

A SCHOOLWIDE MODEL

How to Challenge Gifted Students and Improve Achievement for All

Dina Brulles, Ph.D.
Susan Winebrenner, M.S.
Foreword by Scott J. Peters, Ph.D.

free spirit
PUBLISHING®

Library of Congress Cataloging-in-Publication Data
Names: Brulles, Dina, author. | Winebrenner, Susan, 1939– author.
Title: The cluster grouping handbook : how to challenge gifted students and improve achievement for all : a schoolwide model / written by Dina Brulles and Susan Winebrenner.
Description: Revised and updated edition. | Minneapolis, MN : Free Spirit Publishing, [2019] | Revised edition of: The cluster grouping handbook : a schoolwide model : how to challenge gifted students and improve achievement for all / Susan Winebrenner, Dina Brulles. ?2008. | Includes bibliographical references.
Identifiers: LCCN 2018060610| ISBN 9781631983566 (pbk.) | ISBN 1631983563 (pbk.) | ISBN 9781631983573 (Web PDF) | ISBN 9781631983580 (ePub)
Subjects: LCSH: Gifted children—Education—United States. | Mainstreaming in education—United States. | Group work in education—United States. | Academic achievement—United States.
Classification: LCC LC3993.9 .W556 2019 | DDC 371.2/54—dc23 LC record available at https://lccn.loc.gov/2018060610

Edited by Christine Zuchora-Walske
Cover and interior design by Shannon Pourciau

10 9 8 7 6 5 4 3 2 1
Printed in the United States of America

Free Spirit Publishing Inc.
6325 Sandburg Road, Suite 100
Minneapolis, MN 55427-3674
(612) 338-2068
help4kids@freespirit.com
freespirit.com

FSC
www.fsc.org
MIX
Paper from responsible sources
FSC® C005010

Dedication

We dedicate this book to all educators who share our interest in helping structure and provide gifted-education services for all students, in all schools, as an integral part of the school day. We appreciate your vision and thank you for your efforts.

Acknowledgments

Thank you to Free Spirit publisher Judy Galbraith and her staff, whose support of our learners' social, emotional, and academic needs continues to provide essential resources to educators, parents, and students.

To Dr. Marcia Gentry, director of the Gifted Education Research and Resource Institute (GERI) and professor of educational psychology and research methodology at Purdue University, for her work pioneering gifted cluster grouping as a practitioner, professor, and researcher.

To Karen L. Brown, gifted-program mentor in Paradise Valley Unified School District, whose inspiration, sage advice, and practical understanding of gifted children in school settings guides teachers of gifted learners in our school district and across the country.

To the gifted specialists in Paradise Valley Unified School District, who lead and support the gifted-cluster teachers in our schools.

To Christine Zuchora-Walske, whose expert editing revised and improved this resource.

Reviewers

Richard M. Cash, Ed.D.
President, nRich Consulting

Marcia Gentry, Ph.D.
Professor, Purdue University

Jason MacIntosh, Ph.D.
Gifted Coordinator, Washington Elementary School District, Arizona

Doug Orr
Associate Superintendent, Natomas Unified School District, California

Cheryl McCullough
Supervisor in Arlington Public Schools, Virginia

Joy Davis, Ed.D.
Professor, Virginia Union University

Randi Cutler
Gifted Specialist, Paradise Valley USD, Arizona

Jonathon Plucker, Ph.D.
Professor, Johns Hopkins University

Jack Naglieri, Ph.D.
Research Professor, University of Virginia

Contents

List of Figures

List of Reproducible Pages

These forms are also available in the digital content for this book. See page PNT for information on how to download them.

Foreword by Scott J. Peters, Ph.D.

American schools face a daunting challenge. Students have never been more diverse and have never entered the K–12 system with a wider range of needs. Students are diverse in their preschool education, informal learning experiences, racial and ethnic backgrounds, languages spoken at home, and exposure to trauma and violence—and in countless other ways. We as educators embrace them all and do what we can to help them learn and develop. For the "regular" education classroom teacher, meeting the needs of every child is nearly impossible. The typical classroom includes students who span eight grade levels in their academic readiness. This is just one way in which students vary, and the classroom teacher—often on his or her own—must teach them all.

I was a convert to cluster grouping. Although I studied under Marcia Gentry, one of the leading researchers of cluster grouping, I never saw it as "enough" for gifted students. When I began working with schools and writing *Beyond Gifted Education*, I struggled with the logistics of how to challenge students who were two, three, four, or more years above grade-level content while still maintaining diverse, integrated classrooms. I began to see that there are too many of these students to hire our way out of the problem. If every child who is above grade level needs a separate, full-time gifted teacher, we're doomed to fail. So how do we expand the reach of the classroom teacher in order to challenge the greatest percentage of students possible? This question brought me to cluster grouping.

The Cluster Grouping Handbook is impressively practical. When I first read the book, I was surprised at how specific it was in its attention to every logistical, day-to-day action necessary to make cluster grouping work. As I read further, I began to understand that this level of practicality has come from the authors' decades of experience implementing cluster grouping in school districts, as well as helping others do the same. When you read the pages of this book, you can tell that the authors have worked through every conceivable barrier, teacher concern, parent question, and student case. Specific details, such as how to handle performance pay and how to help building principals see the value of cluster grouping, are the rule rather than the exception. How should you roll out cluster grouping? See chapter 2 as well as the provided presentations and frequently asked questions. How do teachers need to think differently about their lesson planning in a cluster grouping framework? See chapters 5 and 6. *The Cluster Grouping Handbook* is not theoretical; it addresses real challenges in a practical way with abundant suggestions and supports for common pitfalls.

I am often approached by school district leaders wondering how to get started serving advanced learners, or how they can challenge kids who need more while also furthering equity, narrowing achievement gaps, and meeting every state and national mandate. Every time, my answer is the same: cluster grouping and acceleration. Both of these interventions meet the needs of gifted students without additional staffing. Cluster grouping is not a panacea. There will be students who have needs that cannot be met through cluster grouping alone. But when educators implement cluster grouping, then pull-out programming, acceleration, and supporting students with multiple exceptionalities become easier. Cluster grouping is the foundation upon which all other advanced interventions should be built. Cluster grouping seeks to expand the reach, range, and effectiveness of the grade-level classroom, thus reserving more intense, time-consuming, and costly interventions for students who have even more advanced needs. If this sounds too philosophical or unrealistic, don't worry. *The Cluster Grouping Handbook* opens by walking you through all these program interactions in chapter 1.

As you dive into this book, I hope you'll keep in mind that the overall goal of gifted education is the same as that of K–12 education: to challenge as many students as possible as much of the time as possible. Every child deserves to learn something new every day. Cluster grouping is one way to expand the reach of a finite amount of instructional resources and staffing to challenge a wider range of learners in an inclusive and equitable fashion.

McFarland, Wisconsin, 2019

Introduction

The field of education in the United States is coming to the end of decades of reserving advanced learning opportunities only for students who have proven, through some district measure, that they are able to understand material that was designed for older learners. Educators in the United States now realize that the ways in which they have taught gifted students in the past can benefit many other students as well. The current thinking is that rigor must be woven into the majority of school experiences for all students for as much of the time as possible. There is new emphasis on problem-solving in all curricular areas and availability of science, technology, engineering, and mathematics (STEM) and science, technology, engineering, art, and mathematics (STEAM) experiences for all students. More rigorous standards and learning experiences for all students are becoming the norm.

Dr. Jonathan Plucker, gifted education scholar at Johns Hopkins University, applauds the creation of more rigorous, internationally competitive standards in the United States. He explains that when a "low bar" is used to gauge successful student achievement, gifted students might not experience the rigor they need, and their access to appropriate instructional adjustments may be limited. Plucker says that differentiation strategies must be available to students for whom the learning tasks are not sufficiently challenging (Plucker 2015).

In other words, standards-based learning is not automatically challenging enough for gifted learners, and it may not be challenging enough for other learners either. The National Association for Gifted Children (NAGC) recommends the following interventions with any standards-based curriculum:

1. Provide pathways to accelerate standards-based learning for gifted learners.
2. Provide examples of differentiated task models to address specific standards.
3. Create interdisciplinary product opportunities to elevate learning and address multiple standards from various subject areas simultaneously.

We strongly support increasing access to truly challenging learning experiences not only for gifted learners, but also for students who may not have a history of high achievement. This book will help educators stop worrying about which students are truly gifted and instead concentrate on making all learning opportunities available for all students who can benefit from interacting with them. Any option in this book should be available to any student in any class who can demonstrate readiness for more rigorous learning. Students can, perhaps with some adjustments in the presentation of the material, be successful with the compacted and differentiated teaching techniques that have made this book so popular with the teachers and parents of gifted students.

Consider offering all students the opportunity to grow from where they are, not from where your teacher training courses say students should be. You will not harm a student by offering opportunities to complete more advanced work. Informally assessing all students to determine their entry levels into upcoming standards is just good teaching (Davidson Institute, accessed 2019). You will likely encounter students who are mildly, moderately, or profoundly gifted, and you will discover what instructional methods are most effective for varying levels of gifted ability.

A Note from the Authors About This Update

For this revised and updated edition of *The Cluster Grouping Handbook*, we have refreshed its content for a new age of required standards focused on depth and rigor. Cluster grouping used with gifted-education techniques can benefit not only students formally identified as gifted, but all students. In this second edition, we include updated information on the following topics:

- grouping variations in the SCGM
- building a school culture that supports the SCGM
- using Bloom's Revised Taxonomy to create tiered lessons
- differentiating instruction by developing depth and complexity through the Depth of Knowledge (DOK) framework
- providing ongoing professional training through gifted-cluster coaching, developing a gifted resource site, and using social media
- communicating through cluster-teacher email groups and gifted parent newsletters
- the office's role in monitoring teachers' professional growth
- analyzing achievement data and evaluating programs in the SCGM

Why Meet the Learning Needs of High-Ability Students?

On a day-to-day basis, the highest-ability students usually receive the least amount of their teachers' time. Because of their high test scores and grades, these students are expected to make it on their own or with a minimal amount of guidance.

The inequity of this situation, and what can be lost as a result, is strikingly illustrated by a bell curve showing the percentages of students at different ability levels. The bell curve may create unease among some educators, but we use it for one purpose only: to demonstrate that the learning needs of students at both ends of the learning continuum are identical.

Examine the bell curve in **figure 1**. To teach a class of students, effective teachers usually plan the content, pacing, and quantity of instruction based on what is known about typical students of the age and grade for that class. In a mixed-ability classroom, these are the students in the middle of a heterogeneous group—the students of average abilities on the bell curve. In this same classroom, there are some students who come to the grade level missing many of the basic understandings that typically would have been acquired in earlier grades. These are the students to the left on the bell curve. A third group of students are also part of this classroom: those who are ahead of their grade-level peers in what they know and can do. These are the students to the right on the bell curve.

When teachers discover struggling students in their class—those left of average on the bell curve—they make instant adjustments to their teaching methods. They may slow the pace a bit. They may lessen the amount of work for some students. They may change the methods they use to accommodate the learning styles of struggling students. They may change the way in which they interact with the students and pair them with partners who can work well with them. They may adjust the content to reinforce prerequisite concepts not learned in earlier grades.

Teachers make these necessary adjustments because the students' learning needs *differ from the average.* Now imagine folding the bell curve in half, left to right. You will see clearly that gifted students are as far removed from average on the right side of the curve as are struggling students on the left side. This fact alone provides a clear justification for the same intervention to accommodate their needs—an adjustment of pacing, content, workload, and approach to teaching

FIGURE 1 **Percentages of Students at Different Ability Levels (Based on IQ Scores)**

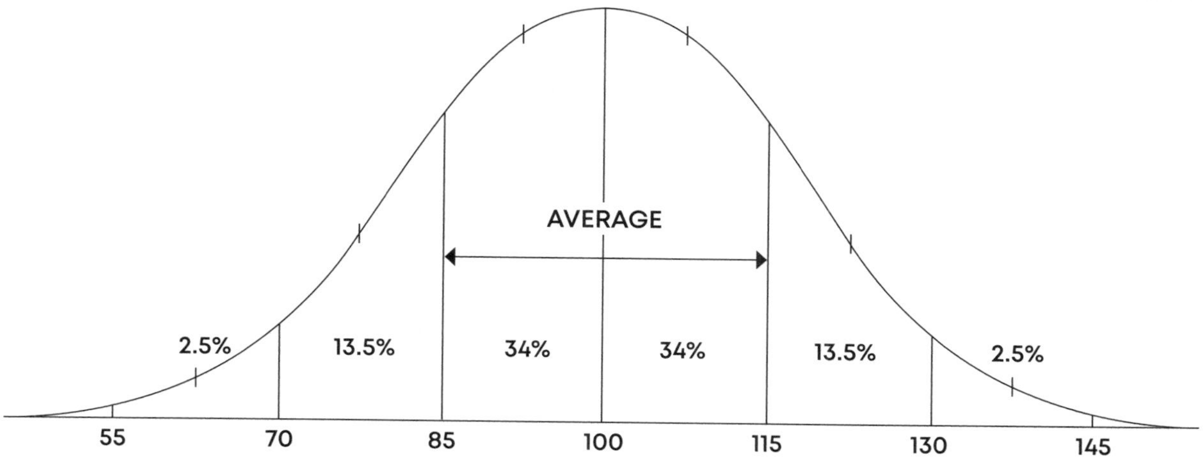

and learning. Gifted students need a faster pace, less practice with grade-level standards, an understanding of their independent work style, a teacher who is comfortable acting as a guide and coach, and opportunities to work with partners who have similar learning ability, style, interests, and preferences. They need this not because they are gifted, but because they are *not average.*

Grade-level standards describe what typical students should be able to learn at a certain age. When we accept the fact that gifted children are able to learn at levels that exceed their chronological age expectations, we immediately understand why grade-level standards must be adjusted for them. We do this because gifted students, like students who struggle to meet the standards, diverge from the norm.

Meeting the Needs of All Students: The Schoolwide Cluster Grouping Model (SCGM)

This book presents a unique approach to help schools meet the needs of all students, including those who are gifted. It is called the Schoolwide Cluster Grouping Model (SCGM). The practice of cluster grouping students has become the most commonly used method for serving gifted students throughout the country. This has occurred most likely because the method can provide full-time academic services to gifted students without major budget implications, and it has the potential to raise achievement for all students in the grade levels that are clustered.

With the SCGM, educators group gifted students into classrooms based on their abilities, while placing all other students according to their achievement levels. Cluster grouping with the SCGM is different from other cluster grouping methods because the SCGM carefully structures classroom compositions with two main goals: (1) to ensure a balance of abilities throughout the grade level *without returning to the practice of tracking* and (2) to reduce the learning range found in each classroom.

Figure 2 on page 4 shows an example of how these two goals can be accomplished by dividing the students at a given grade level into five groups. (For a more detailed explanation of forming clusters and placing them in classrooms, see chapter 1.) In the chart, Group 1 are the identified gifted students, who will be clustered together. Group 2 are high-achieving students who are not gifted but are very capable learners. These students will be clustered and placed in the classes that do not have the gifted cluster. (Clustering gifted students and high-achieving students not identified as gifted in separate classrooms is a key component of the SCGM that has been shown to expand academic growth for both groups.) Group 3 are students with average* academic performance. These are students who typically perform at grade level. Group 4 are students whose performance is below average. These are students who typically perform below grade level. Group 5 are students who produce work that falls considerably below grade-level expectations, or those with significant learning challenges. Students who are identified as twice-exceptional—those who are gifted and also have a learning challenge—are placed in Group 1. So are identified gifted students who are not fluent in English. As shown in figure 2, typical gifted-cluster classrooms will include students from Groups 1, 3, and 4; the other classrooms at the grade level will include students from Groups 2, 3, 4, and 5. Ideally, no classroom will include both gifted students *and* students who perform far below average, so the achievement range in all classrooms will be narrower than that of a randomly heterogeneous classroom.

How does this type of clustering differ from tracking? The two main differences are that, in the SCGM, all classes are heterogeneous, and they provide all students a varied curriculum. Teachers offer opportunities for moving faster or going deeper into the curriculum consistently to the entire class, which means there are times when some students in the gifted-cluster group (Group 1) will be experiencing differentiation and times when they won't. There are also times when students not identified as gifted can benefit from available differentiated learning opportunities.

This is different from a tracking system, in which all students are grouped by ability for much of the school day and are rarely exposed to learning experiences that extend their expected achievement ranges. In a tracking system, students are assigned a set curriculum based on their ability level, and they generally do not veer from that curriculum. With schoolwide cluster grouping, every class in the grade level has students with a range of learning abilities and achievement levels. In order to reach that range, teachers naturally have to modify or extend the grade-level standards.

In the SCGM described in this book, all classes have high-performing students. While one or two classes have a cluster of gifted students, all other classes have a cluster of high-achieving students who, while not identified as gifted, can easily serve as positive academic role models. In a cluster model, learning opportunities are open to all students in the class, and teachers use their students' entry points, or readiness, to determine levels and pace of curriculum. Teachers are

FIGURE 2 **Example of Classroom Compositions for the SCGM (for a Single Grade Level)**

Classrooms	Group 1: Gifted	Group 2: High Achieving	Group 3: Average	Group 4: Below Average	Group 5: Far Below Average	Totals
A	6	0	12	12	0	30
B	0	6	12	6	6	30
C	0	6	12	6	6	30
Totals	6	12	36	24	12	90

*The term *average* is relative and refers to what is average for a school's specific population.

trained in differentiation and curriculum compacting, students receive ongoing assessment, and the results of schoolwide cluster grouping are continually evaluated.

What the Research Says About Cluster Grouping

Research documenting the benefits of keeping gifted students together in their areas of greatest strength for at least part of the school day supports the philosophy behind schoolwide cluster grouping (Brulles 2005; Kulik and Kulik 1990; Rogers 2002; Pierce et al. 2010; Brulles, Cohn, and Saunders 2010). Moreover, the research suggests that all students, including those categorized as average and below average, thrive when placed in heterogeneous classes according to the guidelines of the model (Gentry 1999; Brulles 2005; Pierce et al. 2011; Brulles, Saunders, and Cohn 2010).

The SCGM is an inclusion model that integrates students with exceptional learning needs into mixed-ability classrooms and expects teachers to provide appropriate differentiation opportunities for any students who need them. An inclusion model has already been in use for many years as a method of providing special education services to students who have been identified as having exceptional educational needs. However, it is only when a class has a noticeable group of gifted students—a cluster—that teachers will be most likely to accommodate *their* exceptional educational needs. When there are only one or two gifted students in a class, teachers tend to assume the students are learning as long as they are getting high grades. As a result, teachers may minimize or overlook gifted students' need for expanded learning opportunities. Teachers are also likely to count on these students to help other students with their learning, a practice that robs gifted students of opportunities to move forward in academic areas.

Cluster grouping requires that teachers differentiate instruction. Differentiation occurs when teachers modify the curriculum and their instructional methods in response to the needs, strengths, learning styles, and interests of individual students so that *all* students have an opportunity to learn at their full potential. To be successful, the gifted-cluster teacher must have ongoing training in how to teach high-ability students in the cluster model (Winebrenner and Devlin 2001; Brulles 2005; Brulles, Saunders, and Cohn 2010). The SCGM creates a setting for providing appropriate instruction that is feasible for teachers and for enhancing the likelihood that differentiation will take place.

The SCGM: Who Benefits, and How?

The SCGM offers an educational approach that benefits all stakeholders in the school community—students, teachers, administrators, and parents. Grouping gifted children in a regular classroom can provide academic, social, and emotional advantages to the students and make teaching gifted students more manageable for teachers. Gifted students feel more comfortable when there are other students like them in the class. They are more likely to choose challenging tasks when they can do that work in the company of other students. Teachers attuned to differentiating instruction are more likely to provide appropriate learning opportunities for gifted students and for other students as well. The school is able to provide a full-time, cost-effective program for gifted students, since their learning needs are being met every day. Parents who are satisfied that their children are experiencing consistent challenge at school are more ready to work cooperatively with the school and the teachers and less likely to remove their children from their schools in search of a better option.

Benefits of the Schoolwide Cluster Grouping Model

- serving the learning needs of gifted students in a full-time program that delivers consistent curriculum compacting and differentiation opportunities without major budget implications
- grouping gifted students together in otherwise heterogeneous classes with a teacher who has special training in how to meet their unique learning needs
- facilitating the emergence of new academic leaders in classes that do not contain a gifted cluster
- providing another component to existing services available for gifted students in the school
- improving support to classroom teachers from special education and gifted support staff who have fewer teachers' schedules to work with
- improving student performance by communicating higher expectations for all students, by reducing the range of achievement and ability in all classes, and by providing staff development in gifted education for all teachers on staff
- increasing gifted-education opportunities for primary-grade gifted children, for gifted students who are not fluent in English, and for gifted students who may not be experiencing success in school
- increasing overall achievement at the grade levels that use cluster grouping
- raising expectations for all students by opening access to classroom opportunities historically reserved for identified gifted students only
- retaining families who may otherwise, as a result of feeling that their gifted children's needs are going unmet, choose to remove their children from the school and place them in a different school or provide homeschooling

Impact of the SCGM on Gifted Students

Gifted students who are clustered demonstrate high achievement because they experience more consistent challenge in their learning activities. Their scores on achievement tests show forward progress—rather than lost ground, as has been the case in some schools where gifted students are not placed in clusters or are not consistently challenged in other ways.

When gifted students are purposefully clustered in otherwise heterogeneous classes, rather than split up so that each class has one or two gifted students, teachers are much more likely to notice their learning needs. They also enjoy more attention to their social and emotional needs because of the specialized training the teachers receive.

Cluster grouping also makes it more likely that gifted kids will work to their full potential and take advantage of available differentiated learning opportunities, because they will have other students to work with on these advanced learning tasks. Having serious competition from other students like themselves, they begin to develop more realistic perceptions of their abilities and to better understand and accept their learning differences. With so many opportunities to work and learn together, gifted students become more comfortable working at extended levels of complexity and depth in a given subject or topic. Their willingness to take risks in learning experiences increases when they spend time with others who share the same interests, have similar abilities, and can also benefit from the available differentiation opportunities.

Impact of the SCGM on English Language Learners

Cluster grouping offers exciting opportunities for schools to meet the needs of gifted English language learners (ELL students). When gifted students are served only in a pull-out model, gifted students who are not proficient in English are frequently kept out of gifted services because they cannot work at the same pace and level as the gifted students already proficient in English. With cluster grouping, extended learning opportunities are available in the regular classroom. When ELL students with high learning potential are present in classes that offer consistent challenge, they make faster progress attaining English fluency and academic achievement.

A significant increase in achievement in students of different ethnic groups can also be expected from using cluster grouping (Brulles 2005; Brulles, Saunders, and Cohn 2010). These findings result from classes in which teachers can be more focused and effective in their teaching. Another reason for the achievement gains is that gifted-education training required for gifted-cluster teachers helps teachers set high expectations for *all* students—and students respond positively to these high expectations.

Impact of the SCGM on All Students

Students at all ability levels benefit from the SCGM because in this model, teachers receive more training in how to differentiate the curriculum and the pacing for all types of students, placing learning success within the reach of all. In addition, the SCGM motivates gifted and high-achieving students to work more independently and allows them to spend more learning time on activities that interest and challenge them; this, in turn, opens up more time for teachers to spend with those who need additional assistance.

As teachers become more adept at recognizing giftedness in their students, the number of students they nominate for gifted testing increases yearly in schools that use the SCGM. This is especially noticeable in classes that do *not* have the gifted cluster, demonstrating the benefit of clustering high-achieving children who are *not* identified as gifted in separate classrooms. These classroom structures provide opportunities for the high-achieving students to thrive and emerge as new academic leaders.

Research shows that implementation of the SCGM allows for consistent and comparable levels of achievement growth among students who are not identified as gifted. A 2012 study showed similar achievement gains for general education students (those not identified as gifted) regardless of their placement in a gifted-cluster classroom or another class in the grade level (Brulles, Peters, and Saunders 2012). These results may be attributed to the fact that in the SCGM, classes have a slightly narrowed range of achievement and ability levels.

Achievement Advisory

The SCGM has the potential to significantly improve academic achievement for all students, including English language learners, students from diverse cultures, high-achieving students, and average and below-average learners. Several studies analyzing academic achievement of students in schools that use cluster grouping yield similar results. Marcia Gentry, Mary Rizza, and Steven Owen report statistically significant academic achievement gains in math and reading in a three-year longitudinal study for students in grades three through five (Gentry, Rizza, and Owen 2002). These findings are supported by the research of Dina Brulles, Rachel Saunders, and Sanford Cohn, who analyzed student achievement in mathematics for eleven subgroups at all ability levels in a diverse urban elementary school that used a comprehensive cluster grouping model (Brulles, Saunders, and Cohn 2010). The latter research showed statistically significant achievement gains in mathematics for students regardless of perceived ability levels, gender, ELL status, or ethnicity. Research conducted by Dina Brulles, Scott Peters, and Rachel Saunders shows comparable achievement gains for gifted and nongifted students in this model (Brulles, Peters, and Saunders 2012). (For more details from these studies, see chapter 8.)

Impact of the SCGM on Teachers

Student achievement is positively correlated with effective teaching. The SCGM allows teachers to be more effective because teachers are teaching classes with a smaller range of learning levels. The system provides opportunities for teachers to respond more readily to the needs of all their students, to challenge gifted students clustered together in mixed-ability classes, and to engage in practices that lead to improved academic achievement for students not identified as gifted working at or above grade level. As a result, over time with the SCGM, more students in a school are identified as high achievers and fewer as low achievers.

For a school that already has a pull-out program for gifted students, the cluster model makes scheduling out-of-class activities easier. The resource (pull-out) teacher has to work with only one or two classroom teachers' schedules per grade level instead of the schedules of all the teachers at a particular grade level. The gifted-cluster teacher, whose gifted students venture to another classroom for pull-out services, understands that while they are gone, students who remain should be experiencing activities that reinforce standards the gifted students have already mastered. Therefore, when the gifted students return from the pull-out program, they do not have any missed work to make up, and the teacher does not have additional planning and record keeping that typically comes with makeup work.

When the SCGM is implemented with the goal that all teachers will eventually receive the related staff development, over time it is possible to ensure that all teachers who wish to teach a classroom with a gifted cluster will have that opportunity. At the same time, teachers and students in all classrooms benefit from the teachers' facility with differentiating the curriculum to meet students' varied learning needs.

Impact of the SCGM on Administrators

Schools that use the SCGM find that they can still offer valuable services for their gifted students even with tight budgets or lack of political support. This helps administrators assure parents of gifted students that their children's learning needs will be served. Cluster grouping actually provides full-time placement and service for gifted students in the schools *without* the cost of creating and maintaining a separate gifted-education program. Gifted education becomes part of the school culture.

When schools take the time to implement the SCGM strategically, carefully planning the groups for cluster classrooms, training as many teachers as possible to implement gifted-education strategies, educating parents about how their children's school experience will be affected, and conducting ongoing student assessments and program evaluations, the result is a cohesive and budget-friendly schoolwide approach to gifted education that brings the school community together as it raises student achievement levels.

Impact of the SCGM on Parents

Providing a cluster grouping model announces to the community that the school is committed to recognizing and serving its gifted students and enhancing achievement opportunities for all students. As parents of gifted students come to understand how clustering affects their children's learning opportunities, they see that the school is providing full-time gifted services, that teachers are responding to their children's needs, and that their gifted children spend time learning with other students of similar ability. Parents of students *not* identified as gifted are also likely to appreciate the opportunities the clustering arrangements and differentiation strategies afford their children. When these parents become familiar with the research that shows how the SCGM facilitates the emergence of new leaders in classes that do not have a gifted cluster, they may realize that, for the first time, their children have more opportunities to demonstrate academic leadership. Many students have had this very positive experience as a result of schoolwide cluster grouping.

About This Book and Digital Content

Directed toward administrators and teachers, *The Cluster Grouping Handbook* offers information that will be useful to other school personnel and to parents as well. The book contains precise descriptions of how to develop and maintain a Schoolwide Cluster Grouping Model, specific guidelines administrators and teachers can follow, and suggested criteria for analyzing the level of success of the model in schools. This book gives special attention to how schools can empower gifted English language learners and enfranchise them in gifted-education services. It also includes resources to help parents of gifted and high-achieving students find specific information that will improve their advocacy for the learning needs of their children. Examples throughout the book come from teachers the two authors have worked with, including many examples from the Paradise Valley School District in Arizona, where Dina Brulles works.

Placing gifted students into cluster groups within heterogeneous classes is only the beginning of the SCGM process. Educators must use effective teaching strategies for these students, and administrators must effectively supervise the students and teachers in the gifted clusters. How can schools construct and support the cluster model to serve the learning needs of gifted students effectively and improve achievement for other students as well? What are the critical components of a comprehensive cluster model? What methods can teachers and administrators use to gauge the effectiveness of the SCGM? The mission of this book is to answer these questions.

The book is arranged in three parts:

Part 1: Implementing the Schoolwide Cluster Grouping Model (SCGM). Chapter 1 provides a summary of the SCGM along with detailed information on how to start and maintain a Schoolwide Cluster Grouping Model in your school, with special attention to forming the groups. Chapter 2 details suggestions for building and maintaining support for the SCGM. Chapter 3 presents and discusses both typical and atypical characteristics exhibited by gifted students and suggests specific strategies for identifying students for gifted-cluster groups. Chapter 4 focuses on factors to consider when staffing gifted-cluster classrooms; it also describes the roles and responsibilities of key gifted-education staff within the model.

Part 2: The SCGM in Action: How to Compact and Differentiate Curriculum for Advanced Learners. Part 2 will be especially helpful to classroom teachers. It consists of two chapters that explain and illustrate specific methods for compacting and differentiating the curriculum in order to challenge gifted learners appropriately. The chapters address strategies that will be effective when students have already mastered the curriculum (chapter 5) and when content is new (chapter 6).

Part 3: Sustaining the SCGM. Chapter 7 describes ongoing professional development plans for all staff members working in the SCGM. Chapter 8 offers information about ways to evaluate the model so it can be as effective as possible. It describes the kind of data schools will need to collect from the start of the school year, so educators may find it helpful to read this chapter as the SCGM is getting underway each year.

Throughout the book you will find highlighted information for special audiences and issues. "Supervisor Spotlight" sidebars offer administrators tips and reminders for generating and sustaining support for the SCGM and monitoring how it is being implemented. "Achievement Advisory" sidebars hone in on ways the model can support academic progress for students. The book includes reproducible informational handouts and planning forms, often at the ends of corresponding chapters, and in the downloadable digital content. For information on how to access the digital content, see page PNT.

At the back of the book, you will find information for parents along with a listing of references and recommended books, organizations, websites, and other resources related to each chapter's topic. A glossary of terms related to education—particularly gifted education—is provided as well. Finally, in addition to the book's reproducible handouts, the digital content contains a PDF presentation useful for introducing and explaining the SCGM to the school community.

Let's get started!

Dina Brulles
giftededucationconsultants.com

Susan Winebrenner
susanwinebrenner.com

PART 1

Implementing the Schoolwide Cluster Grouping Model (SCGM)

At the heart of the SCGM are three essential strategies:

- identifying and placing all students in heterogeneous classes that have a slightly narrowed range of student abilities
- ensuring that gifted students experience consistent curriculum compacting and differentiation opportunities
- providing appropriate professional development for staff

To put this model in place in a school or district involves a broad-based, nonlinear process. The four chapters in part 1 combine to lay the groundwork for this process. Chapter 1 details classroom structures and student placement. Chapter 2 describes a two-year timeline for implementing the SCGM. The timeline integrates identification, placement, and staffing with a plan for training teachers in the model and in differentiation strategies, for bringing parents on board, for implementing and maintaining the model over time, and for incorporating ongoing evaluation of how the model is supporting gifted students and raising overall student achievement. Identification of gifted students is the focus of chapter 3, along with information about gifted children's behavior and social and emotional needs. Chapter 4 presents three key staff positions for the model and provides information about selecting teachers for the gifted-cluster classrooms.

1

What Is the SCGM? How Does It Work?

GUIDING QUESTIONS

- What are the components of the SCGM?
- Exactly how should students be grouped in classes to realize the benefits of schoolwide cluster grouping?
- How does the SCGM fit with other gifted-education services?
- How does it fit with other classroom inclusion models?
- Why are identified gifted students and high-achieving students not identified as gifted placed in different classrooms?
- What do parents need to know about the SCGM?
- How can school planners determine whether and when to initiate the SCGM?

Most educators choose careers in education because they care deeply about helping students learn and grow. In today's world, administrators and teachers alike face an almost overwhelming task to be accountable to students, to the communities they serve, and to the performance mandates in place through state and federal education legislation. All educators are acutely aware of the challenges entailed in balancing the needs of teaching the curriculum; reaching diverse learners below, at, and above the norm; and raising the overall rankings of the school as demonstrated in benchmark assessments. Can a model that focuses on gifted students really improve teaching and achievement levels for the broader student population? This chapter will help you understand the SCGM and the role it can play in bringing about this balance.

Overview of the SCGM

The effectiveness of the Schoolwide Cluster Grouping Model depends on the integration of five key components:

1. **Schoolwide implementation.** The SCGM involves the entire school community, including administrators, teachers, professional support staff, students, and parents.
2. **Placement of students.** With the SCGM, all students are grouped into clusters based on their ability and achievement level. The clusters are then placed in classrooms with carefully structured compositions to ensure a balance of abilities throughout each grade level and a learning range within each classroom that is narrower than in a typical heterogeneous classroom.

3. **Classroom strategies.** Teachers use differentiation methods that vary the content, pace, process, products, and learning environment for gifted students and for other students who also benefit from these opportunities. Ongoing assessment and identification of student strengths, abilities, and performance allows teachers to differentiate flexibly and effectively and ensures that all students make continuous progress.
4. **Professional development.** In the SCGM, staff training ensures that teachers learn to recognize gifted behaviors and to differentiate instruction to accommodate the exceptional educational needs of gifted students (students who learn at levels significantly beyond grade-level expectations). When teachers receive appropriate, ongoing training, the SCGM creates an environment that addresses the social and emotional needs of many gifted learners.
5. **Evaluation.** Data collection and evaluation of student and teacher growth are essential. Careful monitoring of progress in the SCGM can demonstrate that cluster grouping is being used effectively, and it can facilitate ongoing success with the model.

The focus of this chapter is on the first two components—understanding the schoolwide structure of the model and configuring the placement of students into cluster groups and classrooms.

A Word About Educational Terminology

Throughout this book, the term *cluster grouping* refers to the Schoolwide Cluster Grouping Model (SCGM). For definitions and explanations of other terms, refer to the glossary on page 246.

Placing Students in Cluster Groups

Cluster grouping occurs when a group of gifted students is placed with groups of other students in a mixed-ability classroom. Ideally, a group of four to ten identified gifted students, usually in the top 5 to 8 percent of achievement potential of the grade-level population, is clustered in a classroom with a teacher trained in how to teach students with exceptional abilities. If a grade level has more than ten gifted students, two or more classrooms may serve as gifted-cluster classrooms.

On page 16, you will find a chart that offers an example of student classroom placements using the SCGM. Prior to placing students into classrooms, educators must assign all students within a grade level to one of the following categories:

Group 1, Gifted. Students in Group 1 are identified as gifted by local criteria, because they have the highest ability in the grade level. This group includes gifted students who are nonproductive or underachievers, culturally diverse learners, English language learners (ELL students), and twice-exceptional students.

Group 2, High Achieving. Group 2 students are highly competent and productive, are working to the fullest extent of their abilities, and are not identified as gifted.

Group 3, Average. These students achieve in the middle (average) range compared to others in their grade level.

Group 4, Below Average. The students in Group 4 may struggle with math or reading and score slightly below grade level, but they can achieve at grade level with some support.

Group 5, Far Below Average. These students struggle with most subject areas and score significantly below proficiency levels on standardized tests.

Educators can determine assignments to the groups by formal and informal gifted-identification procedures. These may combine standardized test scores with teacher or parent observation and other anecdotal data. (Chapter 3 gives a thorough explanation of gifted-identification procedures.) In the SCGM, ability testing is the most significant tool for identifying gifted students. Group 1 includes all students formally identified as gifted, regardless of their achievement levels, including twice-exceptional, ELL, culturally and linguistically diverse, and underachieving gifted students. Group 1 would likely include the top 5 to 8 percent of students in your school in terms of ability or learning potential. Achievement data from the local school population determines student placement into the other four groups. Groups 2 through 5 would include all other students, clustered according to achievement levels. The term *average* in reference to student achievement is relative; it refers to what is average for a school's particular population.

The school's grade-level structure and population influence the number of gifted-cluster classrooms at each grade level. Following is a suggested placement chart. This chart offers an example of three classroom compositions for the SCGM in a single grade level with a total of ninety students. Later in the chapter, you will see several examples that show how the configuration changes based on the number of classes and number of gifted students in a grade level.

The numbers in this chart represent general guidelines, and you should change them according to your school's particular needs. There is no arbitrary limit to the number of gifted (Group 1) clusters your school should have. If your school has identified a large number of gifted students in a given grade level, you can create another cluster. Unless the number of identified gifted students in your school is very small, the SCGM guarantees that there will be no classes in which only one or two gifted students find themselves without a community of other gifted students.

Purposeful Placement of All Students in All Classes

Historically, many districts have spread their gifted students throughout each grade level by placing one or two in each classroom. This is problematic because each teacher ends up with such a small number of gifted students that she or he may not feel the urgency to provide consistent curriculum compacting and differentiation opportunities. Even if the teacher understands gifted students' learning needs, participates in professional gifted-education learning opportunities, and offers extended learning activities, the gifted students have little incentive to partake of those activities if few other students (or none) are doing similarly challenging work. Most students do not want to be observed or perceived as different—it makes them feel uncomfortable.

FIGURE 1-1 **Example of Classroom Compositions for the SCGM (for a Single Grade Level)**

Classrooms	Group 1: Gifted	Group 2: High Achieving	Group 3: Average	Group 4: Below Average	Group 5: Far Below Average	Totals
A	6	0	12	12	0	30
B	0	6	12	6	6	30
C	0	6	12	6	6	30
Totals	6	12	36	24	12	90

In the SCGM, gifted students are clustered together at each grade level. Teachers and principals determine placement of *all* students into *all* classrooms at each grade level, with a goal of creating a balance of abilities and achievement across the classrooms. With this model, if six identified gifted students are entering a grade level that has three classrooms, they are assigned to one teacher, rather than being split up among all available classes. As soon as the gifted students' (Group 1) placement has been determined, students from Group 2 are placed in the other two classrooms. Next, students from Groups 3 and 4 are placed in all three classes. Finally, those from Group 5 are placed in the classes that have Group 2 students. When the grouping is finished, one classroom will include students from Groups 1, 3, and 4 while the other two classrooms will include students from Groups 2, 3, 4, and 5. This creates classrooms where abilities are well mixed, yet the range of student achievement levels in each classroom is narrowed.

A Word About Labels

In this book, we use terms such as *gifted-identified, nonproductive, high achieving,* and *below average* to categorize students' abilities and learning levels. The terms are not intended to stereotype students but rather to give educators readily understandable descriptions that will help them determine placement of students in the cluster classrooms.

When there is a need to create a second gifted cluster at a given grade level, the eligible gifted-cluster students can be placed according to areas of strength. For example, gifted students at a given grade level who have high ability in math can be placed with the gifted-cluster teacher who specializes in teaching math.

Schools with one classroom (or section) per grade level can still implement critical elements of the SCGM, such as learning about the needs of gifted students, using differentiated instructional strategies, and flexibly grouping students for instructional purposes. However, these schools cannot follow the model completely, because the single classroom would contain the full range of ability and achievement levels in the grade level.

When there are no gifted-identified students in a grade level, a gifted-cluster teacher should still be designated for that grade level. This teacher should be invited to participate in the gifted-cluster teacher meetings and other relevant professional development. Having a teacher at every grade level with training or experience in gifted education encourages discussions about the needs of gifted students during grade-level meetings, team planning, and curriculum adoptions. Additionally, when gifted-identified students enroll during the school year, they can be placed with a teacher who has participated in the gifted-cluster teacher training.

Grouping Variations in the SCGM

Establishing the number of gifted-cluster classes at a grade level and then placing students into the various classes involves weighing and balancing various criteria. The number of gifted-identified students and the number of classrooms at each grade level are the primary factors that determine the number of gifted-cluster classes needed in each grade. Because these numbers change yearly, the number of gifted-cluster classes in a specific grade level may also change from one year to the next.

Student populations vary widely from school to school and from grade level to grade level. This variability may call for flexibility and creativity in assigning students to classrooms. The first consideration is the number of classes in a grade level. From there, factors that influence the number of gifted-cluster classrooms and student placements are as follows:

- only one or two classes in a grade level
- few gifted-identified students in a grade level

- too many gifted students for one gifted-cluster classroom
- multi-age classes
- high numbers of both gifted and very low achieving students in a grade

The text and tables that follow provide examples of ways to place students in these scenarios (Brulles and Winebrenner 2011; Brulles and Brown 2018).

THE NUMBER OF CLASSES IN A GRADE LEVEL

The number of classes in each grade level affects the ideal number of gifted-cluster classes to create. The more classes in each grade level, the greater likelihood that an additional gifted-cluster class will be needed. As a general guide, consider the following table:

Classes per Grade Level	Gifted-Cluster Classrooms
2–3	1
4–5	1–2
6–8	2–3

The following scenarios describe placement variations that consider the number of gifted students, the number of classes at each grade level, and other factors.

FEW STUDENTS FOR ONE GIFTED-CLUSTER CLASSROOM

When a grade level contains zero to three gifted students, include some high-achieving students along with the gifted students in the gifted-cluster classroom, as in the following table. This table shows a recommended cluster grouping for a grade level with fifty-five students, among whom are only two gifted-identified students. Remember, the purpose is to create a balance of ability and achievement levels in all classes in the grade, without too wide a range in any particular classroom.

TOO MANY GIFTED STUDENTS FOR ONE GIFTED-CLUSTER CLASSROOM

A large number of gifted students in one class sometimes causes a challenge for the gifted-cluster teacher. When a gifted-cluster classroom has more than ten gifted students, the teacher may spend less time and attention on each gifted student. When a grade level has that many gifted students, educators may want to divide the gifted students into two gifted-cluster classrooms. When there are enough gifted students to form two gifted-cluster classes, there are usually two or more other classrooms in the grade level where high-achieving students are grouped apart from the gifted students. This careful placement ensures a balance of ability and achievement levels in each classroom, without too wide a range in any particular classroom. This balance is critical for implementing and sustaining an effective cluster model.

When educators are dividing gifted students into two gifted-cluster classrooms, they can place the gifted students into the classes based on their learning strengths in math or reading. In Classroom A, gifted students who are strong in math are placed with a teacher who specializes in

FIGURE 1-2 **Recommended Cluster Grouping for Grade Level with Few Gifted Students**

Classrooms	Group 1: Gifted	Group 2: High Achieving	Group 3: Average	Group 4: Below Average	Group 5: Far Below Average	Totals
A	2	7	12	7	0	28
B	0	9	12	2	4	27
Totals	2	16	24	9	4	55

FIGURE 1-3 **Recommended Cluster Grouping for Grade Level with Many Gifted Students**

Classrooms	Group 1: Gifted	Group 2: High Achieving	Group 3: Average	Group 4: Below Average	Group 5: Far Below Average	Totals
A	9	0	11	7	0	27
B	10	0	10	8	0	28
C	0	12	9	0	5	26
D	0	11	10	0	5	26
Totals	19	23	40	15	10	107

math. In Classroom B, the gifted students who are strong in language arts are grouped together with a teacher who specializes in language arts. Similarly, in Classrooms C and D, the students in Group 5 (Far Below Average) are placed according to their needs, which are addressed with relevant resource assistance in those classrooms.

MULTI-AGE CLASSES

Multi-age classes provide an ideal placement for gifted students. In multi-age classes, all students work at varying challenge levels within the same content areas. The teacher provides ongoing formative assessment for all students to create flexible learning groups. This routine practice of pre-assessing students' entry levels in the content areas is ideal for the gifted students in the class.

Figure 1-4 demonstrates how a small school with one and a half classrooms of third grade and one and a half classrooms of fourth grade provides services for its gifted students in the SCGM. The school created one third-grade class, one fourth-grade class, and one multi-age class with both third and fourth graders. The multi-age class is the gifted-cluster class for grades three and four. The school placed high-achieving (Group 2) students in each grade in the other two classrooms.

LARGE NUMBERS OF BOTH GIFTED AND VERY LOW STUDENTS IN A GRADE

Occasionally grade levels will have very large numbers of students who fall into Groups 1 and 5. This scenario necessitates placing some of the students

FIGURE 1-4 **Recommended Cluster Grouping for Multi-Age Classes and Related Grade-Level Classes**

Classrooms	Group 1: Gifted	Group 2: High Achieving	Group 3: Average	Group 4: Below Average	Group 5: Far Below Average	Totals
Grades 3–4 Multi-Age	3 third graders 7 fourth graders	0	4 third graders 6 fourth graders	3 third graders 5 fourth graders	0	10 third graders 18 fourth graders
Grade 3	0	11	10	3	3	27
Grade 4	0	10	11	3	3	27
Totals	10	21	31	14	6	82

in Group 5 into a gifted-cluster class. Assistance from a resource teacher helps the gifted-cluster teacher in that class, who is working with the full range of abilities in one classroom. (Some principals find that the cluster grouping model facilitates the scheduling of resource teachers, because students receiving resource assistance are also clustered.)

When it is necessary to combine students in Groups 1 and 5 in the same class, place both groups of students according to areas of need, such as mathematics. The following table shows how one school divided its large number of students in Groups 1 and 5 in one grade level. The school separated the students in these two groups according to the students' areas of strength or need—in this case, mathematics. The principal then placed the group of students with math strength or need in Classroom B, with a teacher who enjoyed differentiating in math.

Configuring the Cluster Classrooms

Ideally, educators work as a team to create classroom compositions. Teachers from the sending grade levels work with the building principal and the gifted-education specialist or coordinator (when one exists), with assistance from a special education teacher as needed. The placement team can use color-coded cards that represent each of the five SCGM student groups with a designated color. Before the placement meeting, each sending classroom teacher assigns students to the appropriate card colors based on their ability or achievement levels, writing one student's name on each card. (Alternatively, the teachers can use colored dot stickers in conjunction with the school's existing student information cards.)

FIGURE 1-5 **Recommended Cluster Grouping in a Grade Level with Many Students in Groups 1 and 5**

Classrooms	Group 1: Gifted	Group 2: High Achieving	Group 3: Average	Group 4: Below Average	Group 5: Far Below Average	Totals
A	10	0	10	8	0	28
B	7	4	10	0	6	27
C	0	11	6	3	5	25
Totals	17	15	26	11	11	80

FIGURE 1-6 **Sample Completed Grade-Level Data by School Chart**

Current Grades	Group 1: Gifted	Group 2: High Achieving	Group 3: Average	Group 4: Below Average	Group 5: Far Below Average
Kindergarten	2	18	36	17	9
Grade 1	5	16	35	21	8
Grade 2	7	21	32	15	5
Grade 3	8	18	28	16	10
Grade 4	15	20	34	12	9
Grade 5	10	22	25	13	6
Grade 6	9	21	33	13	5
Grade 7	9	19	36	12	7
Grade 8	10	23	31	13	8

Working in grade-level teams, teachers can use school achievement data to indicate the numbers of current students in each SCGM group, using the "Grade-Level Data by School" reproducible chart on page 33. **Figure 1-6** is a sample completed version of this chart.

Using this data, teachers can recommend classroom compositions. At the placement meeting, the placement team combines colored cards for the entire grade level into classrooms following this process:

1. Place all gifted-identified (Group 1) students into designated gifted-cluster classrooms.
2. Cluster high-achieving (Group 2) students into classrooms that have not been assigned a gifted (Group 1) cluster.
3. Distribute average (Group 3) students evenly in all classrooms.
4. Distribute below-average (Group 4) students evenly in all classrooms.
5. Place far-below-average (Group 5) students in the classrooms that have not been assigned a gifted (Group 1) cluster.

It is wise to place one or two more students in the gifted-cluster class(es) than in the other classes, to leave a bit of space in the other classes. This way, new students from Group 2 or Group 5 who enroll during the year will automatically be placed in the classes that have more room and will not be mistakenly placed in the gifted-cluster classroom. See the following table in **figure 1-7**.

FIGURE 1-7 **Sample SCGM Classroom Composition Planning Form**

Classroom (grade, teacher, or other identifier)	Group 1: Gifted	Group 2: High Achieving	Group 3: Average	Group 4: Below Average	Group 5: Far Below Average	Totals
A: Grade 3	5	0	13	5	0	23
B: Grade 3	0	8	10	0	4	22
C: Grade 3	0	7	11	1	3	22
D: Grade 4	9	0	12	6	0	27
E: Grade 4	0	10	11	2	3	26
F: Grade 4	0	9	10	3	4	26
G: Grade 5	10	0	13	6	0	29
H: Grade 5	0	11	12	2	3	28
I: Grade 5	0	11	11	2	3	27
J: Grade 6	8	0	15	8	0	31
K: Grade 6	0	9	15	2	4	30
L: Grade 6	10	0	13	3	4	30
M: Grade 7	9	0	14	8	0	31
N: Grade 7	0	10	13	2	5	30
O: Grade 7	0	11	12	1	6	30
P: Grade 8	9	0	11	9	0	29
Q: Grade 8	0	9	10	4	4	27
R: Grade 8	0	8	11	4	5	28

The configurations shown for grades 6, 7, and 8 in figures 1-6 and 1-7 show how classes in these grade levels might be arranged for K–8 schools. Middle schools that serve grades 6 through 8 or grades 7 and 8 vary drastically in how teams are formed. The numbers of grade-level sections, courses offered, subject areas in which they cluster, schedules, and so on influence how students are grouped. Many middle schools cluster group for English, history, and science and then group according to readiness levels for math.

After the class lists have been assembled, teachers should carefully review them for appropriateness. If it appears that any student placements should be changed, strive to make sure that the trades between classes swap students from the same groups. (For example, exchange a Group 2 student in one classroom for a Group 2 student in another classroom.)

Special Considerations

The following students require special attention when educators are determining classroom placement:

- Gifted students who are nonproductive (underachieving students with high academic ability) are placed in Group 1.
- Students who are both gifted and ELL (English language learners) or former ELL are placed in Group 1.
- Twice-exceptional gifted students—those identified as gifted who also have an IEP (individualized educational program) for special education—are placed in Group 1.
- Students not identified as gifted who have learning disabilities or challenges that significantly compromise their learning ability are generally placed in Group 5, as are students who are scoring well below proficiency levels on standardized tests.
- Ideally, Groups 2 and 5 are placed in classrooms that do *not* have a Group 1 cluster.

While most of the gifted-cluster students are likely in the top 5 to 8 percent of ability in the grade-level population, some may not be achieving at that level. All gifted-identified students at each grade level should be placed into Group 1 regardless of their achievement levels. This placement allows all gifted students access to teachers who have specialized training in gifted education. Working with teachers who understand the unique learning and behavioral characteristics of gifted students can help nonproductive gifted students, as well as gifted students with other types of learning challenges, achieve at higher levels.

Gifted-identified ELL students have the ability to become advanced learners, and therefore benefit from being in a gifted-cluster group. The faster pacing, advanced expectations, and consistent opportunities for higher-level thinking appear to help these students make better progress in their learning than they might make in a class without a gifted cluster (Brulles 2005). For related reasons, twice-exceptional gifted students should also be placed in a gifted cluster.

It is important to note that generally, no high-achieving students—those with above-average performance who are not identified as gifted (Group 2)—are placed into the classrooms with gifted students. The SCGM attempts to separate these two groups because placing clusters of above-average students into the classrooms *without* the gifted clusters ensures academic leadership in every class. Some parents and teachers mistakenly believe that gifted students are needed in all classes as positive learning role models for other students. On the contrary: Because gifted students process information differently from other kids in their class, they are often ineffective when they try to help others learn. Research shows that the difference in learning levels between students should not be too great for a student to be considered an effective role model to another student (Schunk 1987). Students whose performances are higher than average are academic role models for average learners. Average-level students are academic role models for each other and for lower-than-average learners.

SUPERVISOR SPOTLIGHT

When you are making student placements, keep in mind that giftedness spans all cultures. Pay attention to the ethnic representation of the school population and strive for equal representation of ethnic groups participating in the school's gifted services. If there are few students of diverse cultures represented in the gifted population, you may need to seek alternative identification tools to help identify the gifted learners among underrepresented populations in your school. School districts with culturally and linguistically diverse populations need to include assessments that rely less on language abilities and minimize cultural bias. See chapter 3 for information on identifying culturally and linguistically diverse gifted learners.

In a grade level with a large number of high achievers (Group 2) and a small number of gifted learners (Group 1), it may become necessary to place some of the Group 2 students in the same classroom with the gifted-cluster group. However, there will never be a situation where *all* the high-achieving students are placed in classrooms that also have clusters of identified gifted students. That method of cluster grouping is likely to create other classes that have few students who can act as positive academic role models.

There are also several important reasons for not placing Group 5 students into a gifted-cluster classroom. In a classroom with students at both ends of the learning continuum, a teacher's time and attention will be pulled in both directions. As the year progresses, pressure builds for supporting the lowest-performing students to achieve higher scores on critical assessments, and the teacher feels compelled to focus more time on those students. This significantly diminishes the time the teacher can spend with Group 1 students. Keep in mind that all classes in the SCGM have a slightly narrowed range of student ability and achievement, including classes assigned a group of students working far below average. In those classes, students who struggle the most will have a teacher who is not distracted from their needs by the equally intense learning needs of gifted students. These classes also typically have the benefit of resource teachers, special education teachers, or instructional coaches to assist those who need additional support.

In small schools with only two classrooms for a grade level, it may become necessary to place some students from Group 5 in a class that has Group 1 students. In this case, the placement works best when a second adult is sharing the teaching responsibilities—preferably a teacher or an instructional aide with special education training, so that the classroom teacher will have significant time to work with the students in the gifted cluster. It is still preferable to cluster the gifted students together, even if doing so will create a class that has students from both Groups 1 and 5.

Considerations for Middle Schools

The SCGM described in this book is feasible not only in elementary schools but also in middle and junior high schools, which typically use one of two configurations. In the first and most commonly used configuration, gifted students are clustered on a heterogeneous team or in a heterogeneous class. The second configuration creates a team composed entirely of gifted students.

CLUSTERING MIDDLE SCHOOL STUDENTS AS PART OF A HETEROGENEOUS TEAM

When you cluster middle school students as part of a heterogeneous team, use the guidelines described earlier in this chapter, under "Placing Students in Cluster Groups" (pages 15–23). Keep the number of students in the Group 1 cluster to 20 to 25 percent of the entire team enrollment when possible.

If the number of students who need to be assigned to gifted clusters is large, create one cluster of Group 1 students who have exceptional math ability and place them on a team with a strong math teacher. Place another cluster of Group 1 students who excel in reading or writing on a team with a teacher very strong in language arts. Students who demonstrate exceptional ability in both subject areas can be placed in either gifted cluster in order to balance out the groups.

Students assigned to gifted clusters on a team can either be moved from subject to subject as a group or be integrated into mixed-ability groups for part of each school day, as long as the teachers use consistent curriculum compacting and differentiation strategies in all subjects. (Part 2 of this book explains these instructional strategies and provides a wealth of examples.)

CLUSTERING MIDDLE SCHOOL STUDENTS ON A SEPARATE TEAM

Some middle schools opt to create an entire team of identified gifted students. This approach is not technically a cluster model as this book describes it, but it is one way to group gifted students at the middle school level. In this configuration, Group 1 students make up a team, while other teams comprise students from Groups 2 through 5. When you cluster middle school students in this way, it is important to examine whether there are enough high-achieving (Group 2) students to serve as positive academic role models in all the other teams. If the creation of a full-time gifted team robs other teams of academic leadership, assigning gifted students to heterogeneous clusters may be more advantageous for the school as a whole. On the other hand, if having a self-contained team of Group 1 students does not result in other teams that lack academic leadership, this configuration will be effective, as long as the teachers on the Group 1 team consistently provide appropriate compacting and differentiation opportunities for the students.

Other Placement Considerations

Cluster Grouping in Multi-Age Classes

Multi-age classrooms can provide an ideal learning environment for the SCGM's instructional approach, as differentiated curriculum is already a natural part of the instructional repertoire. Teachers who know how to teach multi-age classes are likely to be open to bending the boundaries of grade-level expectations. They are comfortable teaching to individualized levels and modifying their instruction to varying degrees of sophistication. A multi-age setting allows teachers to help students seek work at their *own* level as teachers gain skills in determining academic entry points of the students. The SCGM works particularly well in primary multi-age classes, because there is generally more overlap in required standards in these grades than in older grades.

Serving Kindergarten and Primary Gifted Students

Regardless of whether your school formally identifies gifted students in the primary grades, consider including K–2 teachers in gifted-cluster teacher training. Having a trained kindergarten gifted-cluster teacher in place and ready to work with gifted students provides a structure that will serve gifted kindergartners and ensures that gifted students' learning needs will be factored into planning that occurs during *all* grade levels' team meetings. The same can be said for noticing and serving first- and second-grade students who are clearly gifted.

SUPERVISOR SPOTLIGHT

Parents of high-achieving students (those in Group 2) may be concerned about having their children grouped in a classroom that does not include gifted children. You can remind these parents that this classroom can be highly beneficial to their students. Refer concerned parents to the cluster grouping achievement research results summarized in the introduction (starting on page 5) and remind them that these classrooms will have some assistance provided by push-in or pull-out resource teachers.

When parents question whether their high-achieving children will be challenged in a class without gifted students, take time to meet with them to explain the research that shows how high-achieving students thrive in a setting where they can have positive experiences as academic leaders. Point out the benefits to all students when teachers are trained to modify their instructional plans and approaches to meet various student needs. Refer to page 6 for a concise overview of the benefits of the SCGM. Chapter 2 provides information on using a PDF presentation (included in the digital content) to introduce and explain the model to parents and others in the school community.

All parents need to understand that the school is committed to implementing and sustaining the SCGM with full integrity, which means:

- Teachers are trained to differentiate and compact the curriculum.
- Parents can expect these opportunities in every class.
- Students are not "tracked" together throughout the school day or term, or over the years.
- Regular screening of students allows for newcomers to be appropriately placed.
- Ongoing evaluation ensures that students continue to make progress.

Planning placement of students into the kindergarten gifted-cluster classroom can be tricky and calls for some flexibility. If the kindergarten staff uses a method to assess learning levels of all incoming kindergarten students before school starts, they can use this data for student placement in the same manner as teachers use such data for the other grade levels. Some students may enter kindergarten already having been formally identified as gifted. Although changing classrooms during the school year is generally not advised and can be problematic during the first few weeks of school, it is possible that several noticeably gifted students will emerge and can be regrouped so that they are placed with the gifted-cluster teacher.

Clustering All Special Populations

Some schools expand on the intent of the SCGM by clustering their special education students and their English language learners in the same way that they cluster their gifted students. In this approach, one teacher at a grade level will have the gifted cluster; one will have the special education cluster, and one will have the ELL cluster. In each case, the rest of the classroom will have a heterogeneous mixture of ability and achievement levels.

When New Gifted Students Enroll During the School Year

A procedure for when new gifted students enroll during the school year also needs to be in place. Principals should be involved in determining the classroom assignments whenever possible, to make sure that newly enrolling gifted students are placed in gifted-cluster classrooms. Depending on the criteria set by their state for providing services to gifted students, principals should consider placing students into the gifted-cluster class when students enroll having results of gifted testing that qualify the student for services based on existing state criteria.

SUPERVISOR SPOTLIGHT

Make your office staff aware of the policy on placing new students, so they do not automatically assign incoming students into classrooms with the fewest students without administrative advice. If a parent believes a child is gifted but has no supporting evidence, you may decide to have the student tested according to district policy, or the parents could opt for outside testing from a private psychologist if your school district or state allows for it.

Placing Students Over Time

Cluster grouping creates a system that is structured, yet fluid. School administrators and teachers can adjust the groupings yearly to reflect the needs of the school population, such as when one grade level has a large number of beginning teachers or when one of the cluster groups has an unusually high number of gifted students, or to reflect other factors, such as teacher turnover or schedules.

In this model, once students are identified as gifted, they should remain so. Identified high-potential students are considered gifted regardless of classroom performance, productivity, or behavior. (See chapter 3 for further discussion of these issues.) In the SCGM, gifted students might stay grouped together throughout their years in a school, in a similar manner as in other gifted-program models. Each year, however, they interact with new classmates as the rest of the classroom composition changes. When numbers permit, the formation of a second gifted-cluster class at a grade level can also provide opportunities for gifted students to interact with different students, as it allows for reconfiguring which of the gifted kids are together in a classroom from year to year. The students will be continually regrouped according to the structure outlined in this chapter.

Every year, teachers and administrators work through the appropriate steps to place students for the upcoming school year. Except for identified gifted students, teachers should reevaluate each student's achievement every year to ensure appropriate student placement and a balanced classroom makeup at all grade levels. Students not previously identified who show signs of potential giftedness should be given an appropriate ability test.

What the SCGM Looks Like in the Gifted-Cluster Classroom

Classrooms that contain the gifted cluster appear similar to other classrooms in which teachers actively differentiate curriculum and instruction. The students who are in the gifted cluster will not be grouped together all the time. They are frequently working in flexible groups according to their learning needs, as are all other students in the class. Not all students are working on the same material at the same time. Some students are working individually or in small groups. The teacher might be spending less time on whole-class instruction and more time facilitating learning for students working in small groups.

All differentiation and curriculum compacting opportunities are offered to all members of the class. (Differentiation and compacting, key instructional strategies in the SCGM, are explained in detail in part 2 of this book.) There will be times when some students who have not been identified as gifted are working with the gifted students on differentiated activities. There will also be times when gifted students are working on regular curriculum with students who are working at grade level. All students will move in and out of groups depending upon their needs in relation to the curriculum being taught.

As an example, if a teacher offers a voluntary pretest of a week's work in vocabulary, anyone may volunteer to take the pretest. Only those students whose pretest results demonstrate they are ready for more advanced work that week will be eligible for that advanced work, regardless of their gifted identification. Likewise, gifted students who do not pass the pretest at the required level will not automatically participate in advanced-level differentiation. The teacher, taking into consideration appropriate levels of instruction for all students, then uses continuous assessment and diagnosis to guide instruction. This is exactly what teachers are expected to do constantly for students working below proficiency levels. Doing the same for gifted students is only fair and appropriate.

Clustering Combined with Other Forms of Grouping or Gifted-Education Services

The Schoolwide Cluster Grouping Model offers an effective, budget-friendly method to provide comprehensive, ongoing gifted-education services while simultaneously meeting the learning needs of students at varying ability levels and improving overall achievement. The SCGM can readily mesh with other gifted-education programming, grouping, or inclusion practices a school may have in place or want to incorporate, including pull-out services, content-replacement options, flexible grouping, and content replacement and flexible grouping combined.

SUPERVISOR SPOTLIGHT

In a broad sense, the SCGM may be considered "structured autonomy." School administrators can make the SCGM work within their own systems. The model may look slightly different at schools within a school district, according to the numbers of gifted identified students, classes per grade level, and staff.

These services may already be in place at a school, or they may develop while the SCGM is being implemented. Having the ability to modify how the model looks in your school district helps establish teacher buy-in and strengthens the services for gifted students. Factors that determine variations of the SCGM include the availability of gifted-support teachers in the district, availability of staff assistance (such as specialists in reading, math, media, or technology), grouping practices currently occurring in the school, and other relevant considerations.

Cluster Grouping with Pull-Out Services

Gifted students need time to be together when they can just be themselves, so if a pull-out program is in place, it can be an excellent adjunct to the SCGM. On its own, if a pull-out program is the only available gifted-education service at a school, and if nothing significantly different occurs for the students when they are in the regular classroom during the rest of the day or week, this is not considered a viable gifted-education program. Combining cluster grouping *with* pull-out services ensures consistently challenging learning opportunities for gifted students, with the added benefit of providing opportunities for gifted students to meet together for activities not normally available in regular classrooms. Activities and curriculum that are offered in a pull-out class should be beyond the academic reach of other students at that grade level and might include content replacement in the core subjects for which students receive daily instruction in their advanced group. If the activities offered in the pull-out class are appropriate for all students at a grade level, they should occur in the regular classrooms.

Including pull-out services with cluster grouping benefits the teacher and other students in the classroom as well as the gifted students. When gifted students leave the classroom for pull-out programming with a gifted specialist or resource teacher, the gifted-cluster teacher has fewer students in the classroom and more time to focus attention on the specific skills that the rest of the students need addressed. Since the gifted-cluster teachers use this time to teach material the gifted students have already mastered, there's no need for the students to make up the work upon their return from the pull-out program.

Pull-out programs can provide other benefits for gifted students and their teachers. The gifted students enjoy regularly scheduled time with like-minded learning peers to work in subject areas or on extension activities that are beyond the learning level of their grade-level classmates. The arrangement is mutually beneficial to the pull-out teacher and the classroom teacher. The gifted-cluster teacher is relieved of some of the duties of providing extension activities. The pull-out teacher in turn benefits from having fewer teachers' schedules per grade level to work with (often only one—that of the gifted-cluster teacher).

It remains the responsibility of the gifted-cluster teacher to provide consistent compacting and differentiation opportunities within the classroom and the regular curriculum. The gifted pull-out teacher can be a resource to cluster teachers as they differentiate the curriculum for students who need it.

Cluster Grouping with Regrouping for Content Replacement

Content replacement is an example of a daily pull-out program in which the instruction gifted students receive when leaving the cluster classroom replaces grade-level instruction in one of the major content areas, usually math or reading. In schools using content replacement, all classes at a particular grade level teach math and reading at the same time. Gifted students leave the classroom daily for their math and reading instruction with the gifted specialist or gifted resource teacher.

Cluster Grouping with Flexible Grouping

Another combination schools use with great results is cluster grouping combined with flexible grouping. Flexible grouping mainly occurs for math and reading instruction and requires all teachers at a grade level to schedule the math or reading instruction at the same time. In this variation, the grade-level teachers form flexible groups based on the students' skills-mastery levels. All students in the grade level then change classrooms, or regroup, according to abilities or skills mastered. Forming the flexible groups requires that teachers use ongoing assessment to determine the mastery levels of students. Teachers use school- or district-adopted assessments to pretest students when creating groups and determining placement. Students retest periodically, as a group or individually, to determine if a change in groups is indicated. The teachers at the grade level, or even between grade levels, work together to plan instruction, making flexible grouping truly a team approach. Students change groups based on their readiness and mastery of the specific content being covered at that time.

In this grouping method, the groups are fluid and are not determined by gifted-identification status. With flexible grouping, students are placed into groups based on readiness and skills-mastery levels for a particular subject area only, and then they are regrouped back to their regular cluster class when that subject area instruction concludes. Flexible grouping allows teachers to specifically target instruction to the needs of different groups at different levels. It does not replace the broader arrangements of cluster groups within classrooms, but rather organizes students into flexible groups where students can learn at their current level at any given point in time.

Cluster Grouping with Both Content Replacement and Flexible Grouping

Cluster grouping with content replacement and flexible grouping occurs when gifted students leave the gifted-cluster classroom for math or reading instruction with a gifted specialist or resource teacher. The grade level then forms flexible groups with the remaining students based on mastery of skills being addressed. The system provides smaller class sizes with a very narrow range of ability, allowing instruction focused on the specific needs of the students.

Cluster Grouping with an Inclusion Model

The SCGM is totally compatible with an inclusion model that integrates students with exceptional educational needs into regular classes. Students with special education needs have often been clustered in the same classroom for various reasons. For example, if a school is housing a program for students with hearing impairments, and those students spend much of their time in regular classrooms, it would make no sense to split them up so that each class at a grade level had one or two of the children. When these students are clustered together, their special education teacher, whose expertise is in teaching children with hearing impairments, can work as a coach or co-teacher with the regular classroom teacher. The students themselves feel secure being with other children who have a similar learning challenge. The hearing-impairment specialists have fewer teachers to coach. When we cluster gifted students together, we do so for exactly the same reasons. In their book *A Teacher's Guide to Flexible Grouping and Collaborative Learning,* Dina Brulles and Karen Brown provide additional methods for grouping students.

Questions Teachers, Parents, or Other School Stakeholders May Ask

Why not assign gifted students evenly to all classes? Can I create small groups of at least three gifted students in all classes if I have the numbers to evenly distribute them?

No. When the structure of the SCGM model is changed, the likelihood of experiencing the desired outcomes is greatly diminished. Each teacher would have a fuller range of abilities in the classroom, which would lessen the potential for achievement gains across the board. Opportunities for leadership in gifted education at each grade level would be significantly reduced because there would be fewer teachers who specialize in serving the needs of gifted students. This scenario would result in less accountability for teachers to facilitate academic progress for gifted students. Staff members would not be as likely to identify students as gifted, because a few of these students would be represented in each of the classrooms. When we do not identify students as gifted, we are less likely to recognize, acknowledge, and address their learning and affective needs.

Gifted students benefit from learning together and need to be placed with similar students in their areas of strength. Cluster grouping allows gifted students to learn together while avoiding permanent grouping arrangements for students of other ability levels.

When teachers try to meet the diverse learning needs of all students in totally heterogeneous classes, it becomes extremely difficult to provide appropriately challenging instruction to all students. Often, the students of highest ability are expected to make it on their own. When a teacher has a large group of gifted students in the classroom, taking the time to make appropriate provisions for them seems more realistic.

The research of Marcia Gentry and Dina Brulles shows that gifted students who are clustered demonstrate high achievement because they experience more consistent challenge in their learning activities (Gentry 1999; Brulles 2005). Their scores on achievement tests document significant achievement gains rather than lost ground, as has been the case in some schools where gifted students are not placed in gifted clusters or are not consistently challenged in other ways.

Won't the creation of a cluster group rob the other classes of academic leadership?
No, because the SCGM ensures that *all* classes have academic leadership. When a cluster of gifted students is placed in one class, and a cluster of high-achieving students not identified as gifted is placed in every other class, all classes have students who can serve as academic role models.

High-achieving students in the classes without the gifted students have new opportunities to become academic leaders. When these students are in the same classes with identified gifted students, their achievement potential is often overshadowed by the presence of highly verbal, highly competitive classmates. High achievers can serve as academic leaders and role models for average-performing students in the class, because they usually demonstrate a stronger work ethic to achieve the high grades they earn.

Research on role modeling indicates that to be effective, role models cannot be drastically discrepant in ability from those who are supposed to be motivated by them (Schunk 1987). A familiar analogy can clarify this concept: Imagine your first day of skiing. Because you are a novice, you accidentally get on the wrong lift. It takes you to the top of the "black diamond" ski slope, where only the most daring and athletic skiers venture. You watch the experts for a few minutes as they soar through the air in what appear to be gravity-free gymnastics, land on their skis, and sail down the mountain without even getting any snow on themselves. After watching the experts ski, what are the chances that you will ski today? Probably very low. But if you relocate to the beginner hill and watch other novices try to ski, fall down, get up again, and make gradual progress, the chances of your attempting to ski today are vastly improved. The same principle applies to the way the SCGM places students in all classes. Low-achieving students are more likely to be motivated by others who are competent and hardworking but not gifted.

Won't the presence of the clustered gifted students inhibit other students in that class and negatively affect their achievement?
No. Many cluster teachers report that there is general improvement in overall achievement for the entire class. This suggests the exciting possibility that when teachers learn how to provide what gifted students need and offer modified versions of the same opportunities to the entire class, expectations and levels of learning rise for all students.

How should gifted students be identified for the gifted-cluster group?
Identification should be conducted each spring, using a standardized ability test preferably administered by someone trained in gifted education. Ideally, identification instruments will include verbal, quantitative, and nonverbal identification tools. A combination of traditional measures such as standardized tests, criterion-referenced measures, and end-of-the-year assessments may be used to identify the achievement levels of students in Groups 2 through 5. Schools that use only one instrument for identification run the risk of excluding some gifted students. For example, using only a nonverbal test of intelligence could leave unidentified those gifted learners who are highly verbal and who may not score well at all on a test of spatial abilities. Likewise, the sole use of ability tests that rely on English language proficiency will prevent some gifted students from receiving educational opportunities that are commensurate with their abilities. (Chapter 3 provides an overview of strategies and instruments for identifying gifted students.)

SUPERVISOR
SPOTLIGHT

The SCGM will not work in schools with principals who honor parent requests for teachers. Honoring such requests makes it impossible to maintain a balance of ability and achievement throughout the grade level.

How can gifted students' progress be tracked?
Maintain differentiated education plans (DEPs) for gifted students and file DEPs with these students' other ongoing records. (For sample DEP forms, see pages 221–224 at the end of chapter 8.) In some schools, teachers also develop more generic plans for the gifted-cluster students as a group. Specific plans describing curricular interventions for individual students might also be recorded on compactor record sheets (described in chapter 5). The DEPs note the students' areas of giftedness and briefly describe the modifications planned for the student or the group. It is important to share DEPs with parents during conferences. This information will help students' future teachers know what strategies were successful with the gifted-cluster students and will also provide documentation of learning that subsequent teachers can use to guide future instruction.

Is clustering feasible only in elementary school? Is it mainly for larger schools and districts?
No. Educators may use cluster grouping at all K–8 grade levels, in all subject areas, and in schools of all sizes. However, the structure will vary when incorporated at the middle school level. Gifted students may be clustered in one section of any heterogeneous class or team, especially when there are not enough students to form an advanced section for a particular subject. Cluster grouping is also a welcome option in rural settings, where districts may have a smaller student base, minimal funds allotted for gifted education, fewer programming options, and more multi-age classrooms.

How can we determine whether the SCGM is right for our school?
You will need to consider a variety of factors when you are determining changes to your school's or district's gifted-education services. An informal needs assessment can begin the process that will guide your planning. In your needs assessment, you will want to include the components described in the "Gifted-Education Programming" reproducible form on page 32. Discussing these planning points with a committee made up of teachers, principals, parents, and gifted students will help you determine what you need to accomplish. This chapter and the introduction contain the basic information you will need to decide whether the SCGM is a good match for your school's needs.

SUMMARY

This chapter has set forth the key components of a Schoolwide Cluster Grouping Model that provides full-time services for gifted students while improving student achievement across all classes and grade levels. We have described specific strategies for:

- placing all students in classrooms to reach optimal achievement outcomes
- incorporating the SCGM into other forms of grouping or gifted-education programming
- answering questions and communicating information about the model to teachers and parents
- taking steps to determine whether and how to begin implementing the SCGM

Throughout the chapter, we have reinforced the concept of structured autonomy. The SCGM provides a structure within which schools can make adjustments to best fit their needs.

Gifted-Education Programming

How to Know If Change Is Necessary in Your School

1. Analyze the current situation.

Does your state have mandates or guidelines that govern gifted-education services?

What is considered best practice in the field of gifted education? You may consult the NAGC National Standards in Gifted and Talented Education at www.nagc.org or contact the gifted-education organization in your state.

What gifted-education services are currently taking place in the school or district?

What is working well?

What needs analysis and intervention to work better?

2. Create a vision as a starting point.

What are the short- and long-term goals for the gifted-education program? (Goals should be both ideal and reasonable. Know that the ideal model of services develops over time.)

What are considered acceptable phases to accomplish this goal?

What existing structures or initiatives are in place in the school or district, and how might implementing the SCGM support those structures and initiatives?

3. Define an action plan.

What is the general plan for the gifted-education program?

What is the projected timeline for delivering and implementing the model in your school or district?

Who will be responsible for which parts of the model's implementation?

What are the specific steps necessary for implementation in the short and long term?

Grade-Level Data by School

1. Principals: Ask each teacher to identify the ability and achievement levels of her or his students.
2. Teachers: Working with your grade-level team, use your school achievement data to indicate the numbers of students in each group for your current students.
3. Principals: Combine the data for each grade level and record the total numbers here.
4. Placement team: Use this data to construct balanced classes for next year with the SCGM Classroom Composition Planning Form (pages 34–35).

Current Grades	Group 1: Gifted	Group 2: High Achieving	Group 3: Average	Group 4: Below Average	Group 5: Far Below Average
Kindergarten					
Grade 1					
Grade 2					
Grade 3					
Grade 4					
Grade 5					
Grade 6					
Grade 7					
Grade 8					

SCGM Classroom Composition Planning Form

School Name: ______________________________

Classroom (grade, teacher, or other identifier)	Group 1: Gifted	Group 2: High Achieving	Group 3: Average	Group 4: Below Average	Group 5: Far Below Average	Totals
A:						
B:						
C:						
D:						
E:						
F:						
G:						
H:						
I:						

CONTINUED > > >

SCGM Classroom Composition Planning Form, continued

Classroom (grade, teacher, or other identifier)	Group 1: Gifted	Group 2: High Achieving	Group 3: Average	Group 4: Below Average	Group 5: Far Below Average	Totals
J:						
K:						
L:						
M:						
N:						
O:						
P:						
Q:						
R:						

2

Planning and Introducing the SCGM

GUIDING QUESTIONS

- What are the steps for implementing the SCGM?
- What is the best way to communicate information about the SCGM to staff, parents, and others in the school community?
- How does the SCGM incorporate the essential components of gifted programs?
- How can support for the model be established and maintained?

Once the decision to implement the SCGM has been made, it is a good practice to form a committee to study the needs of the students and school (or schools, if the implementation will be districtwide). Ideally, the committee will consist of one or two parents of gifted students, a parent of a student who has not been identified as gifted, two potential gifted-cluster teachers, and the principal. If it is a district committee, it should contain two school principals from the elementary level, a middle school principal, several potential gifted-cluster teachers, parents of gifted students, parents of students not identified as gifted, gifted specialists or mentors, and the district gifted coordinator or other administrator in charge of gifted education. This committee should plan to meet regularly throughout the school year while developing and implementing the SCGM plan for the school or district. Throughout the process, committee members should communicate concerns of the groups they represent in order to create a plan that can be supported by all parties. The committee should continue to meet periodically following the implementation year to build, support, and strengthen the model. The committee's work will include some or all of the following activities:

- Follow a needs assessment process to determine how the SCGM can best be implemented in that particular school or district.
- Become familiar with all components of the SCGM and their application.
- Determine a timeline for communicating about and implementing the model.
- Develop and implement an evaluation process for the model.

Step-by-Step SCGM Implementation

Making sure that all staff members understand how the model works helps bring people on board and create a system that becomes part of the school culture. Careful scheduling of testing, professional development, and communication facilitates progress. Having the following information planned out in advance shows commitment to creating and sustaining the model in ways that support the education of gifted students and reflect the school's or district's needs:

1. Develop a timeline for implementation similar to the one on pages 37–38.
2. Determine the grade levels to be included year by year.
3. Identify training needed before implementation. (Content from this book can be used for training. In particular, see chapter 3 for background on traits, behaviors, social and emotional needs, and identification of gifted students; see chapters 5 and 6 for differentiation and curriculum compacting strategies.)
4. Determine criteria and a process for staffing (see chapter 4).
5. Develop a plan for staff development and training (see chapter 7).
6. Plan progress evaluation benchmarks for the first three years (see chapter 8).

Developing a Timeline

Many districts will choose to implement the SCGM across all elementary and middle schools. The SCGM may initially be established at one or two schools in a district. This is sometimes a planned pilot study, or it can become an informal one. When other district schools see the pilot school's success, the model typically expands to include schools throughout the district.

FIGURE 2-1 Establishing the SCGM: Year 1—Planning Year

Time of Year	Tasks
August–September	Form committee to determine school's or district's gifted-education needs. Plan parent night seminars for the year (topics and dates).
October–January	Plan with principal(s). Determine the grade levels for initial (and subsequent) implementation. Hold informational meetings about the SCGM for administrators, teaching staff, and parents. Provide professional development: gifted-education basics.
February–April	Make cluster-teacher designations for upcoming year. Provide professional development: cluster grouping book studies, workshops, in-services for cluster teachers. Administer spring gifted testing to identify students for gifted clusters.
May	Make student placements for upcoming year. Set up classes for upcoming fall. Provide professional development: teaching strategies. Plan summer professional development.
June–July	Provide professional development: curriculum development. Schedule gifted-cluster teacher meetings for upcoming year.

FIGURE 2-2 **Establishing the SCGM: Year 2—Implementing Year**

Time of Year	Tasks
August–September	Gifted-cluster teachers meet to plan and share curriculum. Gifted-cluster teachers send welcome letters to parents. Set up gifted-cluster teacher meeting dates for the current year. Begin holding meetings. Arrange and administer fall gifted testing. Provide placement information to office staff. Give cluster teachers guidance on parent communication.
October–January	Collect student identification information for an SCGM database. Provide professional development: offerings in gifted education. Hold monthly gifted specialist meetings and monthly gifted-cluster teacher meetings.
February–April	Provide professional development: cluster grouping book studies, workshops, in-services. Make gifted-cluster teacher selections for upcoming year. Provide additional training for proposed new gifted-cluster teachers. Administer spring gifted testing to identify students for gifted clusters. Hold monthly gifted specialist meetings and monthly gifted-cluster teacher meetings. Plan for creating classroom compositions for upcoming year.
May	Make student placements for upcoming year. Create budget for upcoming year. Plan next fall's professional development. Schedule gifted specialist meetings for upcoming year. Hold monthly gifted specialist meetings and monthly gifted-cluster teacher meetings.
June–July	Provide professional development: curriculum development and teaching strategies. Schedule gifted-cluster teacher meetings for upcoming year. Complete program evaluation.

Regardless of whether implementation is at one school or all, the information in this chapter will help guide the process.

The two charts on pages 37 and 38, one for the year spent planning the implementation of the model and another for when it is in place, describe the sequence of necessary tasks for establishing the SCGM. Use the information in the charts as a guide when creating your implementation plan. Seek feedback and input from the principals and then from teachers when implementing the model throughout the school or district.

You may discover that your school district prefers to follow a longer-term plan to implement the SCGM. If so, begin by spending a full year providing information to administrators, teachers, and parents.

The second year would then be the planning year, as described in the chart on page 37. The planning year would include providing professional learning opportunities, scheduling informational meetings for all stakeholders, planning a timeline for implementation with benchmarks, and beginning the SCGM in at least one school in the district (to serve as a model). Implementation throughout the school district would then occur in the third year. You would continue holding ongoing informational meetings and supporting teachers with professional learning opportunities during this implementation year.

Tools for Introducing the SCGM to Principals, Teachers, and Other Staff

- Use the PDF presentation provided in the digital content to present the model.
- Provide staff with copies of this book. Go through the table of contents, which gives a detailed outline of the model and the book. Focus on the benefits presented on page 6, the overview of the SCGM (pages 14–15), and the example of classroom compositions (page 16).
- Post the "Frequently Asked Questions About the SCGM" (pages 49–50) and make this reproducible available to each staff member.

Sharing Information with Principals, Teaching Staff, and Parents

For a districtwide or schoolwide model, the individuals in charge of gifted education should start providing information about the SCGM to principals and staff early in the fall of the planning year. When the model is being implemented districtwide, schedule time into principals' meetings throughout the year to provide information on cluster grouping. These meetings will give principals opportunities to communicate with their staff and parents about concerns and questions that may arise. Include information regarding the characteristics and needs of gifted learners. Then describe the SCGM and explain how this model addresses the needs of all students, including gifted students.

If your district is considering implementation of the SCGM, help principals and staff members make specific plans for managing the model in their schools. Introduce the model at school staff meetings, and answer questions and provide information so that staff members understand how the SCGM can improve students' experiences and performance at school and what this will mean for teachers. Each school has its own culture, and different staff may react differently to the model. For some, the SCGM will be a mere adjustment of current practices. For others, it will be a significant departure from previous approaches.

Principals should begin identifying which teachers to assign to the gifted-cluster classrooms by early spring if possible. Begin with the assumption that just one gifted-cluster teacher will be needed at each grade level. Others can be added if gifted testing yields large numbers of identified students in a single grade level. Chapter 4 (pages 90–95) includes guidelines for determining who would be good candidates for gifted-cluster teacher positions. Professional development for gifted-cluster teachers should also begin at this time.

Success in the SCGM hinges on the preparation of the gifted-cluster teachers and the classroom placements. Ideally, some professional development will have occurred during the spring of the planning year to prepare new cluster teachers. Principals can assist by arranging gifted-cluster teacher workdays or work periods at a school or in the district office. The summer months are a perfect time for gifted-cluster teachers to work together to develop plans and curriculum for specific grade levels. At these workshops, teachers can combine their knowledge and experience in gifted education, differentiated teaching strategies, and resources to create and share lessons. Encourage and support gifted-cluster teachers by providing professional growth credit for time spent preparing for the upcoming school year.

To build awareness and support from within the school system, provide information to classroom teachers, school counselors, psychologists, administrators, and office staff. These groups need information on the description and benefits of the program for all students, the methods by which gifted students will be identified and served, and staffing details. They need to feel confident that the SCGM provides an appropriate way to serve not only the school's gifted students but all the school's students. Communicating information about these topics to the entire school staff will demonstrate that the SCGM is fair to all students and teachers and will help staff understand how the model can raise student achievement at all ability levels and in all classrooms.

Parents will initially have a number of questions about cluster grouping. Parents of gifted students may wonder if the SCGM is a "real" gifted program. That is, they may wonder if it can engage and challenge their gifted children, if the teachers are sufficiently prepared to teach gifted students in a regular classroom, and how this model will impact their children's learning. Prepare in advance for questions and concerns. Having accurate information for parents and teachers increases the success of the SCGM at your schools. Providing ongoing information and opportunities for parents and teachers to ask questions demonstrates that there has been thorough and thoughtful planning for this model. This facilitates acceptance by all concerned groups.

Parents of students in Groups 1 and 2 are the largest stakeholders in the SCGM. The parents of students in Group 2 may feel that it is in their children's best interest to be placed in the same classroom as the identified gifted students. While parents of students in both of these groups need information about how the model will impact their children, it is not necessary to draw significant attention from the entire community to the SCGM. It is more important to anticipate that there will be requests for information and to have that information at hand to share with concerned parties. Make information about the SCGM available when needed, but do not present it in a way that places undue focus on it. It is not necessary to give this topic any more public consideration than is given to providing ethnic or gender balances in classes. Schoolwide cluster grouping does not represent a drastic difference in the way schools operate. It is a structure that, when implemented conscientiously, ensures an appropriate education for a school's gifted learners while providing academic benefits for other students as well.

Tools for Introducing the SCGM to Parents

- Provide parents a copy of "A Note to Parents" (page 232). This parent note helps parents understand the key principles of the SCGM and encourages their support.
- Share the list of "Frequently Asked Questions About the SCGM" (pages 49–50) with any parent who has questions or concerns.
- Send information to your parents of gifted-identified students explaining the SCGM and welcoming them into their gifted children's school experience. (See sample letter on page 48.)

Developing and Maintaining Support for the SCGM

Historically, school districts offered gifted-education services as a pull-out enrichment program, a content-replacement program in which students studied advanced curriculum, or a self-contained classroom program. By contrast, the SCGM has the advantage of providing full-time services without the costs of additional personnel. Furthermore, gifted students who are underachieving or nonproductive, have learning differences, or are from culturally diverse groups are much more likely to be identified and served in this model. The SCGM provides these full-time services in an inclusion model while costing the school or district little and potentially raising student achievement for all students. These latter two factors—funding and student achievement—are of high priority to all stakeholders and can help develop and maintain support for the model.

Garnering Support for the SCGM in the School Community

As noted earlier in the book, teachers support the model when they realize they are not losing their bright, capable students, because *all* classrooms have either gifted or high-achieving students. Gifted-cluster teachers appreciate that the gifted students are rarely out of their classroom for alternative learning experiences. Once they develop their understanding of how gifted students learn, they adapt their instruction to the appropriate levels and needs. Likewise, in classrooms that do not have a gifted cluster, teachers understand that the narrower range of student abilities in their classrooms allows them more time to address the learning needs of all their students.

School counselors and school psychologists are more likely to support the SCGM when they see improvement in the emotional, behavioral, and motivational issues often associated with gifted students whose learning needs are not being met. Additionally, these professionals appreciate seeing the personal growth that results when high-achieving students take on leadership roles. They understand that when curriculum and instruction are appropriately challenging and when students work together with their intellectual peers, the students are motivated to engage in rigorous learning activities. When counseling staff are informed about how students are identified and placed in the cluster classrooms, these staff can provide valuable support to the classroom teachers and to parents. This is especially true in the case of twice-exceptional gifted students.

Media and library staff members support the SCGM, because they have the opportunity to become an essential resource to facilitate independent study for gifted students. Office staff appreciate the inclusionary aspect of the SCGM, because it means they will never be in the position of having to explain to a parent why a child of high ability has been excluded from gifted-education services. Everyone appreciates that the training needed by gifted-cluster teachers is available for all staff and understands how the strategies presented can potentially benefit all students.

Parents support the SCGM for several reasons. Parents of gifted students appreciate knowing that their children's learning needs are being regularly accommodated without the students feeling uncomfortably singled out. Parents of students who are high achieving and far below average realize that their children may achieve at higher levels when the gifted students are not in the class, because their children have more of the teacher's time and attention. Parents of high-achieving students are also quick to realize that their children have more opportunities to become class leaders than they do when they are mixed with gifted students. Parents of students with learning challenges come to appreciate the fact that their children's teachers have more time to devote to their instruction in this model.

SUPERVISOR SPOTLIGHT

An effective media specialist can support the SCGM by providing assistance for independent study and research projects. Some media specialists may be able to arrange a space in the media center designated for students who are working on independent projects and learning activities.

Compatibility of the SCGM with Essential Gifted-Program Components

To fully support the SCGM, educators and parents of gifted students need to understand the ways in which the model comprises key components and practices of effective gifted programs. The work of Dr. Barbara Clark describes the essential components of a comprehensive gifted-education program: flexible grouping, curriculum differentiation, continuous progress, intellectual peer interaction, continuity, and teachers with specialized training in gifted education (Clark 2013). Each of these six components is present in the SCGM.

1. Flexible grouping. Flexible grouping ensures that students have opportunities to work with their intellectual peers based on areas of interest and levels of readiness. In the SCGM, flexible groups are created in the class and among classes in the grade level, and teachers are trained in various methods of flexible grouping and collaborative learning.

2. Curriculum differentiation. Gifted students generally have advanced learning abilities, making them capable of learning at levels beyond same-age peers and grade-level standards. This usually means that they need differentiated or accelerated curriculum. Differentiated curriculum and instruction address the content students are learning, their learning pace, the processes they use to learn, the products on which they work, the ways in which their work and learning levels are assessed, and the actual learning environment. Differentiation is at the heart of teaching in the SCGM. Effective cluster teachers participate in professional learning opportunities that address how to challenge gifted students through the use of curriculum compacting and differentiation opportunities.

3. Continuous progress. To bring struggling students up to grade-level standards, the teacher starts where the students are and moves them forward, one step at a time, so they experience continuous progress in their learning. Gifted students deserve the same consideration. All students should expect at least one year's academic growth for each year in school. When gifted students begin their school year, they may likely have mastered the majority of the required standards even before instruction on the grade-level curriculum. This makes it impossible for them to continuously progress unless their teacher uses compacting and differentiation strategies.

Within the SCGM, gifted-cluster teachers meet regularly to learn together, troubleshoot problems that emerge, and share information about curriculum and strategies. This practice helps teachers become more flexible and comfortable with differentiated instruction. With this collaboration and peer support, teachers are more likely to support their gifted students' learning needs in all their subject areas and plan so that challenging instruction occurs in a consistent manner.

4. Intellectual peer interaction. Throughout life, we all seek like-minded people with whom to interact, as we are much more comfortable with people who understand us and accept us as we are. Academically, gifted students have little in common with their age peers unless those peers are also advanced learners. Clustering gifted students makes it more likely that they will take advantage of advanced learning opportunities provided by the teacher, since they will have peers with whom they learn. Gifted students become motivated by the challenge of working alongside others with similar abilities. In the SCGM, all students have intellectual peers in *all* the content areas by virtue of the model's structure.

5. Continuity. Some schools provide pull-out gifted programs for as little as thirty or forty-five minutes per week. Other schools have only before- or after-school offerings for their gifted students. Many schools provide services to gifted students only in certain grades. Program options and levels of service may change yearly with new teachers, administrators, and district priorities, which often relate to funding and staffing allocations. In these scenarios, gifted students do not receive continuity in their instruction. Advanced and differentiated instruction for gifted students should occur whenever students are identified as gifted rather than when a particular service is offered by the school.

In the SCGM, cluster grouping can take place in all grades, providing continuity for gifted students. The teachers collaborate as a vertical team comprising the gifted-cluster teachers at all grade levels in the school. This vertical collaboration provides opportunities for teachers to communicate across grade levels and can lead to a smoother transition for students from one grade to the next.

The vertical team, or gifted-cluster strand, understands and accepts that curriculum is not always grade-level specific. The team collaborates so that students can have continuity in their instruction regardless of the grade level from which the content is derived. This team approach ensures that each year, teachers are cognizant of curricular adjustments that were made for students in the previous grade level. Teachers also use cumulative records to determine the type and level of compacting, differentiation, enrichment, and acceleration their current students have had in the past in specific content areas.

6. Teachers with specialized training in gifted education. Educators in most states can receive the highest available degree in education without ever being required to take a class in gifted education. This means that many teachers and administrators know little about how gifted students think, feel, or learn, or about how to provide for their exceptional learning needs. Ongoing, specialized training to work effectively with these atypical learners is essential. In the SCGM, administrators can purposefully plan professional development opportunities that build on teachers' experiences and previous training and can direct that training to the level and needs of the staff. Some schools and districts develop professional learning communities (PLCs) around the topic of challenging their gifted learners.

Teacher Engagement and Growth: Building a School Culture That Supports the SCGM

In this model, all classes are purposefully balanced, so a range of student ability or achievement exists in every classroom. The chart on page 16 clearly illustrates how all students at a grade level can be purposefully placed so that each teacher in the grade level has a more manageable range of student performance than would exist in a totally heterogeneous class. Balancing homeroom classrooms in this way is very comforting to teachers (and to parents). Everyone can see that all classes have strong academic role models with a slightly narrowed range of abilities and achievement levels.

Participation in ongoing school-based study groups empowers teachers to try new strategies and to coach each other toward effective implementation. One particularly exciting approach is classroom action research, a process in which participants systematically and carefully examine their own educational practice using research techniques. Teachers who take part in action research are likely to make lasting changes in their own classrooms and with their own students because of the effects they observe. Action research is an important component of PLCs. Several resources listed on pages 51 and 52 can be helpful in making sure the most effective benefits of collaborative learning approaches are recognized and implemented.

Teacher Rotation

Once a teacher has been designated as a gifted-cluster teacher, she* retains that assignment for two to three years. The first year of any new program requires extra time and attention for the teacher to learn and become comfortable teaching in the model. Many gifted-cluster teachers wish to enjoy the fruits of their labors for at least another year. Some principals elect to rotate the gifted-cluster teacher assignment among those teachers interested and willing to participate in professional learning that is appropriate for teaching gifted students. Bear in mind that professional development in strategies for working with high-ability learners benefits many students, not only those identified as gifted. For that reason, making sure that all teachers have at least some basic training in gifted-education practices will improve teaching and learning for all teachers and students.

Rotating gifted-cluster teachers can be helpful to prevent members of the school community from perceiving that only one teacher at a grade level is capable of teaching gifted students. When gifted students move into the district, principals should be able to reassure parents that compacting and differentiation opportunities are available with all teachers in any classroom. Some teachers may not want to have a class with a gifted cluster in it, and that should be respected when possible. Some teachers who are reluctant to teach gifted students have a special talent in motivating and successfully teaching students who struggle to learn. These teachers may be relieved that their classes do not contain any identified gifted students, so they have more time to work with the students they particularly love to teach. However, these teachers can still benefit from understanding the emotional and behavioral needs of gifted students and from working together with other teachers to learn classroom differentiation strategies. For this reason, we recommend professional learning opportunities in gifted education and differentiated instruction for all teachers over the course of time.

Performance Pay and the SCGM

Some states or districts link teacher pay to student performance. Throughout this book, we have documented the potential for significant achievement gains for *all* students at a school using the SCGM, including students who are not placed in the gifted-cluster classrooms. When performance pay is linked to academic growth for all students at a grade level, rather than just for those scoring below proficiency levels, then performance pay and cluster grouping are completely compatible.

Principals can build school support for the SCGM by encouraging a grade-level team approach when monitoring student achievement. Principals can support this team approach by not comparing individual teachers' standardized student test scores. Administrators should focus instead on a growth model that monitors individual progress for all students, including those who are at the top of their class in achievement. This encourages teachers to support one another toward the common goal of grade-level achievement.

Expectations and Involvement of Parents of Gifted Students

Parents of gifted children commonly seek information about giftedness, gifted education, and resources available to them in their communities. Understandably, they seek this information even more diligently when they perceive that their children are not receiving challenging instruction. Over time, parents can become even more

*Throughout this book, we alternate use of gender pronouns *she* and *he, him* and *her* when describing adults and children. This is for ease of reading only. The information discussed applies to everyone.

knowledgeable about gifted education than their children's teachers are.

Parenting gifted kids is an ongoing challenge and can be emotionally and physically draining. It can be difficult for parents to have to align themselves with school expectations that are in conflict with their children's advanced learning needs. Some parents regretfully find themselves advising their gifted children simply to comply while at school rather than to advocate for themselves. When parents of gifted students find that their child's teacher actually understands this dilemma and provides consistent compacting and differentiation opportunities in the gifted-cluster class, they can breathe a sigh of relief.

Parents have a right to expect that a school's or district's mission statement is intended for their child as well as others. Parents of gifted students should expect those same intentions for their children. For example, if the mission statement promises that all students will be challenged to develop their potential, parents of gifted students have a right to expect those same outcomes for their children.

SUPERVISOR SPOTLIGHT

When holding informational meetings for parents of gifted students, use the tools suggested on page 40 to familiarize parents with the approach of the SCGM and to answer their questions and concerns. Also include the following:

- basic information on what it means to be gifted (Information from chapter 3, pages 55–61, may be helpful.)
- samples of typical extension activities created for differentiation in a gifted-cluster classroom
- a list of resources such as the reproducible one on pages 51–52 (Also include any available local resources.)

One common conflict between parents and the school centers on the issue of whether the gifted students are completing all their schoolwork. Parents and students know that much of the grade-level work is redundant for gifted students. They greatly appreciate consistent opportunities for students to receive full credit for the grade-level standards they have already mastered and for their ability to learn new material much faster than their age peers.

Work proactively with the parents of your school's gifted students. Encourage them to seek additional supports and opportunities for their children. Make copies of the handout on pages 51–52 to provide support for advocacy. Make parents aware of specific resources that are available to help them seek out-of-school experiences for their children too. Take advantage of some of the knowledge and resources parents have discovered by encouraging them to share their findings with school staff.

Invite parents of identified gifted students to an informational meeting about cluster grouping. Make every effort to have the meeting flyers and agenda available in languages appropriate to the school population. Use the PDF presentation in the digital content to describe the model in detail. Parents will appreciate knowing that the school has a vision, a plan, and support for their children's services. Accept that parents may be skeptical when they are told that all necessary differentiation will be available in their child's gifted-cluster classroom. Parents who have had previous experience with a pull-out program or self-contained program may need reassurance that the gifted-cluster teachers have participated in professional development focused on gifted education and differentiating curriculum for gifted learners. At the informational meeting, share professional development plans with parents so they feel confident that their children's teachers are being trained appropriately in how to teach gifted students in the regular classroom. If possible, introduce the gifted-cluster teachers and allow time for parents and teachers to meet and chat.

A national organization called Supporting the Emotional Needs of the Gifted (SENG) provides training for parents and teachers who want to lead support groups for parents of gifted children at their schools. Parents who join the SENG group attend training to understand the social and emotional needs of their gifted children so they can provide support for other parents who are experiencing similar challenges. After the training, SENG groups meet at the school or district sites for a period of eight to ten weeks, during which time they discuss issues such as motivation, discipline, stress management, communication of feelings, and relationship issues within the family. The SENG groups increase parents' awareness that talented children and their families have special emotional needs, and they enhance parenting skills for nurturing the emotional development of gifted children.

An active SENG group supports teachers as well as parents, because it eases some of the responsibility of communicating information about the social and emotional needs of the gifted students they are teaching. By providing parents with opportunities to learn more about these shared concerns of gifted children, SENG groups strengthen relationships between parents and teachers. The reproducible handout on page 51 provides more information about SENG.

Communication to Parents from School Office Staff

Parents routinely call schools to inquire about gifted-education services, and office staff are on the front lines for fielding parents' questions. For this reason, office staffers need to understand the cluster grouping concept so they can enthusiastically support it when they are communicating with parents who are registering their children for school. Give office personnel an orientation in the basics of the SCGM and provide tools that they can use to give accurate information to callers and visitors. Prepare a guide that office staff can use to describe the school's gifted services and the SCGM (see **figure 2-3**). Referring to the prepared information, office staff will be able to address routine questions, such

FIGURE 2-3 **Referrals for SCGM Contact Information**

Office staff should refer callers to:	For information regarding:
The gifted-cluster teacher	How the teacher will address the needs of the gifted students in the classroom
The gifted specialist (gifted mentor)*	What it means to be gifted The school's testing and identification procedures How curriculum is differentiated in the school Parent resources
The principal	The school's gifted-cluster teachers Student placements How the school supports the SCGM
The district gifted coordinator*	How the district supports gifted education The district's testing and identification procedures Professional development for gifted-cluster teachers District and state policies Additional parent resources

* These staff positions are described in chapter 4.

as a description of the SCGM and other gifted services in the school, testing dates, and contact information for others who can answer more in-depth questions. Office staff will appreciate being able to direct parents to the appropriate people for additional information.

Introduction Letters to Parents from the Gifted-Cluster Teachers

Parents of gifted students appreciate hearing from their child's classroom teacher about how their child's learning needs will be addressed during the school day. As the new school year approaches, the gifted-cluster teacher can proactively address parents' questions and concerns by sending home a letter describing how the gifted students' needs will be addressed in the classroom. This letter welcomes the child to the teacher's gifted-cluster classroom and briefly explains how gifted students are served in the SCGM. In addition to explaining how they will differentiate learning for their gifted students, gifted-cluster teachers may also choose to indicate other available supports for gifted students, such as media-specialist services, technology teachers, the school's fine arts program, and extracurricular activities.

A sample teacher's welcome letter is provided on page 48. The letter communicates to parents the following key facts:

- The teacher is aware of the child's gifted-identification status.
- The teacher is taking responsibility for addressing the academic needs of gifted students in the gifted-cluster classroom by using specifically described compacting and differentiation activities.
- The school supports cluster grouping and is making an effort to ensure that gifted students feel welcome and comfortable.

The Critical Role of the Building Principal

The proactive support of the building principal is essential to the success of the SCGM. Principals can actively demonstrate support by arranging time for gifted-cluster teachers to plan together, by providing staff development, and by attending gifted-cluster teacher meetings whenever possible. Principals may want to be made aware of any announcements, newsletters, or flyers that the gifted-cluster teachers send home.

It takes administrative involvement and active participation to support the SCGM. While it may sound like a daunting goal, remember that implementing any program begins slowly and develops over time. The development of the SCGM depends on the staff's experience level and understanding of gifted education. Seeking staff input on how the SCGM will appear at each school strengthens the model and can help ensure its effectiveness. The level of involvement of the school's staff members and the understanding of the parent community can reflect the principal's commitment to schoolwide cluster grouping.

SUMMARY

This chapter has provided specific information about how to:

- use a two-year timeline for planning and implementing the SCGM in a school or district
- describe how the essential components of gifted-education programs are present in the SCGM
- communicate information about the SCGM to all interested parties
- build and maintain a supportive school culture for the SCGM

Student's name: ______________________________

Date: ______________________________

Dear Parent/Caregiver:

I would like to welcome your child and you to my classroom this year. My classroom is identified as a gifted-cluster classroom at our school. Cluster grouping allows a group of gifted students to spend time learning together on a daily basis. Your child has been identified as one of the students who will be receiving gifted services within my classroom and through additional resources provided by gifted-education staff.

Staff work to meet the needs of gifted students in a variety of ways. The curriculum and instruction are *differentiated* within the classroom for each gifted student based on the student's individual strengths and needs. This means that in my classroom, I plan to:

- teach advanced learners at an appropriate pace and depth for them
- give students full credit for what they already know
- provide extension activities to replace the grade-level work students have already mastered
- provide alternative homework and assignments when needed
- provide time for work on independent projects and activities
- use critical and creative thinking activities
- teach students how to self-evaluate their learning

Gifted students are challenged in all areas of the curriculum. Gifted-cluster teachers from all grade levels work together to support one another's efforts by sharing resources and activities that will further benefit students. Additionally, after-school activities, such as

______________________________,

will be offered to enrich your child's school experience this year.

Homework for the gifted students in my classroom may be modified according to the ways in which the curriculum is differentiated for them. On some days, they will not bring home the same homework as other students. On other days, they may not have any homework.

Sincerely, ______________________________

Frequently Asked Questions About the SCGM

The Schoolwide Cluster Grouping Model (SCGM) provides a comprehensive way to serve gifted students on a full-time basis while enhancing achievement opportunities for all students. The information on this form answers common questions about the SCGM.

What does it mean to place students in cluster groups?
A group of gifted-identified students is placed ("clustered") into a mixed-ability classroom with a teacher who is trained to differentiate curriculum and instruction for gifted students.

Isn't cluster grouping the same as tracking?
No. In tracking, students are grouped into classrooms with others of comparable ability and remain together throughout their school years. Curriculum is based on the ability of the average students in the class.

When clustered, all classes have a range of abilities. Teachers modify or extend grade-level standards according to the students' needs and abilities.

Why should gifted students be placed in a cluster group instead of being assigned to all classes?
Gifted students need to spend time learning with others of like ability to experience challenge and make academic progress. Gifted students better understand their learning differences when they are with like-ability peers. Teachers are more likely to differentiate curriculum when there is a group of gifted students in their classroom.

What are the learning needs of gifted students?
All students deserve consistent opportunities to learn new material. With gifted students, this means having opportunities to engage in intellectually stimulating endeavors that go beyond or deeper into grade-level curriculum.

Why not create small groups of gifted students in *all* classes?
This approach greatly diminishes the desired outcomes of the SCGM because:

- Teachers have students with a range of abilities that is too broad.
- There are no opportunities for gifted-education leadership at the grade level.
- There is less accountability for teachers to facilitate progress of their gifted learners.
- Teachers may feel a decreased need to identify gifted students.
- Students' learning needs are less apparent.
- Providing appropriate teacher training becomes difficult.

Won't the creation of a gifted-cluster group rob the other classes of academic leadership? Aren't gifted students needed in all classes so they can help others learn?
In this model:

- All classes have a group of gifted students *or* a group of high-achieving students, so every class has academic leaders.
- High-achieving students have new opportunities to become academic leaders.
- Gifted students make intuitive leaps and, therefore, do not always appear to have to work as hard as others. This means that gifted students are not always the best academic leaders for other students.

CONTINUED > > >

Frequently Asked Questions About the SCGM, continued

How does the SCGM fit with other inclusion models?
The SCGM is compatible with other inclusion models schools have historically used, such as grouping students who need language acquisition services and services for special education. For ease of scheduling and to ensure that students receive appropriate instruction by properly trained teachers, schools commonly cluster special education students according to the services they require. Gifted students' unique learning needs can be readily served by the SCGM in the same way.

Gifted students are no more special than any other student. They simply have learning needs that differ from those of other students, and therefore gifted students need to be grouped with teachers who have specialized training, similar to English language learners and students receiving special education services.

Will the presence of gifted students in the classroom inhibit learning for other students?

- Not when the gifted cluster is kept to a manageable size. The recommended gifted-cluster size is four to ten students.
- New academic leadership is present in all classes, which actually raises the numbers of high achievers in the classrooms and the school.
- When learning extension opportunities are offered to all students in the class, expectations and levels of learning rise for all.

Are gifted-cluster groups "visible" in the classroom?

- Gifted-cluster groups are rarely distinguishable from other groups of students in the classroom.
- *All* students move in and out of groupings according to interest, ability, and pace regarding different topics.

How are records kept of the progress made by gifted-cluster students?
Gifted-cluster teachers keep differentiated education plans (DEPs) for their gifted students. DEPs are simple checklists and narratives that suggest differentiation strategies teachers can use when planning instruction. They indicate students' areas of strength and challenge and document students' progress using the targeted strategies.

What are some advantages of cluster grouping?

- Grouping all gifted children in a regular classroom provides social, emotional, and academic advantages to students.
- Teachers can focus instruction to better meet all their students' academic needs.
- Achievement rises for most students.
- Schools provide full-time gifted services with little additional cost.

Gifted-Education Resources That Support the Schoolwide Cluster Grouping Model (SCGM)

Organizations

National Association for Gifted Children (NAGC) • www.nagc.org. A national advocacy group of parents, educators, and researchers united in support of gifted education, NAGC offers a wealth of information and services to members, including professional development opportunities, youth enrichment programs, legislative updates, and publications such as *Parenting for High Potential* and *Teaching for High Potential.* NAGC sponsors national and regional conferences on gifted education. Visit the site to find information for your state's affiliate organization, such as a state gifted conference, local workshops, and parent events.

Supporting the Emotional Needs of the Gifted (SENG) • www.sengifted.org. With a focus on the unique social and emotional needs of gifted children, SENG provides summer conferences for parents and teachers, along with a program for gifted students themselves. SENG also provides publications and training for parents who want to lead a support group for parents of gifted children in their home district.

Information on Giftedness

Council for Exceptional Children (CEC) • www.cec.sped.org. The largest international professional organization dedicated to improving outcomes for individuals with exceptionalities, CEC offers publications about children with learning challenges that help in understanding twice-exceptional learners. This site is also the source for ERIC Digests on gifted education—a collection of professional literature, information, and resources on the education and development of persons who are gifted.

Davidson Gifted Database • www.davidsongifted.org/Search-Database. Sponsored by the Davidson Institute for Talent Development, this website offers articles, discussion forums, news, resources, and state-by-state policy information related to giftedness and gifted education.

ERIC Institute of Education Sciences • www.eric.ed.gov. Formerly the ERIC Clearinghouse on Disabilities and Gifted Education, ERIC is no longer funded by the US government. Many of the site's research summaries on pertinent topics are still helpful and informative.

Hoagies' Gifted Education Page • www.hoagiesgifted.org. This comprehensive website is a favorite for teachers and parents of gifted children. It contains many helpful links.

International Baccalaureate Organization (IBO) • www.ibo.org. Growing in popularity in the United States, the IBO offers focused, high-quality programs to schools all over the world.

Kidsource Online • www.kidsource.com. Source for excellent articles on gifted education. On the menu at the top left, choose "Education."

Uniquely Gifted • www.uniquelygifted.org. This website provides many resources to help parents and teachers understand and address the special challenges faced by twice-exceptional children.

CONTINUED > > >

Gifted-Education Resources That Support the Schoolwide Cluster Grouping Model (SCGM), continued

Teaching Resources

Center for Gifted Education (CFGE) Curriculum Resources. The CFGE at the College of William and Mary has a large roster of classroom resources that can be ordered at education.wm.edu/centers/cfge. Choose "Curriculum" on the menu; then choose "Curriculum Materials."

National Association for Gifted Children (NAGC) E-Learning On-Demand. Visit www.nagc.org. Choose "Professional Learning" on the menu, then choose "E-Learning On-Demand."

Publishers

Free Spirit Publishing • freespirit.com. A publisher of nonfiction resources for children, teens, parents, educators, and counselors, Free Spirit provides research-based and user-friendly materials covering gifted education, learning differences, social and emotional concerns, and school success.

Great Potential Press • www.greatpotentialpress.com. Great Potential produces books for parents, teachers, counselors, and educators of gifted and talented children on a wide range of topics, including the social and emotional needs of the gifted, creativity, college planning, legal issues, and more.

Prufrock Press • www.prufrock.com. Find innovative books, magazines, and software in virtually all content areas, as well as a host of professional development resources.

Zephyr Press • www.chicagoreviewpress.com. Choose "Imprints" on the menu, then choose "Zephyr Press." Zephyr produces instructional materials that integrate high-level thinking, problem-based learning, and multiple intelligences theory in the classroom environment. Practical and easy to use, these materials enable educators to teach to students' individual needs.

Programs and Research Institutions

Davidson Institute for Talent Development • www.davidsongifted.org. A foundation with a focus on profoundly gifted children, this institute offers scholarships, free academic services, and summer institutes for gifted students as well as the Educators Guild, a free online community for educators committed to meeting the unique needs of the gifted. Visit the website to access online research reports, resources, and news for teachers and parents.

Johns Hopkins Center for Talented Youth (CTY) • cty.jhu.edu. CTY identifies top academic students and provides fun and challenging educational programs for students in grades kindergarten through twelve. Its offerings include summer residential programs, distance education, and family academic programs.

Summer Institute for the Gifted (SIG) • www.giftedstudy.org. SIG facilitates day programs and residential sessions offered by educational institutions in several states.

3

Identifying Students for Gifted-Cluster Groups

GUIDING QUESTIONS

- What criteria should be used to identify students for gifted clusters?
- What are typical characteristics and behaviors of gifted students?
- How can giftedness be recognized in very young students, students who have learning challenges, or those who are not fluent in English?
- How does perfectionism impact the thinking and performance of gifted students?
- Can a student whose productivity is very limited be considered gifted?
- What social and emotional challenges do gifted middle school students experience?
- What procedures are needed to conduct formal testing for giftedness?

What does it mean to be gifted? The National Association for Gifted Children (NAGC) offers this definition: "Children are gifted when their ability is significantly above the norm for their age" (NAGC, accessed 2019). NAGC goes on to explain that people may show giftedness in one or more domains, such as intellectual, creative, artistic, or leadership, or in a specific academic field, such as language arts, mathematics, or science.

Most states have specific regulations or guidelines for identifying students for gifted-education services. These guidelines typically prescribe the types of assessments schools can use and the various data points needed to qualify as gifted in the state. Districts and individual schools typically have their own practices as well. Selection almost always involves testing students—but who will be tested, when will they be tested, by whom, and with what tests? A group-administered ability test that relies heavily on English language fluency will certainly identify some gifted students, but using this type of test alone will *not* ensure that all gifted students are identified, especially those who are not fluent in English. Likewise, a nonverbal test could fail to identify some highly verbal gifted students. Teachers, administrators, and parents need to be able to recognize the diverse characteristics and behaviors that can indicate giftedness. For this reason, schools must make multiple pathways available for nominating students and use multiple measures for gifted identification. These tools should incorporate batteries of tests that measure verbal, nonverbal, and quantitative areas.

Parents, teachers, administrators, school support staff, and the students themselves should have the opportunity to nominate students for gifted testing. Different people may recognize different strengths and abilities in children based on their roles in the children's lives. The best process for determining whether a student should be tested for the gifted cluster involves gathering information from several sources, including:

- teacher observations
- parent nominations
- performance-based evidence (such as portfolio samples)
- achievement tests
- previous intelligence or ability tests

SUPERVISOR SPOTLIGHT

Schools typically schedule testing for gifted identification one or more times a year. Because student placements into the gifted-cluster classroom are determined by gifted identification, and since class placements commonly occur in May, principals will want to have all students identified for placement in Groups 1 through 5 by the end of April. This requires scheduling comprehensive gifted testing early enough in the spring to have the information you will need for class placements. Invite nominations from teachers and families well ahead of scheduled testing dates. Chapter 2 has more information regarding a timeline for implementing all aspects of the Schoolwide Cluster Grouping Model (SCGM).

The behaviors and characteristics described in this chapter apply across grade levels, cultures, and student exceptionalities. Teachers who have some background or training in gifted education are generally more accurate in the identification process than those without this experience. Teachers in general tend to most readily recognize potential strengths in students who are highly verbal and perform well in class and those from the teachers' own culture group. While such students may be gifted, others who exhibit different traits may be gifted as well.

A typical procedure for determining which students are gifted starts with gathering information from teachers and parents. This information can help determine which children should be given formal ability testing and what type of testing (for example, verbal, quantitative, or nonverbal) will most likely yield the best information about the child's potential. Parents are instrumental in the nomination process, since they observe their children in other situations than teachers do. Parents can also observe their children's attitudes toward school, schoolwork, and learning in general. Therefore, carefully consider information that parents provide.

This chapter describes an array of characteristics and behaviors associated with giftedness, along with suggestions for informal and formal methods of recognizing giftedness in high-ability students who also have learning differences, language barriers, low productivity, or behavioral challenges. At the end of the chapter is a list of identification instruments recommended for testing and a set of informational handouts and checklists teachers and parents can use to nominate children for gifted testing. Whenever possible, forms and other communication tools should be made available in the primary languages spoken in the school community.

Note: The information in this chapter can be used to identify students who will make up the gifted clusters—students who are placed in Group 1 of the SCGM. Chapter 1 describes the guidelines to be used for students in Groups 2 through 5.

Recognizing the Traits of Giftedness

Many characteristics are present among gifted students consistently and intensely over time. The following list can serve as a guide to noticing students who may be gifted. To be considered gifted, it is not necessary for a student to exhibit all the listed characteristics; some gifted students also exhibit characteristics that are not on this list. However, students who consistently demonstrate a good portion of these characteristics are likely to be gifted.

Gifted Students' Learning and Behavioral Characteristics

Gifted children may:

- be intensely curious about many things
- learn and easily comprehend new material much faster than age peers do
- know a lot about many things, often without direct instruction, and may love to share their knowledge
- have a vocabulary that is significantly advanced for their age
- be able to clearly express their ideas
- be able to process information with great speed and understanding
- sustain longer periods of attention and concentration than age peers can
- be more independent and less concerned about peer approval than age peers are
- make intuitive leaps in understanding concepts
- have difficulty following prescribed step-by-step procedures for doing expected tasks
- remember forever what they have learned one time
- be able to operate on several tasks simultaneously without losing track of any
- routinely have exceptional insights
- think with depth and complexity
- show a ready grasp of underlying principles
- make valid generalizations about events, people, or objects
- enjoy learning tasks that reflect critical thinking and allow for creativity
- appear to have more energy than other children their age have
- seem to require little sleep
- display heightened levels of sensitivity and empathy regarding justice and fairness in personal and societal events
- demonstrate an advanced sense of humor
- relate more easily to older students or adults than to age peers
- have some anxiety about fitting in
- feel the need to be perfect and first in all their endeavors
- exhibit high expectations of others in their lives
- express skepticism, criticism, and judgment of people and situations
- act bossy or take charge with others
- often prefer to work alone

Some gifted students have advanced academic ability across all subject areas; some demonstrate greater strengths in only some academic areas. In either case, they are considered gifted. Gifted children also vary in their learning, their processing, and their expressions that reflect their high ability. This makes it especially important for parents and teachers to recognize the wide range of traits and behaviors that can indicate possible gifted abilities in a student.

SUPERVISOR SPOTLIGHT

Help teachers understand that the behaviors and traits described in this chapter are characteristics of giftedness, even though they may not be correlated with achievement. Consult the "References and Resources" section on pages 235–245 for materials that will help you, your staff, and parents understand and nurture gifted students who learn in unconventional ways.

Giftedness in Creative Thinking and Production

Some gifted persons have advanced abilities in creative thinking. Students such as these may:

- routinely express original ideas and plans
- make connections between broad ideas
- enjoy complexity in ideas and activities
- tolerate ambiguity and delay of closure
- create unique solutions to problems and obstacles
- be intensely aware of beauty and other aesthetic phenomena
- take risks without regard to consequences
- lack inhibitions and say whatever they are thinking
- challenge existing ideas and practices
- delight in nonconforming behavior
- blissfully ignore disorder or messiness

Students who are very creative may appear to be nonconformists. They may perceive things in ways that others, including their teachers, do not instinctively comprehend or appreciate. For this reason, they may prefer to work independently when others are involved in group work. These students can become intensely absorbed in the process of learning and may modify the teacher's plans without seeking permission first. Highly creative students sometimes generate interesting and unique ways to pursue learning. They may enjoy the process so much that they do not complete their work or projects. Some creative students may pay attention to fine details in their work and ignore neatness in other areas.

A typical illustration of a very creative individual can be seen in the student who is completely oblivious to something that is holding the attention of all her classmates. The student might simply be lost in her own thoughts. This child might not adjust easily to changes in routine or transitions in the classroom.

ACHIEVEMENT ADVISORY

With the SCGM, teachers learn not only to recognize creatively gifted students but also to adapt teaching strategies to help these students use their natural behaviors in productive ways. By finding out what motivates the students and encouraging their interest and intensity, the teacher can allow students to address the desired learning outcomes through those interests. When cluster grouped, these highly creative and productive gifted students can inspire one another further by spending time working together on extension activities and independent projects.

Gifted Students in the Primary Grades

Many schools do not formally identify gifted students until the third grade, based on the schools' identification procedures and possibly a misconception that identification of primary-age students is unreliable and difficult. The resources listed on pages 239–240 describe several reliable tools that identify gifted behaviors in very young students. Using these tools, it is quite easy to spot precocious abilities in thinking, reasoning, conversing, and creative processing in very young gifted students simply by noticing the ways in which their words and behaviors resemble those of older children.

Gifted Culturally and Linguistically Diverse (CLD) Students

Students who are English language learners (ELL students) and those from diverse cultures are referred to as culturally and linguistically diverse (CLD) students. CLD students are underrepresented in many (if not most) schools' gifted programs. This is a source of ongoing frustration in the field of gifted education. A language gap often interferes with CLD students' ability to understand content and express thoughts and understandings clearly. CLD gifted students may not have acquired the level of English language proficiency to be able to demonstrate their abilities in English. But many behavioral characteristics common to gifted students cross cultures, and characteristics known to describe gifted students in general will also describe CLD gifted students. It is important to recognize the behaviors as indicative of gifted abilities, despite the fact that students may not be achieving at grade-level standards.

Even when schools are able to identify ELL or CLD gifted students, the dilemma has been that those students are often not skilled enough in English language learning to be able to function well in the school's existing gifted programs. Pull-out and self-contained programs that are based upon acceleration in language-rich content areas may unintentionally exclude gifted CLD students. Lack of fluency in English prevents many of these students from achieving at the level, pace, and rigor of other gifted students who speak fluent English. The SCGM provides the opportunity for gifted CLD students to have their intellectual needs met *as they assimilate* the language, so it is critical that school staff make an effort to notice and recognize behaviors and characteristics that indicate high potential.

SUPERVISOR SPOTLIGHT

CLD and ELL students identified as gifted based on local identification practices are placed in the gifted cluster regardless of their achievement. This placement removes barriers that have historically kept these students from receiving gifted-education services. These students will make much faster academic progress when they are in a gifted-cluster classroom.

Traits to Look for in Culturally Diverse Students

Characteristics that indicate the gifted potential of ELL and CLD students include:

- ability to learn English quickly
- articulation in role playing and storytelling
- richness in imaginary and informal language
- high interest in certain topics
- quick grasp of new information
- evidence of creative ability in thinking or problem-solving
- ability to see relationships and make connections
- ability to improvise with everyday objects
- exceptional ability in any of the fine arts
- exceptional talents in areas valued by their culture
- high standards for themselves
- curiosity
- persistence
- independence
- highly observant nature
- self-direction
- preference not to stand out in a group

- tendency to find and correct their own mistakes (but not others' mistakes)
- ease in adapting to new situations
- ability to carry responsibilities well
- originality and imagination

ACHIEVEMENT ADVISORY

Clustering is especially compatible with the values of many immigrant parents. Hispanic families, for example, generally want their children to fit into the mainstream culture. Because they do not want their children to stand apart, or to seem or be viewed as "superior" to others, many parents of CLD students are likely to decline traditional types of gifted-education services, such as pull-out programs, for their children. In the SCGM, gifted services are provided in the regular classroom, so parents of CLD students are more likely to support their children's placement in a gifted-cluster classroom.

Students Who Are Twice-Exceptional

Some students are clearly gifted in some areas while experiencing learning challenges in other areas. Are they gifted, do they experience learning challenges, or both? One example is a student who can verbalize beautifully but "refuses" to write down anything. This student actually may not be able to record his thoughts because of a writing-related disability. Another example is a gifted student with dyslexia who is unable to decipher or decode words, yet—because of her high intelligence—may have taught herself to "read" by memorizing words. This student's exceptional abilities may not be apparent to some teachers because her pace may *appear* slow due to the process she goes through when reading. However, the student's thinking and information processing may occur at very high levels.

The term *twice-exceptional* (sometimes referred to as 2e) refers to gifted students who also have learning or behavior challenges. In school programs, their gifted potential may be overlooked, or not addressed, in favor of focusing on their areas of weakness. Conversely, their ability to "get by" due to their high intellect may mask their disabilities. The students often develop compensatory strategies that hide their disabilities, yet the disabilities nonetheless may prevent them from achieving at high levels on conventional measures such as classwork and testing.

Twice-exceptional students are commonly screened out of participation in gifted programs because their learning difficulties often lead to lower achievement test scores than their gifted potential would suggest. These students may be perceived as not being able to work at the same advanced level of others in the gifted program. Intelligence quotient (IQ) tests administered to document a learning disability may also indicate advanced learning ability. Once an advanced IQ has been documented, the student should be considered gifted and should be placed in the gifted-cluster group (Group 1). (For additional information on IQ testing, see pages 66–67.)

It's critical for classroom teachers to be aware of twice-exceptional gifted students' areas of strength, so they do not inadvertently focus only on the students' challenges. A gifted learner who also has a learning difficulty will become disillusioned with schooling if the bulk of his school time is spent remediating his area(s) of weakness. Twice-exceptional students are as gifted in their areas of capabilities as any other gifted students are. Therefore, when it comes to their areas of strength, they should enjoy the same learning opportunities as do students who are gifted in many areas. At the same time, they need modifications and support in their areas of difficulty, which a differentiated cluster classroom readily provides.

Dr. L. Dennis Higgins created the chart in **figure 3-1** to compare the characteristics of gifted students with or without disabilities.

Gifted students diagnosed with attention deficit hyperactivity disorder (ADHD) can also be considered twice-exceptional. Because behaviors of ADHD and giftedness can appear so similar, it

FIGURE 3-1 **Characteristics of Gifted Students**

Without Disabilities	With Disabilities
Able to learn basic skills quickly and easily and retain information with less repetition	Often struggle to learn basic skills due to cognitive processing difficulties; need to learn compensatory strategies in order to acquire basic skills and information
Have high verbal ability	Have high verbal ability but difficulty in English language arts (ELA); may use language in inappropriate ways and at inappropriate times
Develop reading ability early	Frequently have reading problems due to cognitive processing deficits
Highly observant	Have strong observation skills but often have deficits in memory skills
Have strong critical-thinking, problem-solving, and decision-making skills	Excel in solving real-world problems; have outstanding critical-thinking and decision-making skills; often independently develop compensatory skills
Have long attention span and persistent, intense concentration	Frequently have difficulty paying attention but may concentrate for long periods in areas of interest
Creative in generating thoughts, ideas, actions; innovative	Have unusual imagination; frequently generate original and at times rather bizarre ideas; extremely divergent in thought; may appear to daydream when generating ideas
Take risks	Often unwilling to take risks with regard to academics; take risks in non-school areas without considering consequences
Have unusual sense of humor	May use humor to divert attention from school failure or to create distractions
May mature at different rates than age peers	Sometimes appear immature, since they may use anger, crying, withdrawal, and so on to express feelings and to deal with difficulties
Independent	Require frequent teacher support and feedback in deficit areas; highly independent in other areas; often appear to be extremely stubborn and inflexible
Sensitive	Sensitive regarding disability area(s); develop protective excuses
May not be accepted by other children and may feel isolated	May not be accepted by other children and may feel isolated; may be perceived as loners since they do not fit typical model for either giftedness or learning disability
Exhibit leadership ability	May exhibit leadership ability, but the disability may interfere with ability to exercise leadership skills; may be leaders among nontraditional students
Have a wide range of interests	Have a wide range of interests but handicapped in pursuing them satisfactorily due to processing or learning problems
Have very focused interests	Have very focused interests that are often not related to school subjects

Reprinted with permission of L. Dennis Higgins, Ed.D.

can be difficult to determine if a child is gifted or has ADHD or both. **Figure 3-2** describes specific behaviors exhibited by gifted children that may look similar to behaviors that are present in students with ADHD. The left column describes characteristics of children with ADHD, and the right column describes characteristics of gifted children.

Some gifted students do have ADHD. The information in the next section, "Behaviors That May Indicate Twice-Exceptionality," may be helpful in recognizing these students.

Within the group of gifted students considered twice-exceptional, there exists a small group of gifted students with autism spectrum disorder (ASD). Gifted students on the autism spectrum may possess very high cognitive abilities while at the same time experiencing behavioral, communication, and social challenges. Sometimes giftedness is mistaken for ASD, and sometimes ASD is mistaken for giftedness. Sometimes the two conditions mask one another. While it's rare for a child to have both, this can and does happen.

ASD is considered a disability under the Individual Disabilities Education Act (IDEA), a federal law enacted to ensure free and appropriate public education (FAPE). Therefore, a comprehensive professional examination is needed to diagnose ASD and to determine how to best support this twice-exceptional student's learning needs. Like all twice-exceptional students, gifted students with ASD need educators to address both their strengths and their weaknesses.

Behaviors That May Indicate Twice-Exceptionality

Some gifted kids may have some form of learning disability, yet few of these students are typically identified as gifted, in part because their learning challenges may depress their exceptional learning ability into the normal range. Parents often are more attuned than teachers are to the intellectual strengths of a gifted child who also has a learning difficulty. The following learning challenges can be indications that a child with a learning difficulty might also be gifted. The student may:

- have a large vocabulary that is deficient in word meanings and the subtleties of language
- be reading below grade level but have a deep or broad understanding of some topics

FIGURE 3-2 Characteristics of Students

Who Have ADHD	Who Are Gifted
Are inattentive in almost all situations	Are inattentive and bored and tend to daydream in specific situations
Have difficulty persisting at tasks with no immediate consequences	Have difficulty persisting at tasks that seem irrelevant
Are impulsive and have trouble delaying gratification	Have judgment that lags behind intellect
Have trouble following commands to regulate or inhibit behavior in social contexts	Have a high level of intensity, which may lead to power struggles with authorities
Are more active and restless than typical children	Are highly active and energetic, may need less sleep, love movement, and need physical action
Have difficulty following rules and regulations	Question rules, customs, and traditions

Adapted from "Similarities Between ADHD and Gifted Behavior" in *Misdiagnosis and Dual Diagnoses of Gifted Children and Adults* by James T. Webb et al. (Scottsdale, AZ: Great Potential Press, 2016).

- have the ability to express herself verbally or create complex work but an apparent inability to write down any of her ideas
- excel at abstract reasoning but seem unable to remember small details
- seem bright and motivated outside of school but have difficulty with traditional school tasks
- have a slow reaction time that results in incomplete work and low scores on timed tests
- have a general lack of self-confidence that manifests as inflexibility, inability to take risks, supersensitivity to any type of criticism, helplessness, socially inadequate behaviors, stubbornness, and other behaviors that distract others from her learning inadequacies
- lack effective organization and study skills; may complete work but not be able to locate it when it is time to turn it in to the teacher

These challenges are real, yet they are not insurmountable. When placed in a gifted-cluster classroom with a teacher who understands giftedness, twice-exceptional students can thrive. Exposure to higher-level activities and flexible learning opportunities, coupled with the gifted-cluster teacher's willingness to allow students to work through their interests and express themselves through their preferred learning styles, can make all the difference for the twice-exceptional gifted learner.

ACHIEVEMENT ADVISORY

Students who *are* gifted and do *not* have ADHD will respond positively to compacting and differentiation opportunities such as those described in chapters 5 and 6. Children *with* ADHD who are *not* gifted will not be likely to benefit from compacting experiences.

Understanding the Social and Emotional Aspects of Giftedness

Gifted children experience uneven social, emotional, and intellectual development. Because their mental age exceeds their chronological age, they are often more socially competent with older students. Any social problems with their age peers should not be perceived as general social dysfunction. Their chronological age should not prevent them from experiencing challenging curriculum or from being placed with older students for certain classes if and when the teachers form flexible groups beyond grade levels.

Regardless of the areas in which gifted students are identified, many have unique social and emotional needs that teachers must understand in order to help the students work to their potential. Not all students experience these challenges to the same degree—some gifted kids, in fact, have few adjustment problems—but many experience some or all of a distinctive set of emotional needs and resulting social challenges:*

Feeling different. Like members of any special needs group, gifted students may feel insecure just because they are different from the norm. Sometimes gifted kids are *very* different; they may feel isolated and alienated and act quirky as a result. Their self-image and self-esteem can suffer, as can their relationships with other students.

Heightened perceptions and sensitivities. Gifted children are often highly perceptive to the sounds, sights, smells, touches, tastes, movements, words, patterns, numbers, and physical phenomena of daily life. Gifted individuals also perceive greater levels of complexity in the world around them. They may feel physical and emotional sensations more intensely. Many gifted kids are more sensitive to ethical issues than their age peers are.

*Some of the descriptions of the social and emotional challenges of giftedness presented in this section are adapted with permission from *When Gifted Kids Don't Have All the Answers: How to Meet Their Social and Emotional Needs* by Judy Galbraith, M.A., and Jim Delisle, Ph.D. (Minneapolis: Free Spirit Publishing, 2015), pp. 60–67.

They may be highly moralistic and quick to judge others. At the same time, despite their intellectual advancement, they can be emotionally immature.

Heightened response to stress. Challenges to emotional peace often occur when a student's intellectual abilities are out of sync. For example, a student who has strong conceptual and mathematical skills but also has a reading disability may feel quite frustrated with regular schoolwork. Someone with strong spatial ability but weak writing skills is likely to be similarly stymied. There is also stress associated with asynchrony—the observable difference between advanced intellectual abilities and typical or even below-level abilities in other areas. One example might be the student who has the ability to read and understand books written for much older students coupled with an inability to perform in physical education tasks and games.

Perfectionism. Although some adults may perceive perfectionism as a positive quality, it can have a negative impact on learning. Perfectionism means that you feel you can *never* fail; you *always* need approval, praise, or recognition. Gifted people of all ages are especially prone to perfectionism. This may be rooted in the awareness of quality—gifted people know the difference between mediocre and superior. Perfectionism can lead to anxiety and pressure and can result in being obsessively focused on getting things "right," in procrastinating, or in being paralyzed into nonproductiveness. See page 63 for more information about perfectionism.

Characteristics That May Create Challenges in the Classroom

Some gifted students display characteristics that are contrary to what many understand as giftedness. These behaviors may confuse teachers when they are making recommendations for gifted testing, because the students can appear to be intentionally disruptive and challenging in the classroom. These behaviors are not what teachers normally expect from gifted students. However, the negative behaviors can greatly diminish when teachers understand the causes behind them and modify the students' curriculum and instruction accordingly. Educational consultant Roger Taylor describes several characteristics that tend to screen students out of gifted programs. Teachers may encounter gifted kids who:*

- are bored with routine tasks and refuse to do rote homework
- seem unwilling or unable to move into another topic
- are self-critical and impatient with failures
- are critical of others and of teachers
- often disagree vocally with others and with the teacher
- make jokes or puns at inappropriate times
- are emotionally sensitive—may overreact, get angry easily, or seem ready to cry if things go wrong
- are not interested in details; hand in messy work or none at all
- refuse to accept authority; may appear nonconforming or stubborn
- tend to dominate others

Gifted students' learning characteristics and social and emotional stresses can create challenges at school, including the following:

- impatience with the pace of curriculum and instruction at school and the learning time needed by classmates
- impatience with routines and rules
- frustration that topics and issues they consider important are not included in school curriculum

*Adapted with permission from "Characteristics of the Gifted That Tend to Screen Them Out of Programs" by Dr. T. Roger Taylor.

- a tendency to show off as a means of receiving validation for their advanced abilities
- reluctance to complete assignments related to grade-level standards, but ability to do well on assessments and standardized tests
- difficulty in social relationships with age peers; tendency to appear bossy and demanding
- the appearance of daydreaming and apparent ambivalence toward required lessons
- unwillingness to move past topics that intrigue them, and frustration when there is not enough time to work on what interests them

With these possible challenges that gifted students face, it is not surprising that for some, school can be a daily reminder of not belonging. Insight into these behaviors can help teachers more readily recognize ability and potential in students whose social and emotional challenges may at times be more noticeable than their intellectual exceptionalities. As with gifted CLD and twice-exceptional students, gifted students with intense affective challenges can benefit greatly from being placed together in a gifted-cluster classroom, where a teacher trained to work with these students can guide them to:

- understand and appreciate their own differences and accept the differences of others
- cope with heightened sensitivities
- deal with stress from themselves and from their world
- develop a tolerance for frustration and willingness to work on challenging learning tasks
- understand how perfectionism impacts learning and behavioral challenges
- learn to feel worthwhile even when they are not always the best or the first

In addition, the compacting, acceleration, and student-directed learning experiences that students experience in a gifted-cluster classroom allow them to work with high-ability peers in ways that are comfortable and productive. This can ease many of the social and emotional stressors that typically accompany giftedness.

The Challenge of Perfectionism

One of the more challenging manifestations of giftedness in the school setting for many gifted children is perfectionism. When gifted children experience easy successes over time with little or no effort, they may conclude that the difference between very smart people and others is that smart people always just "get it." They may come to fear that unless they always demonstrate that their work is easy, observers may conclude that they are not really all that smart.

A healthy striving for excellence is different from perfectionism. As Dr. Tom Greenspon, a psychologist specializing in the emotional needs of gifted children, explains, "Trying your hardest, going all out, extending yourself beyond your usual limits, and even overdoing it are not perfectionist behaviors in themselves. The difference is that perfectionists set *unrealistically* demanding goals, and when they fail to achieve these goals, they feel *unacceptable* and personally *worthless*" (Greenspon 2012, 22). Striving for excellence on a particular project or assignment is desirable and worthwhile. Needing to be perfect at all times and in all learning situations is harmful and can be debilitating.

The fears that accompany perfectionistic thinking may be viewed when a student:

- shows reluctance to begin a task; procrastinates endlessly because if he never starts, no one will be able to judge the product
- starts work over often; destroys work rather than handing in an imperfect product
- works very slowly to avoid making mistakes
- has a huge need for constant teacher assistance and reassurance

- cries when things do not go smoothly
- argues regarding teacher comments or criticism
- brags about his accomplishments

Some teachers believe that gifted students' work should always be exemplary, neat, and beautiful and wonder how a student whose work is far less than perfect could be considered gifted. Perfectionism is often the root cause of a lack of productivity in gifted students. Careless work may also be a sign of frustration over being expected to complete classwork that presents no challenge. It is important that teachers keep an open mind so they can notice gifted characteristics even in nonproductive students.

Nonproductive Gifted Students

Many gifted students who do not demonstrate high achievement at school have been labeled "underachievers." We prefer the term *nonproductive*. Nonproductive gifted students may have high scores on ability tests but low grades in school.

When gifted students are not demonstrating high achievement or productivity, power struggles can ensue among home, school, and student. When a teacher notices that a gifted student is not completing schoolwork, she might assume that the student is lazy or unmotivated. This judgment may be mistaken. The student may simply not be motivated by the material being taught in the regular classroom because it does not capture his interest, because the content is not new or is not challenging, or because he learns in unconventional ways. Gifted students may be more productive when they are working on tasks that create excitement and involve challenge. Once the schoolwork is streamlined through compacting and differentiation, power struggles over work completion typically abate.

Gifted students achieve at higher levels when they are exposed to challenging curriculum. When gifted students are not challenged, they may languish academically and even score below their grade-level expectations. As a result, they then may be excluded from their school's gifted program, the precise remedy for their academic languishing.

Placing nonproductive gifted students in gifted-cluster classes can help motivate them in several ways. Being offered regular opportunities to make meaningful choices and receiving full credit for previously mastered standards can be highly motivating for a nonproductive learner. Engagement in activities of the child's choosing encourages creativity and critical thinking, which further motivate the learner. Students in an effective gifted-cluster classroom have more opportunity to self-select books, projects, and avenues of study. Their teachers are more likely to give options and to recognize students' knowledge of content. Nonproductive gifted students respond in productive ways when the classroom teacher understands what motivates them.

Gifted Students in Junior High or Middle School

Gifted adolescents may exhibit most of the behaviors described in this chapter and are as likely as younger gifted kids to experience unique social and emotional challenges. In addition, some adolescents have asynchronous experiences in school as they deal with glaring differences between themselves and their age peers. Gifted middle or junior high school students may be able to engage in abstract reasoning at a level that surpasses their classmates by two or three years. This is why grouping for peer support and gifted students' collaborative learning is so important.

Unless these students are purposefully grouped with like-minded learning peers, their frustration may lead to behaviors that make them appear lazy or disinterested in school. They may experience pressure from teachers and parents to just do what is asked of them; they get the message that everyone has to go through the motions of doing tedious required work during their lifetime, and middle and junior high school may be one of those times. Frustration from being misunderstood, along with the pressure to conform, can lead to depression, anger, and even rage. When gifted adolescents are purposefully clustered together in teams and placed with teachers who know how to motivate and challenge them, they are more likely to feel as though they fit in and are more likely to enjoy school.

During the middle school years, some students decide to discontinue participation in gifted services for various social and emotional reasons, the most prevalent of which is the need to belong or fit in. Placement in a gifted-cluster group automatically creates the conditions for fitting in with like-minded peers. Willingness to participate in extended learning activities increases when one has the company of other students working on similar tasks. Therefore, cluster grouping adolescents is a highly effective method for delivering gifted-education services to this age group. In the SCGM, tailoring curriculum and instruction to the needs of the gifted learner occurs in all classes and in all content areas, providing opportunity for advanced learning even if the student does not seek out advanced courses.

Teacher and Parent Nominations

Using multiple criteria when identifying students for cluster classes makes it more likely that students with different learning needs and styles will be included in the identification process. In the SCGM, teachers are trained to recognize the traits that can indicate giftedness. To assist in focusing on and harnessing this information about individual students, school administrators can create testing nomination packets for parents and teachers. Pages 77–89 provide sample forms that can be used or adapted to fit an individual school's or district's criteria for formatting and language. This kind of input from teachers and parents, along with additional evidence from grades, scores on achievement tests, and student portfolios, provides information to help identify which students should take ability tests to determine whether they are gifted.

Recommended Forms to Include in a Teacher Nomination Packet

Teachers who recognize signs of giftedness in a student in their classroom can use these forms to determine which students should be tested for gifted services:

- a letter explaining the purpose of the nomination packet, such as the "Teacher Letter" on page 81
- information that may help teachers better understand what it means to be gifted, such as "Differences Between the Bright Child and the Gifted Learner" on page 75 and "Characteristics of Giftedness That Present Challenges" on page 76
- a screening form that lists traits and characteristics and allows teachers to note students who come to mind for each description, such as the "Teacher's Class Screening Form for Nominating Students for Gifted Testing" on pages 82–83
- a second form that lists traits and characteristics and allows teachers to rate how often and to what degree an individual student exhibits characteristics of giftedness, such as the "Rating Scale for Gifted Services" on pages 84–86
- a permission form similar to the "Permission to Test" form on page 80

Recommended Forms to Include in a Parent Nomination Packet

When parents ask about having their children tested for giftedness, give them an information packet to help them determine whether testing is appropriate. Include the following:

- a letter explaining the purpose of the packet, such as the "Parent Letter" on page 77
- information that may help parents better understand what it means to be gifted, such as "Differences Between the Bright Child and the Gifted Learner" on page 75 and "Characteristics of Giftedness That Present Challenges" on page 76
- a checklist of traits and characteristics typical of gifted students that parents can complete, such as "Parent Information Form: Gifted-Education Services" on pages 78–79
- a form giving the school permission to test a child for qualification for gifted services, such as the "Permission to Test" form on page 80

Processing Nomination Information

Carefully reviewing nominations from parents and teachers prior to scheduled testing can ensure that testing is appropriate for those students who are nominated. Some parents and teachers mistakenly believe that high-achieving students are gifted or that all gifted students are able to demonstrate high achievement. Ability or potential should not be confused with achievement. A team consisting of a gifted specialist, gifted coordinator, gifted resource teacher, classroom teacher, and principal—or any variation thereof—is recommended for evaluating nominations. Depending on the students' areas of strengths and challenges, you might also consider seeking input from the school counselor, school psychologist, media specialist, or special education teachers.

Standardized Tests

Characteristics discussed in this chapter should help teachers recognize which students would likely perform well on tests used to identify gifted potential. Gifted identification draws teachers' awareness to students' potential that may have previously gone unnoticed. It also provides documentation to support the need for modified instruction. Schools use gifted-testing results to help advocate for appropriate educational accommodations, such as acceleration, enrichment, and placement into a gifted program.

Schools must routinely test students on mastery of grade-level standards for accountability purposes. Many use benchmark achievement tests to help guide instruction for individuals and groups. These achievement tests do not show whether a child is gifted, but achievement tests *can* be used as one factor in deciding if a child should be tested for gifted services. School benchmark assessments provide teachers with information on how the student is mastering specific content related to grade-level work. Some gifted students have the ability to master new content with ease. Teachers should consider nominating those students; however, they should not limit their nominations to those students who demonstrate academic achievement.

Ability and Achievement Testing

Ability tests and achievement tests measure different things. Ability tests measure a student's potential and capability to learn. Ability tests most commonly used for gifted identification include the *Cognitive Abilities Test (CogAT)* and the *Naglieri Nonverbal Ability Test—Third Edition (NNAT3)*. Some states and districts use IQ tests. An IQ test is another type of ability test; it is individually administered by a psychologist.

Schools administer achievement tests to document what the children *have already learned.* Achievement tests gauge where the students are in their acquisition of knowledge of specific information. District benchmark assessments, state standardized achievement tests, and textbook assessments are examples of achievement tests.

Because not all gifted children are achieving at levels commensurate with their abilities, some gifted students score very high on ability tests, yet demonstrate average performance on achievement tests. Gifted students certainly have the *ability to excel* when appropriate instructional interventions are in place. Having test data from both ability and achievement assessments helps schools plan and guide instruction for the students. In the SCGM, students are placed in the gifted cluster (Group 1) based on ability, not achievement. Students who score high on achievement tests but are not identified as gifted based on local standards are placed in Group 2.

SUPERVISOR SPOTLIGHT

Check with your department of education for information on testing and requirements for reporting to parents. Many states have gifted-testing guidelines that require schools to use certain tests and to provide an exact number of testing opportunities or specific areas that must be tested. Start your search by looking for a person who is the designated state director of gifted education or for an active state organization in gifted education.

Some gifted-identification tools specify that they be administered individually, and some are designed for group administration. Regardless of whether ability tests are administered individually or in a group, a standardized ability test will not yield a false identification—it will not identify as gifted someone who is, in fact, *not* gifted—provided the test was administered according to the publishers' guidelines. If a student scores exceptionally well on any measure, the gifted potential is present. Use the results of these tests as guidelines, but never eliminate a child who has been nominated as gifted because of *one* test score that is below the accepted guidelines. If a student misses the qualification cutoff by a point or two, many schools offer an approved backup, or secondary test, for the student to take. This second test may confirm or override the results of the first test. See "Tests for Identification" on pages 239–240 for descriptions of different ability and IQ tests.

Intelligence tests and ability tests yield different, but related, information. Although IQ tests yield much more specific information about how a child learns and processes information, valid IQ tests require administration by specially trained professionals or psychologists. They are expensive and time-consuming to administer. The expense, along with most school districts' limited number of trained professionals available to administer the IQ tests, prevents them from being widely used. Parents can pursue this option on their own. Appropriate outside testers can be located in psychology departments of universities, through college programs for kids, through regional educational service centers found in some states, and through state gifted associations. If a child has had outside testing administered by a psychologist, those scores should be considered for the child's potential placement into the gifted-cluster group.

Different Measures of Ability

Ability tests used to identify giftedness measure general ability. There are a number of reasons why some gifted students may not qualify as gifted on a specific test or test battery—often because of language barriers, cultural differences, social and emotional impediments, or a learning difficulty or difference. For this reason, ability tests and test batteries are available that can identify gifted students through various types of measures. Some ability tests have different batteries: verbal, quantitative, and nonverbal. Others measure ability in just one or two of the areas. Many gifted students have advanced abilities in a combination of the three areas. Some have advanced abilities in one or two areas, but not another. This means that a wider range of test batteries will identify giftedness in a wider range of students.

It is the construct of the test item that makes it verbal, quantitative, or nonverbal. These three areas on an ability test constitute the vehicle through which a child is identified as gifted. Identification in one of these areas does not describe a specific way of thinking or learning.

Giftedness Identified on Verbal, Quantitative, and Nonverbal Assessments

Gifted students identified in the verbal area typically have an advanced vocabulary and an advanced ability to learn and use words. They may love songs, music, or poetry, and some enjoy learning world languages. They understand and use metaphors and analogies and appreciate subtleties of language, skills that relate to learning in all subject areas. These students are especially likely to exhibit strengths in language arts and social studies. Because classroom instruction relies heavily on the written and spoken word, these students usually feel very comfortable learning in the school setting.

Gifted students identified in the quantitative area understand advanced mathematical concepts, enjoy mathematical reasoning, use logic to solve math and life's problems, and appreciate the more esoteric topics in math. They may be very accurate in computation or may make careless errors because they are less interested in accuracy than in the big ideas. They make intuitive leaps in their mathematical thinking and are often unable to explain just how they arrived at an answer or solution. They appreciate receiving credit for having mastered required standards with less practice than their classmates and prefer self-paced instructional programs.

Gifted students identified in the nonverbal area have an innate, advanced ability to make and see connections and relationships. They are skilled at abstract reasoning and problem-solving. In the classroom, relationships exist within each subject area and across subject areas. Because of their abilities to make relationships between ideas and content, nonverbally identified gifted students may enjoy and be interested in computer programming, coding, artificial intelligence, virtual reality, puzzles, and assembling and creating things. They are also very observant about changes in the environment around them. These students may or may not be fluent with language-based tasks. Some nonverbally identified gifted students demonstrate what they have learned most effectively through interactions, demonstrations, hands-on activities, and presentations.

Students may, for example, be identified as gifted on the verbal battery of an ability test. These students have strengths in reading and writing. Others may be identified as gifted in their scores on the quantitative battery; these students have strengths in mathematic reasoning. Students identified as gifted on a nonverbal assessment, or on the nonverbal battery of an ability test, may have advanced abilities in a variety of areas.

Awareness of this is important because many educators unwittingly harbor a bias, assuming that students who do not exhibit strength in the verbal area are not likely to be gifted. That is a myth, and it prevents many high-ability students from receiving the gifted-education services they need in order to fulfill their potential, especially gifted ELL students or those with cultural or learning differences. Whether students are capable of expressing themselves in English or understanding grade-level curriculum in English is not the essential issue. The point is that students identified on a nonverbal assessment have as much advanced learning potential as students identified by verbal or quantitative assessments. Some students identified as gifted on a nonverbal assessment may actually have very advanced abilities in the language arts and in mathematics.

Giftedness, when identified in any area or on any assessment, involves an advanced ability to see connections and make relationships. Making relationships between existing knowledge and new ideas is a fundamental part of learning. In school, this relates to all content areas: reading, writing, math, social studies, science, and the fine arts.

Administering Ability Tests

Schools and school districts usually determine which people administer the gifted-identification tests based on the test administration requirements in their area and the availability of trained personnel. Teachers, school administrators, and other school professionals can conduct the group-administered ability tests most commonly used to identify gifted students in the schools, although this takes time away from their other responsibilities.

Another method for testing, which provides more consistent results and costs the school or district very little, involves hiring testing technicians instead of using teachers to administer the test. We suggest hiring retired teachers or other experienced certified teachers who are not seeking to teach. These teachers usually have experience administering tests and can be trained quickly on the administration procedures for the ability test the school district uses to identify giftedness. Retired teachers also have experience interacting with school personnel, and their knowledge of school procedures and schedules helps them complete testing with the least amount of disruption in the school. The district gifted-program coordinator can train the testers.

Generally, each testing technician is assigned a group of schools. One technician for twelve to fifteen schools is recommended. School districts that use gifted-testing technicians structure the testing schedule according to the number of technicians available and according to the state's testing requirements. Most states require that districts provide two or three testing dates each year.

School districts incorporating this system pay the testers the same rate they pay substitute teachers to cover classes for the gifted-cluster teacher or gifted specialist when these teachers provide the testing. Benefits to the school are several: Teachers remain in the classroom teaching, so instructional time is protected. A set schedule is created. (See **figure 3-3**; a similar reproducible scheduling form is on page 74.)

FIGURE 3-3 **Sample Gifted Testing Schedule for a School District**

Testing Period: Fall   Testing Technician: Ms. Merry Tester   Test: CogAT

Week	School
Aug. 28–Sept. 1	School A
Sept. 5–8	School B
Sept. 11–15	School C
Sept. 18–22	School D
Sept. 25–29	School E and School F
Oct. 2–6	School G
Oct. 9–13	School H
Oct. 23–26	School I and makeups
Oct. 30–Nov. 3	School J
Nov. 6–9	School K
Nov. 13–17	School L
Nov. 27–Dec. 1	School M
Dec. 4–8	School N
Dec. 11–15	School O
Dec. 18–21	School P and makeups

Procedures for the administration, evaluation, and reporting of gifted testing are consistent across the school and district. When trained testers are employed, the data are deemed reliable regardless of which technician administered a given test. See the following sample guidelines for creating consistent testing procedures throughout a school district. The guidelines describe steps to consider when you are creating your own testing procedures.

EXAMPLE OF TESTING PROCEDURES FOR GIFTED SPECIALISTS/ CLASSROOM TEACHERS

1. Your school's testing schedule is posted to your Google Classroom. Please confirm the testing dates no later than ______________. Be sure the dates are on your school's master planning calendar. (Makeup testing and IEP/504 testing take place in June, when the school year concludes.)
2. Create a Google Doc for each testing session, and be sure to share the document with your tester and school principal.
3. Review characteristics of nominees for gifted testing with your staff.
4. Begin the nomination process at your school and collection of parent "Permission to Test" forms early to allow time for parents to return the forms. (If you like, use parent-teacher conferences to obtain parent signatures on the forms.) Your testing technician will pick up signed permission forms two weeks before testing.
5. Turn in all permission forms to your school's testing technician, including those that indicate students have IEPs or 504 education plans. Your tester will check for special testing accommodations (such as individual or small-group testing needs) and will schedule accordingly.

EXAMPLE OF TESTING PROCEDURES FOR GIFTED-TESTING TECHNICIANS*

1. Pick up permission forms two weeks prior to your scheduled testing. A couple of days before this, contact the gifted department office for the students' birthdates and previous testing results. (These are used for age norming and to determine if the students have already qualified as gifted in one area.)
2. After collecting the permission forms and while you are still at the school, check to see if any children have an IEP or 504 education plan indicated on their permission form. If so, ask the school nurse for copies of the necessary accommodations, then schedule testing as appropriate. If an IEP is noted, inform the gifted department office. The office will check with the special education department to determine the appropriate testing environment and will provide you a copy of the needed accommodations.
3. While you are at the school, request a copy of the lunch, special area classes (such as music, art, and physical education), and recess schedules along with a school map.
4. Create your testing schedule using Google Sheets. Attempt to work around special area classes. Determine if a student has previously qualified as gifted in any area(s). Do not test students in area(s) in which they have already qualified. Instead, cross out that portion of the test on the answer sheet so the scorer will be aware that the student already has been identified as gifted in one or more areas of the test.
5. Check to ensure students who will be testing have not been tested (using the same test) within the last twelve months.
6. Schedule morning testing for kindergarten through second grade over three days (Monday, Tuesday, and Wednesday). Schedule testing for third through sixth grades in the

*Used with permission from Paradise Valley Unified School District.

afternoons of those days or over the two remaining days (Thursday and Friday). A three-day testing schedule is as follows: day 1—verbal, day 2—quantitative, and day 3—nonverbal. A two-day testing schedule for grades three through six is as follows: day 1—verbal and nonverbal (one hour and forty-five minutes), day 2—quantitative (fifty minutes). Here is a suggested three-day testing schedule:

- Kindergarten: 8:55–9:45 a.m. (fifty minutes); groups of five to eight students
- First grade: 9:55–10:50 a.m. (fifty-five minutes); groups of six to ten students
- Second grade: right before or after lunch (one hour); groups of fifteen students
- Grades three through six: any time after lunch (one hour); larger group of students (up to thirty)

7. At least one week prior to testing, email your school's administrative assistant to request a testing room. Provide the office with your testing schedule and the number of desks or tables and chairs you will need, so the office can assign an appropriate room.

8. Email the testing schedule to the school's gifted specialist one week prior to testing, so the specialist can forward it to the students' teachers. Include your list of students being tested, so there are no discrepancies on testing day.

9. On testing day:

- Try to arrive with plenty of time, especially the first day.
- Sign in at the front office.
- Prepare the testing room.
- Pick up students from their classes.
- Introduce yourself and explain to the students why they are being tested. Let them know results will be mailed to their home in approximately three weeks.
- Set guidelines for testing, such as "No talking during testing; eyes on your own paper (use privacy folders if necessary); drinks and bathroom breaks need to occur between testing sessions."
- Never leave students in the testing room by themselves.
- After testing, walk younger students back to class.
- If a student is absent one testing day but returns before you are finished testing at the school, attempt to complete as much of the student's testing as possible while you are at the school. If the student is absent the entire time, or you don't have time to make up testing for this student, inform the teacher about makeup testing in June. Be sure to indicate the absence on the record sheet so the scorer will know that the child wasn't tested.
- When you are finished testing, file the tests in alphabetical order by grade level. Return the tests to the gifted department office after you are finished at each school. Try to return tests on the last day of testing.

10. Here are the supplies you will need:

- plenty of sharpened pencils
- scratch paper for students in grades three through six and paper markers for students in kindergarten through second grade
- privacy folders
- tissues
- a sign reading "Testing—do not disturb"
- an extra test for each level and answer sheets in case of last-minute additions

11. Follow these instructions for labels:

- Use the student testing record sheet for all the necessary label information (student names, identification numbers, birthdates, teacher names, and so on).

- Use the chronological age chart for norming to determine each student's age.
- Affix labels that include the students' names, identification numbers, grade levels, and classroom teacher names on the test booklets for grades kindergarten through two and on the answer sheets for grades three through six. This information is typically provided by the administrator who oversees gifted education at the district office.

12. After testing is completed, fill in student testing record sheet using the same information found on the labels. Write the student names alphabetically by grade level.
13. For students with an IEP or 504 education plan, call parents if June testing is needed, so they can schedule a testing time.
14. When you are testing students with an IEP or 504 education plan, write out a description of how the accommodations were met during the testing. Sign and date this description, then attach it to the parent "Permission to Test" form.

SUPERVISOR SPOTLIGHT

Whatever procedure you follow for testing, make sure teachers and parents are aware of the testing timeline so students are present and prepared for those assessments.

Special Considerations When Identifying CLD Gifted Students

As we have noted earlier, schools should adopt identification procedures and assessments that appropriately identify *all* gifted students. Nonverbal assessments or batteries are essential in this process. Many CLD students are identified as gifted on nonverbal assessments, which require students to rely on the advanced reasoning and problem-solving skills that clearly define giftedness in any population.

To see how effective a school's identification methods are in recognizing and serving giftedness across cultures, look at the percentage of gifted-identified students from each demographic group, and compare this to the percentage of all students from that demographic group in the school. For example, if 45 percent of the students in the school are Hispanic students, approximately 45 percent of the students identified as gifted should be Hispanic. If this is not the case, it may be necessary to look at alternatives for identifying CLD gifted students.

Parent Notification

Parents should be notified of the results of the gifted testing. Pages 87 and 89 present two reproducible notification letters, one for parents of students who qualify for gifted-education services and one for parents of students who do not qualify.

When parents receive initial notification that their child has qualified for gifted services after testing, they may have some immediate questions. They may be concerned that their child will be pulled out of homeroom class or be sent to a different school. Sending out a letter introducing the SCGM (see the reproducible letter on page 88) alleviates apprehension and builds reassurance with parents. We recommend sending this SCGM introductory letter *along with* the letter informing parents that their child qualifies for gifted services. Be sure to provide suggestions about where they can seek additional information.

SUMMARY

In this chapter, you have learned to recognize the behaviors that identify students as gifted. We have paid special attention to identifying gifted children among English language learners (ELL students) or students who are culturally or linguistically diverse (CLD students). We have provided information about:

› characteristics of giftedness that impact students' thoughts and behaviors

› special considerations when you are working with students who are twice-exceptional or not very productive with their work

› perfectionism and how it explains many of the most challenging behaviors of gifted students

› specific methods to use to identify gifted students for gifted-cluster classes

Gifted Testing Schedule

Testing period: ______________________________

Testing technician: ______________________________

Test: ______________________________

Week	School

Differences Between the Bright Child and the Gifted Learner

All descriptors represent a continuum of behaviors rather than extremes.

Bright Child		Gifted Learner
Knows the answers	→	Asks the questions
Is interested	→	Is highly curious
Is attentive	→	Is mentally and physically involved
Has good ideas	→	Has wild, silly ideas
Works hard	→	Plays around, yet tests well
Answers the questions	→	Discusses in detail, elaborates
Is in the top group	→	Goes beyond the group
Listens with interest	→	Shows strong feelings and opinions
Learns with ease	→	Already knows
Requires 6–8 repetitions for mastery	→	Requires 1–2 repetitions for mastery
Understands ideas	→	Constructs abstractions
Enjoys peers	→	Prefers adults
Grasps the meaning	→	Draws inferences
Completes assignments	→	Initiates projects
Is receptive	→	Is intense
Copies accurately	→	Creates a new design
Enjoys school	→	Enjoys learning
Absorbs information	→	Manipulates information
Is a technician	→	Is an inventor
Is a good memorizer	→	Is a good guesser
Enjoys straightforward sequential presentation	→	Thrives on complexity
Is alert	→	Is keenly observant
Is pleased with own learning	→	Is highly self-critical

Adapted with permission from "Differences Between the Bright Child and the Gifted Learner" by Janice Szabos Robbins.

Characteristics of Giftedness That Present Challenges

Characteristics that may keep a student from being recognized as gifted
A gifted child exhibiting any of these traits may not be readily identified for gifted-education services:

- is bored with routine tasks, refuses to do rote homework
- has difficulty moving into another topic
- is self-critical, impatient with failures
- is critical of others, of teachers
- often disagrees vocally with others, with the teacher
- makes jokes or puns at inappropriate times
- shows intense emotional sensitivity—may overreact, get angry easily, or be quick to cry if things go wrong
- is not interested in details; hands in messy work
- refuses to accept authority; is nonconforming, stubborn
- tends to dominate others

Characteristics of gifted students who are bored
A gifted child who is bored may exhibit any or all of these traits:

- has a poor attention span
- daydreams frequently
- has a tendency to begin many activities but to see few through to completion
- development of judgment lags behind intellectual growth level
- has an intensity that may lead to power struggles with authorities
- has a high activity level; may seem to need less sleep
- has difficulty restraining desire to talk; may be disruptive
- questions rules, customs, routines, and traditions
- loses work, forgets or doesn't do homework, is disorganized
- has apparent carelessness
- has high sensitivity to criticism

Adapted with permission from "Characteristics of the Gifted That Tend to Screen Them Out of Programs" by Dr. T. Roger Taylor and from "Dual Exceptionalities" by Colleen Willard-Holt (ERIC Digest E574, 1999, ERIC #ED430344).

Student's name: ______________________________

Date: ______________________________

Dear Parent/Caregiver:

You or your child's teacher has requested that your child be considered as a candidate for gifted-identification testing. To determine whether you believe testing is appropriate for your child, please follow this brief procedure:

1. Read the information provided in "Differences Between the Bright Child and the Gifted Learner" and "Characteristics of Giftedness That Present Challenges."

2. Complete the "Parent Information Form: Gifted-Education Services." If you have questions about gifted-education services, gifted testing, or about whether gifted testing is appropriate for your child, please contact the school's gifted specialist at ______________________________.

3. After completing the information form, if you wish to have your child take part in testing for gifted identification, please complete the "Permission to Test" form.

4. Return the "Permission to Test" form to ______________________________ on or before ______________________________.

If you complete and return the "Permission to Test" form, you will be notified of the testing date. Thank you.

Gifted-Education Services Coordinator: ______________________________

Phone and email: ______________________________

Parent Information Form

Gifted-Education Services

The purpose of this form is to help you determine whether it is appropriate for your child to take part in testing that identifies students for gifted-education services. It is for your information only and should not be turned in to the school.

Criteria	Not at All	Sometimes	Often	Very Often
1. Does your child use a lot of sophisticated or adult words?				
2. Does your child want to know why things are the way they are? Does he/she want to know how things work or why people say or do certain things? Does your child want to know what makes things or people tick?				
3. Does your child notice likenesses and differences between people, events, or things?				
4. Is your child a keen and alert observer? (For example, does she/he seem to get more out of a TV show, game, or experience than other children of the same age?)				
5. Is your child interested in "adult" social problems such as world hunger, pollution, or war?				
6. Does your child explain things well and relay messages accurately?				
7. Does your child suggest a better way to do something if he/she isn't satisfied with the way it's being done?				
8. Is your child extremely curious? Does she/he ask many questions about all kinds of things?				
9. Does your child think through his/her decisions more than most children of the same age do?				

CONTINUED > > >

Adapted from "Elementary Parent Nomination Checklist" with permission from the Austin, Texas, Independent School District Gifted and Talented Program.

Parent Information Form, continued

Criteria	Not at All	Sometimes	Often	Very Often
10. Does your child imagine things to be different from the way they actually are? Do you hear her/him saying, "What if . . . ?" or "I wonder what would happen if . . . ?"				
11. Does your child feel comfortable with situations that may not have one right answer?				
12. Does your child stick to a job or problem until it is completed or solved to his/her satisfaction?				
13. Is your child sensitive to the needs and feelings of others?				
14. Does your child frequently have unusual ideas?				
15. Does your child seem to look for challenges?				

Adapted from "Elementary Parent Nomination Checklist" with permission from the Austin, Texas, Independent School District Gifted and Talented Program.

Permission to Test

Student: ______________________________

Date: ______________________________

School: ______________________________

Grade/class: ______________________________

Teacher: ______________________________

__________ I give permission for my child to be tested for school-based gifted-education services.

__________ I DO NOT give permission for my child to be tested for school-based gifted-education services.

I understand I will receive written notification of my child's status following evaluation.

Signature of parent/guardian: ______________________________

Permission to Test

Student: ______________________________

Date: ______________________________

School: ______________________________

Grade/class: ______________________________

Teacher: ______________________________

__________ I give permission for my child to be tested for school-based gifted-education services.

__________ I DO NOT give permission for my child to be tested for school-based gifted-education services.

I understand I will receive written notification of my child's status following evaluation.

Signature of parent/guardian: ______________________________

Student's name: ____________________

Date: ____________________

Dear Classroom Teacher:

The school is beginning the process of identifying students who qualify for gifted-education services. Use the forms in this packet to assist you in recommending those students for whom gifted testing is appropriate. Please follow this brief procedure:

1. Read "Differences Between the Bright Child and the Gifted Learner." Use this information to help you place students in your classroom in the appropriate category.

2. Read "Characteristics of Giftedness That Present Challenges." Use this information to help you recognize students whose exceptional abilities may be masked or overlooked due to behavioral issues.

3. Complete the "Teacher's Class Screening Form for Nominating Students for Gifted Testing" as it applies to students in your classroom. (Do not include students who are already identified as gifted and are presently receiving gifted-education services.)

4. Complete a "Rating Scale for Gifted Services" form for each student whose name appears **six or more times** on the screening form.

5. Those students who rate predominantly in the "Often" and "Almost Always" columns of the rating scale should be nominated for gifted testing. Submit individual rating scales to ____________________
on or before ____________________.

6. Send a "Permission to Test" form home for parent signature for those students you consider to be candidates for gifted testing. Return any signed "Permission to Test" forms to
____
on or before ____________________.

Teacher's Class Screening Form for Nominating Students for Gifted Testing

Teacher: ______________________________

Grade/class: ______________________________

School: ______________________________

Date: ______________________________

Please use this form to identify students who are strong candidates for gifted-education services. For each description, write the first and last names of **up to three students** who **first** come to mind. The same student may be listed multiple times. You need not fill in every space if no students, or fewer than three, come to mind for a particular quality. Complete a "Rating Scale for Gifted Services" form for those students whose names appear **six or more times** on this class screening form.

1. Learns rapidly and easily

   ____________ ____________ ____________

2. Offers original, imaginative responses

   ____________ ____________ ____________

3. Is widely informed on many topics

   ____________ ____________ ____________

4. Is self-directed and has a long attention span

   ____________ ____________ ____________

5. Is inquisitive, skeptical

   ____________ ____________ ____________

6. Uses an extensive vocabulary

   ____________ ____________ ____________

7. Constantly asks questions; is curious about many things

   ____________ ____________ ____________

8. Seeks out challenging work or changes simple tasks into more complex tasks

   ____________ ____________ ____________

9. Associates often with other smart children, even if they are older or younger

   ____________ ____________ ____________

CONTINUED > > >

Adapted with permission from *The Survival Guide for Teachers of Gifted Kids* by Jim Delisle and Barbara A. Lewis (Minneapolis: Free Spirit Publishing, 2003).

Teacher's Class Screening Form for Nominating Students for Gifted Testing, continued

10. Has an advanced sense of humor; understands adult humor

_______________ _______________ _______________

11. Is easily bored; argues that she/he does not need to do some of the assigned work

_______________ _______________ _______________

12. Has intense emotions; cries easily when frustrated; is empathetic to people and events

_______________ _______________ _______________

13. Understands concepts easily and quickly

_______________ _______________ _______________

14. Challenges the teacher's knowledge base

_______________ _______________ _______________

15. Does not accept things at face value

_______________ _______________ _______________

16. Dislikes arbitrary decisions

_______________ _______________ _______________

17. Is seen by other children as "smart"

_______________ _______________ _______________

18. Produces original ideas and projects

_______________ _______________ _______________

19. Uses logic to solve problems

_______________ _______________ _______________

20. Is intrigued by abstract ideas

_______________ _______________ _______________

Adapted with permission from *The Survival Guide for Teachers of Gifted Kids* by Jim Delisle and Barbara A. Lewis (Minneapolis: Free Spirit Publishing, 2003).

Rating Scale for Gifted Services

Teacher: Complete this rating scale *only* for students whose names appear six or more times on the "Teacher's Class Screening Form for Nominating Students for Gifted Testing." Complete one form for each student.

Student: ______________________________

Date: ____________ ID no.: ____________________ Birthdate: ______________

School: ______________________________

Grade/class: ______________________________

Teacher: ______________________________

Referred by: ❑ **Parent** ❑ **Teacher** ❑ **Student Self-Referred** ❑ **Other**

Rating Scale	Rarely or Almost Never	Sometimes	Often	Almost Always
1. Has unusually advanced vocabulary for age or grade level				
2. Possesses a large storehouse of information				
3. Has quick mastery and recall of factual information				
4. Demonstrates insight into cause-effect relationships; the how and why of things				
5. Realistically understands events, people, and things				
6. Relates similarities and differences in events, people, and things				
7. Has keen sense of humor and sees humor in situations that may not seem humorous to others				
8. Judges and evaluates ideas, events, and people				
9. Separates parts, reasons, and sees logical answers				
10. Is a keen observer; recalls details				

CONTINUED > > >

Adapted from *Scales for Rating the Behavioral Characteristics of Superior Students* by J. S. Renzulli, L. H. Smith, A. J. White, C. M. Callahan, R. K. Hartman, K. L. Westberg, M. K. Gavin, S. M. Reis, D. Siegle, and R. E. Sytsma Reed, 2013, Waco, TX: Prufrock Press. Copyright 2013 by Prufrock Press. Adapted with permission.

Rating Scale for Gifted Services, continued

Rating Scale	Rarely or Almost Never	Sometimes	Often	Almost Always
11. Raises probing and relevant questions (as distinct from informational or factual questions)				
12. Becomes absorbed and involved; is persistent in completing tasks and acquiring information				
13. Has good problem-solving skills; identifies problems and seeks solutions				
14. Reads a great deal on his/her own; likes challenging materials				
15. Is internally motivated and self-directed				
16. Is self-confident with peers and adults				
17. Adapts easily to new situations and to change				
18. Is self-assertive and individualistic; persistent in his/her beliefs				
19. Works independently				
20. Is responsible and can be counted on to do what she/he has promised and usually does it well				
21. Works with peers cooperatively; shares; expresses ideas willingly				
22. Is very curious and interested in a variety of things				
23. Explores ideas and solutions to problems, questions				
24. Is innovative; produces unusual, unique, clever responses and products				
25. Frequently takes risks				
26. Is eager to do new things; enjoys complex situations				

CONTINUED > > >

Rating Scale for Gifted Services, continued

Rating Scale	Rarely or Almost Never	Sometimes	Often	Almost Always
27. Displays intellectual playfulness; fantasizes, imagines ("I wonder what would happen if . . .")				
28. Manipulates ideas; seeks solutions by adapting, organizing, improving, and modifying				
29. Is sensitive to beauty; displays a natural wonderment				
30. Uses colorful language when speaking and writing				
31. Organizes and adapts ideas through structure				
32. Creates new ideas; eagerly seeks knowledge				
33. Is excited and adventurous; likes to make discoveries				

Adapted from *Scales for Rating the Behavioral Characteristics of Superior Students* by J. S. Renzulli, L. H. Smith, A. J. White, C. M. Callahan, R. K. Hartman, K. L. Westberg, M. K. Gavin, S. M. Reis, D. Siegle, and R. E. Sytsma Reed, 2013, Waco, TX: Prufrock Press. Copyright 2013 by Prufrock Press. Adapted with permission.

Student's name: ____________________

Date: ____________________

Dear Parent/Caregiver:

Your child has recently completed testing and qualifies for gifted-education services. Your child's test scores are recorded at the bottom of this letter. The test results show your child's ranking within the national percentile for verbal, quantitative, and nonverbal reasoning.

It is important to note that the state-approved test cited below measures a student's reasoning ability and is *not* indicative of student achievement. A percentile rank is not the same as the percent correct. Percentile ranks provide a comparison of your child's performance to that of a national sample of students in the same grade, ranking students on a scale of __________ to __________. In accordance with the state gifted mandate, students who qualify at or above the __________ percentile in any area of the test qualify for gifted-education services in this school district.

Our district provides gifted-education services in a Schoolwide Cluster Grouping Model (SCGM). The enclosed sheet provides information about this model.

Please complete and sign this form in the space indicated below and return it to your child's teacher. A duplicate copy has been enclosed for your records. If you have any questions, please contact the gifted specialist at your child's school.

Sincerely,

Gifted-Education Coordinator

- -

Student: ____________________

School: ____________________

Grade	Testing Date	Verbal Test/ Level	Reasoning Percentile	Quantitative Percentile	Nonverbal Reasoning Percentile

I give permission for my child, ____________________, to receive gifted-education services.

Signature of parent/guardian: ____________________

Date: ____________________

Student's name: ____________________

Date: ____________________

Dear Parent/Caregiver:

You have received notice that your child qualifies for gifted-education services. These services will be provided through the Schoolwide Cluster Grouping Model (SCGM) that is being implemented at your child's school this year.

In the SCGM, all gifted children at each grade level are clustered together into an otherwise mixed-ability classroom with a designated gifted-cluster teacher. Gifted-cluster teachers provide individualized instruction or extended and accelerated learning opportunities as determined by the needs of the student. Gifted-cluster teachers receive specialized, ongoing training in the areas of gifted education and differentiated instruction—special teaching strategies for modifying curriculum content, pace, process, products, assessments, and learning environment to meet individual gifted students' needs. This training prepares the teachers with an understanding of how gifted children learn and gives them the tools they need to provide appropriate teaching strategies for their gifted students. The school's gifted specialist and the district gifted coordinator serve as resources and support to the gifted-cluster teachers.

Our school is very proud to implement this gifted-education service model in the fall of the upcoming school year. It allows us to provide full-time services for your child and other gifted students without the interruption of out-of-class programs. For further information regarding gifted education and the Schoolwide Cluster Grouping Model, please visit the district website (____________________) or contact your school's gifted specialist.

Sincerely,

Gifted-Education Coordinator

Student's name: ______________________

Date: ______________________

Dear Parent/Caregiver:

Your child has recently completed gifted testing. Based on the test results recorded at the bottom of this letter, your child does not qualify for gifted-education services at this time.

The test results show your child's ranking within the national percentile for verbal, quantitative, and nonverbal reasoning. It is important to note that the state-approved test cited below measures a student's reasoning ability and is *not* indicative of student achievement. A percentile rank is not the same as the percent correct. Percentile ranks provide a comparison of your child's performance to that of a national sample of students in the same grade, ranking students on a scale of __________ to __________. Scores in the __________ to __________ percentile range are considered to be average; scores in the __________ to __________ percentile range are considered to be higher than average. In accordance with our state and district gifted mandates, students who qualify at or above the __________ percentile in any area of the test qualify for gifted-education services in this school district.

If you have any questions, please contact the gifted specialist at your child's school.

Sincerely,

Gifted-Education Coordinator

- -

Student: ______________________

School: ______________________

Grade	Testing Date	Verbal Test/ Level	Reasoning Percentile	Quantitative Percentile	Nonverbal Reasoning Percentile

4

Staffing the SCGM

GUIDING QUESTIONS

- How are teachers selected for gifted-cluster classrooms?
- What are the roles and responsibilities of the gifted-cluster teacher?
- What other staffing positions support the SCGM?
- What are the budget implications of staffing and training with the SCGM?

The success of the SCGM depends on how it is implemented by the teaching staff. To be effective, gifted-cluster teachers need to genuinely enjoy working with gifted students, have a flexible teaching style, and be open to collaborating with colleagues. They will be expected to take part in ongoing professional development that helps them understand the social and emotional needs of gifted children, helps them find ways to work effectively with these students, and helps them learn instructional techniques for meeting their unique learning needs.

Getting Started: How to Determine Who Should Teach the Gifted-Cluster Classrooms

The best time to identify teachers for the gifted clusters is prior to setting up classes for the coming year. Teachers always appreciate knowing the particulars about their students and classes well before school begins in the fall. Many teachers take advantage of the summer break to create lessons and learning centers for the upcoming year.

In choosing gifted-cluster teachers for the first year of the SCGM, principals may consider designating teachers who have had some gifted-education training or experience for this role. Although few states require any such training, some teachers have attended workshops, certification programs, or university classes to learn how to challenge gifted students in their classes.

Teachers who are parents of gifted children often make outstanding gifted-cluster teachers because they have firsthand daily experience with gifted children. They understand the critical need to differentiate curriculum and instruction in response to these students' diverse learning needs, because many of these teachers have found themselves advocating for more challenging curriculum for their own children. They also may have a high appreciation for their gifted students' quirkiness, sense of humor, and other personality traits common in gifted students.

Teachers who work well with gifted students are comfortable with versatile teaching practices.

They:

- understand and enjoy teaching gifted students
- are willing to participate in ongoing professional development to facilitate their ability to consistently differentiate the curriculum for advanced learners
- readily manage flexible grouping and learning opportunities
- encourage students to work independently or in small groups
- support student work on student-directed learning
- possess a playful sense of humor and appreciate that same quality in students

SUPERVISOR SPOTLIGHT

Since flexibility is such a critical characteristic for successful teachers of the gifted, anything you can do to demonstrate flexibility in your leadership will provide great role modeling.

It can be beneficial to consult with gifted specialists or the district program coordinator in making gifted-cluster teacher selections. Give more credibility to the presence of the necessary skills than to tenure and length of service. Do not, however, assign a beginning teacher, or someone without the necessary qualifications, to a gifted-cluster classroom.

Gifted-cluster teachers ideally will keep the position for at least two or three consecutive years. Teachers spend the first year learning how to do the job and the second year really enjoying it. Rotating teachers into the gifted-cluster classrooms every two or three years helps develop the school's ability to serve all students. Many schools choose to have their gifted-cluster teachers remain in the role for several years instead of rotating, since the teachers learn and build their instructional skills and practices in the position.

Preparing Teachers for Gifted Education: A Benefit to All

All students deserve to have teachers who are qualified and prepared to address their learning needs. Because school is structured for the average student population, teachers must plan education interventions in order to serve adequately the populations that fall outside the average range. The bell curve on page 3 serves as a reminder that gifted students are as far removed from average as students at the other end of the curve are, and therefore are equally entitled to whatever differentiation is necessary to engage and challenge them. This requires specialized training for teaching staff.

Expanding professional learning opportunities in gifted education to all teachers on the staff will have a positive impact on the entire school. With more information provided to the schools about the characteristics and needs of gifted students, school administrators and teachers will identify qualities in existing staff members who respond well to the needs of gifted students. The skills and instructional practices teachers acquire will allow them to bring the strategies into their own classrooms, where all students can benefit from instructional techniques that enable them to progress at their own rate. This in turn will improve overall class achievement.

Having all teachers trained in gifted education and differentiation will also reduce the number of parents making requests to have children who are not identified as gifted placed into the gifted-cluster classrooms. It will send two important messages to the parent community: that there are many teachers in the school qualified to teach gifted students *and* that the school is not assigning only the "best" teachers to the gifted clusters.

Chapter 2 discusses how to introduce the SCGM to the teaching staff. See chapter 7 for information about ongoing professional development for teachers in the SCGM.

Some teachers need encouragement to teach in a gifted-cluster classroom. They may be reluctant because they have no prior experience working with gifted students. This reluctance alone should not prevent a teacher who possesses the necessary characteristics and skills from being designated as a gifted-cluster teacher. It is the ongoing training and peer support that are critical to the teacher's success.

If only one teacher in the grade level agrees to participate in professional learning opportunities in differentiation and gifted education, it is advisable to keep all the gifted-identified students in that teacher's classroom—even if doing so means that the cluster of gifted students makes up more than 20 to 25 percent of the classroom population. It is not generally effective to insist that teachers take on a gifted cluster when they are not ready to do so, or to spring the assignment on teachers shortly before school starts in the fall. Instead, encourage teachers to develop an interest in teaching gifted students by providing them with information and training.

Roles and Responsibilities of the Gifted-Cluster Teacher

The primary responsibility of the gifted-cluster teacher is to teach all the students in the class. This requires the teacher to create a learning environment that challenges all students and respects differences in learning needs. Gifted-cluster teachers should know how to recognize and nurture behaviors usually demonstrated by gifted students. Each gifted-cluster teacher should be able to:

- understand and accommodate the exceptional learning needs of gifted students
- consistently offer compacting opportunities for content and pacing
- differentiate curriculum and instruction for students who are gifted
- complete differentiated education plans (DEPs) for gifted students
- assess gifted students' growth in an ongoing process before, during, and after instruction to ensure continuous progress
- participate in monthly gifted-cluster meetings at the school
- participate in staff development at the site and district level
- invite testing nominations from other teachers at the grade level
- disseminate information about identification of gifted students to other teachers
- help parents of gifted students provide academic and emotional support for their children

The gifted-cluster teacher also serves as a resource to other teachers when students are identified as gifted during the school year. Assistance can take the form of:

- providing teachers with information about the needs and characteristics of gifted children
- sharing lesson plans and resources with colleagues regarding extension and acceleration strategies

Roles and Responsibilities of Support Specialists

Gifted specialists and program coordinators can be very helpful in supporting gifted-cluster teachers. A gifted specialist, or gifted mentor, may already be in place in schools with other gifted-education services; if not, it is possible to recruit a qualified teacher from existing staff to work with and support the gifted-cluster teachers. A gifted coordinator to serve all the district's schools is a role that either stands alone or is taken on by another school administrator, such as a principal or the district's director of special education, curriculum, or student services.

Gifted Specialist or Gifted Mentor

A gifted specialist, or gifted mentor, is a staff member who has experience and training in working with gifted students. In most cases, the gifted specialist is a gifted-cluster teacher or another full-time school staff member such as the media specialist, a teacher mentor, a gifted pull-out teacher, or a building administrator.

The gifted specialist supports the gifted-cluster teachers in their efforts to serve their gifted students. He provides professional development for gifted-cluster teachers that is geared toward the specific needs of the school, the teachers, and the students. He might model some differentiated lessons and provide coaching to the gifted-cluster teachers. Gifted-cluster teachers view him as a resource and a leader of the school's gifted services.

Responsibilities of the gifted specialist vary among school districts. If there is no district-level gifted coordinator when the SCGM is implemented, the gifted specialist may take on some of the program administration responsibilities normally handled by a gifted coordinator. School administrators should be careful not to let administrative duties, such as testing and reporting of scores, take away instructional time from students or coaching time from teachers.

The gifted specialist should be able to:

- oversee nomination, administration, and reporting for gifted testing
- preside over monthly gifted-cluster meetings at the school
- provide staff development opportunities for the school
- provide coaching for gifted-cluster teachers
- attend monthly meetings with school gifted specialists from the district
- complete a yearly summary report, including program evaluation data
- communicate with parents of the schools' gifted students

Figure 4-1 shows an example of a posting for the position of gifted specialist in a school.

FIGURE 4-1 **Sample Posting to Invite Applications for the Position of Gifted Specialist**

Qualifications:	Certified teacher Gifted endorsed Experience teaching gifted students
Supervisor:	Building principal, gifted coordinator
Responsibilities:	Oversee nominations for gifted testing Administer and score testing Preside over monthly gifted-cluster meetings at school Attend monthly district mentor meetings Provide staff development opportunities for the school Attend district staff development opportunities Communicate with parents Hold parent-night events Gather data for program evaluation purposes

There is one gifted specialist position per school. To apply, please inform your building principal with details regarding your education, endorsements, and experience in differentiating curriculum.

Some districts hire a full- or part-time gifted specialist who is assigned to more than one school. Ideally, no gifted specialist should be responsible for serving more than four or five schools, but in practice, that might not be realistic. This specialist's task is to train gifted-cluster teachers in how to work with gifted students in their classrooms. He may model lessons, work with teachers on developing differentiated lesson plans, or provide other professional development for the gifted-cluster teachers as needed. Additionally, he oversees the identification process at the schools he serves. The gifted specialist is the link among the parents, teachers, school administrator, and district office.

Gifted Coordinator

The gifted coordinator is a district-level administrator. In some districts this staffer is called the gifted facilitator or gifted director. While it is ideal to have this as a stand-alone position, many gifted coordinators have other responsibilities in the area of special education, curriculum planning, or student services. Some school districts implementing the SCGM do not create the position of gifted coordinator until the need is established. If your school district does not have a gifted coordinator or does not see the immediate need for this position, we suggest building the need by establishing the SCGM first. As the model grows in your district, the need for someone to coordinate the model at a district level will emerge.

The primary responsibility of the gifted coordinator is to support the gifted specialists. Working as a liaison between the schools and the district, this person brings continuity and consistency to all aspects of the program. Specifically, she oversees the district's testing procedures, student placements, professional development, program evaluation, and communication with parents. The gifted coordinator must advocate for district resources and attention directed toward gifted students and programming. This person's involvement at the district level in areas such as curriculum adoptions, report card committees, and scheduling can positively impact the SCGM.

The gifted coordinator should be able to:

- distribute information to the public regarding district gifted services
- provide training for gifted specialists and gifted-cluster teachers
- provide information about the SCGM to the school community
- provide training on the administration and scoring of assessments as needed
- research assessment tools for addressing the diverse needs of the district
- facilitate district parent meetings regarding gifted-education opportunities
- coordinate testing schedules
- be available for modeling differentiated curriculum and instruction within the classroom
- be available for teacher consultation
- assist with parent communication as related to gifted services
- respond to requests for gifted students' records from other schools
- lead monthly meetings of the district's gifted specialists
- collect data to present a year-end report to the school board
- maintain professional growth opportunities at the district level
- assist administrators in developing and supporting schools' gifted-cluster classrooms
- ensure district compliance with the state mandate (when one exists)
- maintain a gifted-student database
- provide schools with gifted students' academic achievement
- monitor representation of the district's demographic groups in the gifted-identified student population
- assist principals in the selection of gifted-cluster teachers

Budget Concerns

While many schools and districts might perceive that they cannot adequately fund services for gifted students, the SCGM need not overstretch already tight budgets. It helps to keep in mind that gifted students count in the school district's average daily attendance (ADA), which determines the amount of funds schools and districts receive from the state (if your state provides funding for gifted students). This means that funding for a schoolwide program supporting achievement for all students is compatible with present funding practices.

The good news is that with the SCGM, the only additional funds needed are directed at staff development that benefits all teachers and all students. In other gifted-program models, additional salaries would be needed for hiring specialized teachers or purchasing a separate curriculum. In most cases, these services would come at considerable cost, yet would not be considered full-time attention to gifted students' education. With the SCGM, full-time staff members are already in place to provide comprehensive gifted education within the cluster classrooms. Therefore, additional costs will be minimal and can be incurred gradually.

Principals or district administrators may need to reallocate existing discretionary funds for training and professional development of gifted-cluster teachers. Since most administrators have limited resources to direct toward professional development, many choose to provide training in gifted education first to the current or prospective gifted-cluster teachers and then to the rest of the staff. Some additional funds may also be needed to pay a stipend to an existing staff member who takes on the role of the gifted specialist (if your school district supports paying stipends to teachers who take on additional responsibilities). As noted earlier, the hiring of a district-level coordinator, if one is not already in place, can wait until a need emerges.

SUMMARY

This chapter has described the traits, attitudes, and skills required of gifted-cluster teachers. It has also explained the specific roles and responsibilities of the gifted-cluster teacher, the school gifted specialist, and the district gifted coordinator.

The information in the chapter can help you:

- select staff and create clear job descriptions for each role in the SCGM
- implement the model with minimal budget strain

The four chapters in part 1 have presented key information for getting started with the SCGM. Looking ahead, part 2 details hands-on strategies teachers can use to differentiate and compact the curriculum to meet the needs of gifted students. Part 3 addresses planning and arranging professional development and establishing a system for ongoing evaluation of schoolwide cluster grouping.

Responsibilities of the SCGM Staff Members

Key Responsibilities of the Gifted-Cluster Teacher

- Differentiate curriculum for students who are gifted.
- Complete differentiated education plans (DEPs) for gifted students.
- Participate in monthly gifted-cluster meetings at the school.
- Participate in staff development at the site and district level.
- Invite testing nominations from grade-level teachers.

Key Responsibilities of the Gifted Specialist

- Oversee nomination, administration, and reporting of gifted testing.
- Preside over monthly gifted-cluster meetings at individual schools.
- Provide staff development opportunities for the school.
- Provide coaching for gifted-cluster teachers.
- Attend monthly meetings with school gifted specialists from the district.
- Complete a yearly summary report.
- Communicate with parents of the schools' gifted students.

Key Responsibilities of the Gifted Coordinator

- Provide training for gifted specialists and gifted-cluster teachers.
- Provide training on the Schoolwide Cluster Grouping Model to school staff.
- Coordinate testing schedules.
- Facilitate district parent meetings.
- Be available for teacher consultations.
- Lead monthly meetings of the district's gifted specialists.
- Collect data to present a year-end report to the school board.
- Maintain professional growth opportunities at the district level.

Titles Schools Can Use for Gifted-Education Staff

Classroom Level	Site Level	District Level
Gifted-Cluster Teacher	Gifted Specialist Gifted Mentor	Gifted Coordinator Gifted Facilitator Gifted Director

PART 2

The SCGM in Action: How to Compact and Differentiate Curriculum for Advanced Learners

Part 2 of *The Cluster Grouping Handbook* describes in user-friendly detail classroom strategies that will support your efforts to help all students actualize their learning potential. Many students with high ability decide not to show how advanced they really are because they're concerned that adults and other students will expect them to perform at exceptionally high levels all the time.

The compacting and differentiation methods presented in chapters 5 and 6 describe essential techniques gifted-cluster teachers will want to incorporate into their teaching in order to support the gifted students in their classrooms and ensure that the Schoolwide Cluster Grouping Model benefits all learners. Chapter 5 addresses strategies teachers can use to give students credit for required standards they have already mastered and to provide alternate learning experiences that extend grade-level content. Chapter 6 presents methods for extending learning for advanced learners who need less time to master *new* content. Both chapters offer a range of ideas for differentiating instruction with all students who need it and for building and sustaining a unified classroom learning community.

Written with gifted-cluster teachers in mind, part 2 nonetheless applies to all teachers who seek to differentiate the curriculum to meet the needs of every student in their classrooms. While many of the strategies described are designed for use with gifted learners, teachers will usually find other students in their classes who can benefit from these same learning opportunities.

Although we have written these chapters directly to teachers, the information will be of value to administrators, parents, and other educators as well.

5

Compacting and Differentiating Curriculum That Students Have Already Mastered

GUIDING QUESTIONS

- What learning opportunities do teachers need to offer highly capable students so they can be productive and challenged?
- How can teachers find the time and materials to support differentiation efforts for students who need to experience challenge beyond the grade-level parameters?
- How can the teacher manage a classroom in which students are simultaneously working on different learning tasks?
- How does compacting work with standards-based learning, STEM and STEAM instruction, and problem-based learning methods?
- What can the teacher do to build a unified learning community in which all students feel part of the whole class and feel as important as their classmates regarding needed differentiation opportunities?

Gifted students often are extremely frustrated by the amount of time they have to spend in school "learning" content they have already mastered. A typical skill taught in the early grades is revisited and built upon each year throughout a student's elementary and middle school experiences. This practice of spiraling curriculum content is based on the assumption that students need multiple repetitions to learn new concepts. However, gifted students usually learn after one exposure to a concept or skill. Each time they are expected to revisit that concept through the years, their frustration grows and their productivity dwindles.

ACHIEVEMENTADVISORY

Providing all students open access to available compacting and differentiation opportunities sets the stage for higher test scores throughout the class. By inviting all students to participate, teachers are setting very high expectations, and consistently high expectations raise students' confidence levels and increase the potential for greater achievement.

The presence of a cluster of identified gifted students in the class makes the availability of regular compacting and differentiation opportunities imperative. Gifted students are able to do things most other students can't do:

- They learn new material in a much shorter time than age peers do.
- They usually remember forever something they have learned only once, making most review and reteaching unnecessary.
- They multitask with ease. Gifted students do not have to see the teacher in order to hear her. They can easily monitor the teacher's direct instruction lesson even if they are working simultaneously on independent learning activities.

This chapter describes specific strategies to use when teaching content that students have already mastered and presents ways to create consistent interaction between the identified gifted students and the rest of the students in your class. The strategies are useful both in classrooms that have a gifted cluster and in those that do not. They revolve around the concept that once students have documented mastery of a specific skill they are allowed to spend their in-class learning time on extension activities that motivate and challenge them. Chapter 6 describes specific strategies for differentiating content that is *new* to students and explains ways to access and use extension materials.

When you are incorporating new teaching methods, start small and build slowly. Try one strategy at a time, and work with one subject area or class period at a time. Move on to other subjects or classes only when you and the target students are comfortable enough to do so. Be proactive about meeting with other gifted-cluster teachers on a regular basis to share useful methods and avoid potential pitfalls.

Five Elements of Differentiation

Five essential elements of differentiation must be present if the daily learning experiences of gifted students are to be motivating and challenging: content, process, product, learning environment, and assessment. Paying attention to these elements helps you ensure that you consistently meet the learning needs of students of high ability in your classroom.

1. **Content.** Content is differentiated when students spend in-class time working on either accelerated or extended content that moves them ahead in their own learning. Differentiated content should be connected to the required standards but not confined to them. For example, if the class is learning about multiplication of two-figure numbers, students experiencing differentiated content might be learning about multiplication of decimals or working on real-life applications of the multiplication process.
2. **Process.** Process is differentiated by the methods gifted students use to make sense of what they are learning. Compacting, which is giving students full credit for what they already know at the beginning of a unit or chapter, is one important component of differentiated process. Other elements include higher-level or critical thinking, opportunities for meaningful ongoing research, and skills to facilitate those processes. Gifted

students' research should be focused on inquiry rather than simply on finding information. It should also help them understand the processes used by adult professionals.

3. **Product.** Products are differentiated when students are encouraged and allowed to go beyond the written tasks to create actual artifacts, exhibitions, or performances. Products may also be differentiated to accommodate students' preferred learning styles.
4. **Learning environment.** The learning environment is differentiated as students interact with others inside and outside the classroom, as determined by the content being learned. Environment is also impacted when students experience differentiated expectations, flexible time limits, opportunities to work with mentors, and coaching assistance. These factors help students make consistent progress toward being able to operate effectively with independent study and research.
5. **Assessment.** Assessment is differentiated when gifted students are allowed to document their mastery of certain standards *before* that material is taught to the class or when students who learn very quickly work through the required standards at their own pace. When students move through the curriculum at a faster pace or study concepts at a deeper level than the standards dictate, their assessment is differentiated in two ways. First, they are not held to the learning pace of classmates who are age-appropriate learners. They are not required to slow down their learning just because classmates may not be ready for a particular assessment. Second, they are encouraged to develop alternative assessment methods to evaluate the quality of their independent study work, such as student-created rubrics or performance-assessment options.

A Word About the Strategies

The strategies described in this chapter were originally designed for gifted students. In practice, however, they motivate and involve many other students as well. The basic principles of how to teach gifted students effectively are very similar to the principles of good teaching in general: identify a student's entry level with a certain standard, teach him in such a way that he is likely to move forward in his own learning, and continue to monitor his progress. For this reason, all teachers in a school will benefit from learning strategies that are effective with gifted students. Any sound teaching strategy has the potential to positively impact students at all levels of achievement.

How Compacting Meets the Needs of Gifted Students

Gifted students appreciate opportunities to receive full credit up front for any content standards they have already mastered. They also appreciate opportunities to learn curriculum that is new and challenging to them at a pace commensurate with their advanced ability. Beyond appreciating such opportunities, gifted students, like all students, *need and deserve* to have their learning needs met. When working with struggling learners, teachers adjust the content, process, product, means of assessment, and learning environment to ensure that the students make continuous progress in their learning. Gifted students, too, need teachers to constantly assess their entry level, teach from there, and assess their progress—not because gifted kids are any more special than any other students, but simply because their advanced competence in learning grade-level material makes curriculum designed for age peers unchallenging, repetitive, and often boring.

Students might actually be reluctant to experience challenging work when they are always admonished to "do their very best." This expression often serves as a disincentive for advanced learners to work hard. Gifted students may resist challenge because they fear that working hard will lead others to doubt their intelligence, having observed throughout their school years that grade-level peers, teachers, and parents expect them to be *always* at the top of their group in productivity and grades. Instead, adults will want to encourage students to focus on effort. This sends the message that the *process* is even more important than the product. Learning to work hard throughout one's school experience is the best route to lifelong achievement. Once students learn to concentrate on the process rather than the end product and to take satisfaction in having worked hard to get from point A to point B, they will be more motivated to tackle challenges. (For specific tips to encourage all students to work hard at all times, search the internet for videos and other information about Dr. Carol Dweck's work on "growth mindset.")

No state actually requires teachers to *teach* all standards to all students. State laws simply require teachers to document that all students assigned to them have *mastered* the required standards. Documentation of exactly *when* students reach mastery is not legislated, nor is it legislated that all students must show mastery at the same time. Once a student has documented her mastery of a required standard, she should also be allowed to use her learning time in a different manner to work on extension activities while teachers are working with students who need more direct instruction.

Compacting the curriculum allows gifted students to be credited for what they already know and to move forward from there. It *is* appropriate and legitimate, according to district and state expectations, to document which standards students have already mastered *before* directly teaching them. It *is* appropriate for gifted students to be allowed to learn new standards at their advanced learning level. It *is* appropriate for students who have documented previous mastery to spend their school time learning content that moves them forward and allows them to consistently experience challenging and meaningful learning activities.

Another practical benefit of providing compacting and differentiation for advanced learners is that it actually opens up opportunities for teachers to support struggling students. When they know that advanced students are working on challenging tasks, teachers have more freedom to spend as much time as needed with students who are having trouble learning particular topics.

A Few Words About Extra Credit, Enrichment, and Extensions

All students need direct instruction when learning at their personal challenge level. Advanced students, however, often catch on quickly to new content and are ready to work independently sooner than age peers. When this occurs, many teachers offer extra-credit work and are perplexed and frustrated when some gifted students do not take advantage of that opportunity.

How effective is the practice of offering extra credit? Think about it. The only students who ever get to work toward extra credit are those who have more than enough credit already. And the students who could really benefit from some extra credit aren't eligible for it, because they don't have enough of the regular credit. On top of that, students who easily complete work discover that their reward is to get to do more work than other students. No rational person, at any age, willingly does more than others simply because more is better. Rather than completing extra-credit assignments, students should be working on *extension activities* at levels that allow them to progress in their own learning every day during regular school time. Such extensions are far more interesting and worthwhile.

We speak about *extensions* in place of the more commonly used term *enrichment*. All students deserve an enriched curriculum, but only gifted students require teachers to *extend* the parameters of the grade-level standards in order to provide challenging learning opportunities. After they have demonstrated mastery of the grade-level work, the extension activities become students' regular work.

Beyond Learning Extensions: Acceleration in or out of the Classroom

When students need acceleration of content in addition to, or in place of, extensions—such as in subjects that are sequential, like reading or math—a different type of intervention is indicated. Sometimes, when we try to compact to determine where a student's instructional level is, we discover that the student has already mastered so much of the required curriculum that there is very little new grade-level material for him to learn. In such cases, students may be regrouped to work on advanced curriculum. They may be allowed to work with a group of students from a higher grade for the subject areas in which they are significantly advanced. In rare cases when a student's entire learning level is significantly advanced from age peers, radical acceleration or grade skipping is another option.

When allowing students to work on content assigned to a higher grade level, a multiyear plan should be in place that includes the student's parents, future teachers, the principal from the next-level school, and other interested parties in the planning process. The *Iowa Acceleration Scale Manual* (see "Resources" for chapter 1 on page 236) is a book that provides step-by-step support to help educators and parents decide which students should experience acceleration of content and to determine how to facilitate that process. Plans must be made for what will be taught, who will do the teaching, what will happen when students need to go to another location for advanced classes, and who will provide the transportation. If such a plan is not possible, teachers will need to use advanced materials from other sources or consider blended learning, an instructional model that combines traditional classroom methods with digital resources and tools.

Essential Teaching Skills for Gifted-Cluster Teachers

The basic skills you need to make sure that gifted students are consistently challenged are compacting grade-level standards, differentiating curriculum, forming and managing flexible groups, and providing ongoing assessment opportunities.

Curriculum Compacting

Curriculum compacting, a term coined by Dr. Joseph Renzulli, means finding ways for gifted students to spend less time with the curriculum designed for age peers and more time working on curriculum that challenges them. The term itself is designed to shock us into action, because the more generally understood use of *compacting* applies to trash. At most grade levels, gifted students have already learned more than 50 percent of a year's curriculum at the beginning of the school year. They could throw it away as trash and never miss it, because they already have so much of it mastered. Just as a trash compactor compresses garbage so it takes up less space, curriculum compacting compresses a semester's or year's curriculum into a shorter time period by giving students full credit for prior mastery or by allowing them to learn new standards in a shorter time than age peers do. After a trash compactor has done its work, it creates more space for more trash. When you compact the curriculum, you create more learning time for students to work on extension tasks that move them forward in their learning.

In skill areas such as math, reading or language arts, spelling, and vocabulary, the goal is to compact the amount of *practice* kids have to do. This chapter presents three strategies for compacting already-mastered content in this manner: Most Difficult First (described beginning on page 107), pretests with extensions (page 109), and learning contracts (page 111). In content areas where the material may be new for students, teachers can compact the amount of time students must spend learning the required standards. Chapter 6 describes strategies for compacting time. Creative teachers always find ways to mix and match elements from all strategies they learn, and you are invited to do just that!

Curriculum Differentiation

Curriculum differentiation includes any learning activity that is different from what you would teach to the entire class as a direct instruction lesson or practice. Therefore, you can consider differentiation to be anything you do with a small group or individual students that allows them to work on tasks that are not the same as what students in the larger group are doing. You are probably already differentiating to some extent. However, gifted students should be spending most of their school time on differentiated activities rather than working on grade-level standards. Students who are working independently experience the same assessments of grade-level standards at the same time and in the same manner as the entire class, but they spend their time between assessments working independently on topics that extend the required standards.

Flexible Grouping Using Formative Assessments

In gifted-cluster classes, the grouping is flexible and may change daily, weekly, or monthly. Students are placed in learning groups according to common interests, achievement levels, need for differentiation, or even personality characteristics. Students often move between groups. For example, if a spelling pretest on Monday is voluntary, any student who wishes to try to demonstrate that she has already mastered the week's words is free to take the test. All students who pass the test with no more than one or two words spelled incorrectly will be grouped together for that week to work on differentiated activities in spelling or other language arts. The following week the group will change to consist of students who have passed that particular week's pretest.*

During the time when students are working toward mastery of new standards, formative assessments are used along the way to guide and direct instruction. When teachers want to document that students have learned everything they should know by the end of a unit or chapter, teachers use summative assessments. With gifted students, as with all students, teachers are expected to provide ongoing evidence from formative and summative assessments to justify that students are learning at their challenge level. To ensure consistent forward progress in learning, teachers preassess, teach, assess, reteach, provide summative assessments—and then repeat the entire process.

Making Compacting and Differentiation Work Smoothly

You may be concerned that students who do not regularly experience compacting or differentiation opportunities will feel bad about that. You may wonder if you should not even make the opportunities available for gifted students for that reason. Consider that you would never keep a vital learning opportunity away from a special education student because other kids might feel unhappy that they don't get to use certain technology or have a full-time aide helping them with their work. Similarly, it is not acceptable to keep appropriate compacting and extension opportunities away from gifted students.

When you face this dilemma, determine the reasons why some students might be feeling bad

*Flexible grouping is also present when teachers regroup students by achievement levels between sections of a grade level or even across several grade levels. For more on flexible grouping, see pages 28–29 and 42.

and respond to those concerns. For example, if students object that they always have to do all the problems, you might suggest they choose odd or even problems. If they complain that they never have time to work on extension activities, provide that time for all students once or twice each week for twenty to thirty minutes during the regular instructional period. Embedded in extension activities are many previously learned skills, so this is time well spent.

Refrain from making compacting or differentiation opportunities sound so special that students who do not get to experience this will feel that they have missed out on something valuable. As you explain the opportunities, keep your voice and inflections calm and matter-of-fact.

You may experience frustration when you offer compacting opportunities, because some students who should participate choose not to. To entice students to try the compacting opportunities, offer and explain the following two essential guarantees:

1. Students who are successful with the compacting opportunity will not have to do more work than other students. They will spend the same amount of class time on a subject as other students do, but the work they do will be more advanced. Therefore, be careful to avoid the use of the terms *extra* or *extra credit.* The differentiated work gifted students are doing *replaces* the grade-level work they don't need to do. Since it extends the grade-level parameters, it is called extension work.

How Differentiation Communicates Respect for Individual Differences

Whenever students are in classes where differentiation is noticeable, the message they get is that it is perfectly okay if students are different from each other. When students are in classes where the entire class is taught as one group and all students are expected to do the same task at the same time, the message students get is that the teacher prefers it when all students are exactly the same. Providing differentiated tasks when they are needed is one way to teach respect for individual differences. When teachers respect those differences, students are more likely to respect them too.

Consider this example: A fourth-grade teacher, Ms. Olivier, received a complaint from a student named Jason about the spelling pretests. Jason, who was not usually a pretest candidate, felt that spelling pretests were unfair and should be stopped. His teacher used the following scenario to help him understand why it was okay to continue to offer the pretest opportunity.

Ms. Olivier suggested, "Jason, let's exchange shoes for a few minutes. I'll wear yours and you wear mine. Let's see how far we can walk in each other's shoes."

Jason chuckled and said, "That won't work, because our shoes don't fit each other."

Ms. Olivier responded, "That's right! And that's exactly why all kids in this class don't get the same work as all other kids. Each student needs different-size 'shoes' for spelling, math, writing, and other subjects. My job is to make sure all the 'shoes' I give to all my students are a good fit in whatever subject area we're learning."

"So then, what's my job?" Jason inquired.

"Your job is to let me know if the spelling or reading or writing 'shoes' I give you aren't a good fit. But your job is *not* to question the spelling or reading or writing 'shoes' I give to any other student."

Jason thought for a few moments, nodded his head, and walked away.

About a month later, Xavier was sitting at the same table as Jason and noticed that their work assignments were not the same. "How come I'm not doing the same work as you?" Xavier asked.

Jason glanced at Xavier's work and responded, "It's not your size!"

Imagine classrooms in which students accept individual differences as a matter of "size" rather than in terms of greater or lesser abilities. Teachers who regularly differentiate the curriculum for students who need this are "walking the talk" that individual differences should be respected and accommodated.

2. Students must be able to understand that they will never receive a recorded grade that is lower than the grade they would most likely have earned if they had worked on the regular lesson. They should understand why this is the case and how the grading will work. Specific techniques to accomplish this are described in "Grading Extension Work" on page 118.

Strategies for Compacting and Differentiating Previously Mastered Skill Work

Teachers compact previously mastered curriculum by allowing students to demonstrate, before a concept is taught, that they have already mastered it. Teachers use the same assessment for this option that they plan to use with the whole class as a final assessment. When students can demonstrate that they have mastered upcoming material, they are allowed to work on extension activities for part or all of each instructional period.

Renzulli suggests that you think of your lesson planning as budgeting the amount of time that typical students at your grade level need to master required standards. When students demonstrate that they need less direct instruction time than you have budgeted, they "buy back" the remaining time for activities they choose. This concept of buying back time is very enticing for students.

As noted earlier, you can use three strategies to compact curriculum students have learned before: Most Difficult First, pretests with extensions, and Learning Contracts. Generally with these strategies, do *not* review the content with students before the preassessment. Preassessments are not used to discover which students are quick learners, but rather to discover which students already have mastered the material you are about to teach.

Most Difficult First: Compacting and Differentiating One Lesson at a Time

The Most Difficult First strategy is designed to work with one lesson at a time. Students are required to pay attention to the direct instruction during the first part of the instructional period, which optimally takes no more than twelve to fifteen minutes. As you assign some practice items, you indicate which are the most difficult items in the whole assignment. The strategy allows students who demonstrate mastery of one day's content in one subject area to receive full credit quite quickly. The students can then spend the balance of their class time working on designated extension tasks instead of being required to participate in further instruction, because they have demonstrated they do not need further explanation about these particular concepts. The reproducible form on page 122 provides directions for students on how to participate in Most Difficult First.

Before you begin each lesson, decide which problems or exercises represent the most difficult part of the entire practice activity. After you have explained the concepts from the day's lesson, and before students begin practicing what they have learned, describe the Most Difficult First option to everyone. Explain that you can't tell by looking at students just how much practice each person needs to achieve mastery. Tell them that you expect many students may need all the assigned practice. However, if they believe they need less practice to demonstrate they completely understand the concepts, they may try the most difficult problems first, before the other ones. Anyone who gets four or five of these problems or examples correct in fifteen minutes, and whose work is clearly legible for the person who will check it, is considered finished with the regular work. (Don't ask for 100 percent accuracy, because you don't want students to think that you expect them to be perfect at all times.) Those students receive full credit for the entire assignment and may spend the balance of their time in that subject working on "choice work" (differentiated extension activities). Students who begin Most Difficult First, but are unable to finish it in fifteen minutes, continue to participate in the teacher-directed lesson for the remainder of the class period in order to receive more instruction and practice with the concepts being taught.

The first person who completes the four or five questions correctly and brings them to the teacher becomes the checker for the rest of the instructional period. The reproducible form on page 123 provides directions for the checker to follow. If the student does not want this assignment, keep checking other students' papers until one agrees to be the checker.

Once you have announced the checker's name to the class, students who want their papers checked give a signal and wait for the checker to come to their desk. A student may serve as the checker only once each week; on other days, the student should spend the time he "buys back" working on his own extension activities.

At the end of the first practice period, the checker will give you the papers he has collected. Put them aside until you have collected the regular work from the other students the following day. That way you can enter everyone's grade for the day's lesson at the same time, without creating any extra paperwork for yourself. Ask the checker to write the word *checker* and the date on the top of his paper so you will be able to monitor that no student becomes the checker more than once each week. As you enter the grades, do a spot check for accuracy on the part of the checker.

In the primary grades, where children are often seated together at tables, some teachers appoint the first person to finish correctly at each table to be the checker for that day, keeping in mind that a student should only be a checker once a week. Serving as a table checker may be easier for a younger student to manage than assuming a checker role for the entire class.

Students who are successful with Most Difficult First choose from extension activities you make available. Remember that the activities should belong to the same subject area on which the whole class is working, but they are not confined to the standards being taught. Students who work independently must understand and follow the "Five Essential Rules for Working Independently" described in the reproducible handout on page 124. Primary grade students may work on learning one rule at a time.

At the beginning of each chapter of skill work, select two or three activities to use as extensions. Offer activities that appeal to different sensory learning modalities, including visual, auditory, and kinesthetic. You may be able to use material you have enjoyed using with your students in the past but are no longer using because it is not part of the required standards. These activities can now become extensions. If you need answer keys, use those provided by publishers or ask students or parents to prepare them before you make the activities available. Most textbook publishers provide extension or enrichment ideas in the teacher's manual or supplementary materials. Often students who need compacting in language arts just want lots of extra time to read, and that should be provided as long as they are keeping simple records of their reading activities (see pages 116–118 for more on record keeping). Beyond this, you most likely already own, or can easily find in your school, dozens of activities that would serve well as extensions. Invite a few colleagues from your grade level and from higher grades to eat lunch with you in your room and bring materials they think would work for extension activities. (If you provide chocolate, they will come!) For suggested extension activities, see the reproducible forms on pages 125–126 in this chapter and the information on extension activities provided throughout chapter 6.

If your gifted-cluster students attend a pull-out class, use Most Difficult First when they return. It is not fair for these students to have to make up everything they missed while they were gone, since they were working on learning activities in their other setting. At the same time, you probably need some documentation that they have mastered the required standards. Most Difficult First is the perfect solution for this dilemma.

Most Difficult First should be used as a separate strategy for no more than one or two weeks. After that it can be combined with the Learning Contract (page 111) or other compacting options. If you use Most Difficult First alone, students won't be experiencing content at their challenge level, which can postpone their own experience with stimulating learning opportunities. This situation is an unhappy one for parents as well as students.

Using Most Difficult First as a first attempt at compacting will help you see that your gifted students are happy to choose their own extension activities from those that are already available in your class. When you learn to combine it with other strategies, it can be used all year, and you can direct your students to choose extension activities in the same subject area from which they bought the time.

Pretests with Extension Activities: Compacting and Differentiating One Week at a Time

The pretest strategy allows students who demonstrate they have already mastered an upcoming week's worth of material—such as spelling, vocabulary words, or any other work with basic skills—to work on extension tasks instead of the grade-level work. Since the opportunity to demonstrate prior mastery is offered to all students, there is very little, if any, resentment from other students toward students who are experiencing compacting on a regular basis.

As a specific example, consider the use of the pretest strategy with spelling. (If you don't teach spelling as a list, substitute the word *vocabulary* for *spelling* in this example.) On Monday, give all students a minute to look over the list of assigned words. Explain that some students may already know the required words. Reassure everyone that it's fine if they don't know them and it is fine if they do. Invite all students who think they could take the test immediately and score 90 percent or higher to come to a designated area so you can dictate the test to them. Correct the tests. Then, for anyone who meets the criteria, offer a choice of extension activities for students to work on Tuesday through Friday. The activities should be from the same general subject area that is being taught but need not be confined to the standards required for that week. Students who earn the required percentage on Monday are excused from the regular spelling activities and are not required to take the final test. Their A from Monday could be entered into all available spaces in the grade book for that week, or students could receive equivalent credit for their extension work. (For more about grades, see "Grading Extension Work," page 118.)

You might wonder what to do with advanced learners on Monday who choose *not* to take the pretest. Two options are possible. The first is to expect students to begin the required week's work immediately. The second is to offer those students a choice of a few activities that review previously mastered standards and that are perceived as fun. We recommend you choose the second option, because then all students would be looking forward to pretest day, since they would either be trying to demonstrate that they don't need to practice the week's work or they would be spending time on a pleasant related activity. In this way, even students who never take or pass pretests are happy that the opportunity is available. The rest of the week, students will be working either on the assigned lessons or on the differentiated activities.

Some teachers worry that once students know the pretest will be available, they might take their books or lists home over the weekend to study. We don't think that's such a bad thing. Imagine parents seeing their kids choosing to study spelling or vocabulary at home rather than choosing screen time. It's a good bet that parents would not be upset about that.

Please refer to the reproducible handout on page 127 titled "Teaching Skills to Students in Mixed-Ability Classes for Already-Mastered Content." This handout describes the process the teacher can use, along with suggestions on how to incorporate pretesting into your classroom practices.

Compacting and Differentiating for Students in Grades K–2

For at least a few months at the beginning of a school year, students in the primary grades might feel uncomfortable about working away from the teacher and other students. Many primary teachers are concerned that their students are too young to be able to work independently.

Remember that the very definition of giftedness indicates that these kids are thinking like older kids in many ways. They can be taught to work independently with direct instruction in how to do so. Some primary students are able to enjoy more independent work within several months, either alone or in groups with like-minded peers. Eventually, they can participate in Most Difficult First and other compacting opportunities when they are ready. Until they are ready, try the following:

1. During lesson planning, create practice work on two levels: entry and advanced.
2. Expect gifted students to pay attention to the introduction of the lesson content—but limit that lesson to ten to fifteen minutes.
3. When students are ready to practice what you have taught, assign them to places where you have already set out their practice work. Direct students who need entry-level tasks to the desks or tables that contain those tasks and students who need advanced tasks to the tables that contain those tasks.

For example, on Monday, the entry-level tasks can be on tables that have a red token in the center, and the advanced tasks can be at tables with a blue token. On Tuesday, the colors are switched, and the red-token tables have the entry-level tasks while the blue-token tables have the advanced tasks. In this way, children will not associate a token of a certain color with a specific task level. When students notice that all kids aren't doing the same task and ask why that is so, use that opportunity to validate the importance of respecting individual differences.

As the school year progresses, some primary-age gifted students become impatient with large-group activities. They may linger at some activity before joining the larger group. They may inch away from the group toward an activity they were doing previously. These behaviors indicate that they may be ready to use Most Difficult First or the pretest strategies and, with teacher guidance, should be able to learn how to handle the record keeping and behavioral expectations that accompany more independent work.

FIGURE 5-1 **Examples of Entry-Level and Advanced Tasks for Primary Students**

Entry-Level Tasks	Advanced Tasks
Write numerals 1–10.	Make a chart with Arabic numerals on the left side and corresponding Roman numerals on the right side.
Make a list of five words in a rhyming word family.	Create a poem, chant, or rap using rhyming words.
Make an addition/subtraction fact family for two sets of numbers.	Make a multiplication/division fact family for as many numbers as time allows.
Listen to a story about community helpers. Then talk with a partner about the job of each one.	Listen to a story about community helpers. Then, with a partner, list and describe the jobs of four other community helpers not included in the story.
Draw and label a picture of the solar system.	Draw and label a picture of the solar system. On the drawing, include how many days it takes each planet to orbit around the sun.

The following are some guidelines to consider when using compacting strategies in grades kindergarten through two with gifted students who are learning how to work independently:

- Do kid watching to find students who catch on quickly to new material, who appear to know much of the grade-level standards already, or who have a wide storehouse of general knowledge. Always give students full credit for what they have already mastered. Do not expect them to finish the regular work before working on extension activities.
- If gifted students want to participate in direct instruction, keep them there. However, plan seatwork at two levels: grade-level and advanced. Dismiss students from direct instruction by sending advanced students to tables that offer the advanced tasks.
- Use Most Difficult First whenever possible. Gifted students rarely need the same amount of practice as other students. Choose the most difficult items or indicate students can do the last line of each page instead of the entire amount. Offer this option to all students.
- Use the Name Card Method with the whole class. (This is described in chapter 6. See page 154.)
- Teach kids how to get help and how to keep records of their extension work. (Record-keeping advice is provided on page 142 in chapter 6.)
- Provide differentiated learning activities (color-coded) in learning centers.
- Allow plenty of time for students to read books of their own choosing.
- Allow gifted students to work with each other often; assign them as discussion buddies for each other too.
- Do not expect gifted students to tutor or help weaker students—this postpones their own experience with challenging learning.
- Interview parents and students to find students' areas of passionate interest. Allow students to explore those topics in the classroom when they finish assigned work ahead of others.
- Model and encourage respect for individual differences so all students believe they are accepted just the way they are, and gifted students do not feel they have to pretend to be less capable in order to fit in.
- Explore the book *Teaching Gifted Children in Today's Preschool and Primary Classrooms* by Joan Franklin Smutny, Sally Yahnke Walker, and Ellen I. Honeck (see page 242). It contains many ideas for challenging preK and primary-age gifted students.
- Use ideas from discussions in gifted-cluster teacher meetings.

Learning Contracts: Compacting and Differentiating One Chapter or Unit at a Time

The third compacting and differentiation strategy to use for previously mastered curriculum is the Learning Contract. Some teachers may have had unpleasant experiences with contracts at some time in their career, but this particular type of Learning Contract method is easy to use, fair for all students, and highly valued by the students who are ready to use a contract.

Before beginning to teach a new chapter, prepare a Learning Contract similar to the example in **figure 5-2**. (You will also find a reproducible Learning Contract form on page 128.) Each contract has two or three sections. The required standards are listed at the top of the page either as page numbers in a text or as concepts to be mastered. The center section lists possible extension activities along with places for record keeping. The bottom section explains the working conditions. The working conditions may be displayed as a wall chart instead of being listed on the contract. Adjust the working conditions to be compatible with specific needs and expectations.

FIGURE 5-2 Learning Contract

For: Math chapter 4

Student's name: Emma

	Page/Concept		Page/Concept		Page/Concept
	60	✓	64	✓	68
✓	61		65		69
	62	✓	66—Word problems	✓	70—Review (even only)
	63		67	✓	Posttest

Extension options: (Record your extension activities on the lines below.)

VersaTiles

Write story problems

Cross-number puzzle

Your idea:

Working conditions:

1. If a page is checked, do not work on it independently. Wait until it is taught to the whole class.
2. Do not bother anyone or call attention to yourself or the different work you are doing.
3. Work on the task you have selected for all available time during this period.
4. Keep accurate records of your extension work.
5. Do not lose your contract.

Teacher's signature: Mr. Schumacher

Student's signature: Emma

On the first day of the new chapter, invite all students to survey the standards by looking through the content, page by page. Ask students to notice how much of the content they believe they already know. Tell them to indicate whether they already know the content on a given page by silently nodding yes if they do or no if they don't. Next, show students the preassessment. Use the same assessment you plan to use with the entire class at the end of the chapter, or you can use either a chapter review or a chapter test if they are both included in the materials you are using. It is not worth your time to create your own alternative assessment for the pretest.

Invite all students who think they could take the pretest today, finish it in forty-five minutes, and get a specific number correct (such as eight out of ten, or sixteen out of twenty) to sit in designated areas. We suggest requiring competency at a B (85 percent) or higher. Reassure students that it is okay to either take the test or not take it, and that their grade for the pretest will not be entered formally into your grade records. Explain that students who already know the required number of concepts will be able to use a Learning Contract throughout the chapter. Students must hand in their work by the designated time, or they can discard it if they believe they have not met the minimum score.

Note: This method is different from the Most Difficult First and pretest options in that students are not given automatic credit for the concepts they miss on the test. They will always participate in direct instruction lessons on the days you are teaching the concepts they missed on the pretest.

Supporting Primary-Age Students' Independent Work

All students doing independent work need high-quality teacher time to help them learn how to work independently and how to keep records of their extension work. All students need lots of encouragement in order to feel good about working with challenging learning tasks and to take satisfaction from their hard work, rather than simply seek consistently high grades. Most students don't want to find themselves in a situation where they are not getting enough of the teacher's time. Regular short meetings with kids working independently will demonstrate that you care about what they are doing and that their work is important to you. Gifted primary kids are really thinking like older kids, so they *can* learn how to work independently if you take the time to teach them the necessary skills.

Suggested Student Study Sites

The following list of interactive websites can provide students with opportunities to work alone or in small groups on a myriad of topics. The sites help develop critical thinking skills, encourage creativity, and can provide lesson extensions in the content areas.

- 101 Questions—www.101qs.com
- Adapted Mind—www.adaptedmind.com
- Byrdseed—www.byrdseed.com
- Code.org—www.code.org
- Khan Academy—www.khanacademy.org
- Knoword—playknoword.com
- LearnZillion—learnzillion.com
- Mathalicious—www.mathalicious.com
- National Library of Virtual Manipulatives—nlvm.usu.edu/en/nav/vlibrary.html
- OneLook Thesaurus—www.onelook.com/reverse-dictionary.shtml
- ReadWriteThink—www.readwritethink.org
- Root Word Dictionary—www.macroevolution.net/root-word-dictionary.html
- Scratch—scratch.mit.edu
- Show Me—www.showme.com
- Study Jams—studyjams.scholastic.com/studyjams
- TEDEducation—ed.ted.com
- Tynker—www.tynker.com
- VirtualNerd—virtualnerd.com
- Visuwords—visuwords.com
- Wonderopolis—wonderopolis.org
- Word Hippo—www.wordhippo.com
- Young Minds Inspired—ymiclassroom.com

Collect and correct the pretests. Do not enter students' pretest scores in the grade book. Use that data to decide which students will be eligible to use the Learning Contract method. Prepare a

Learning Contract only for students who met the expected criteria. On the contract, check the pages or concepts a student *missed* on the assessment, because some direct instruction on those concepts is clearly needed. All students on a Learning Contract will take the posttest for each chapter, just to be sure there has been no loss of concept mastery since the unit began.

Teachers who use traditional hard-copy grade books can use a red-box symbol. In the grade book, draw a red box around each square that indicates a specific page or concept you have checked on students' contracts—the concepts they have mastered. Do not yet enter a grade for these mastered concepts; those will be entered for these students at the same time they are entered for all other students. You will always know which students have contracts and which concepts are checked on their contract, because those pages or concepts are the only ones with red boxes.

If you use an electronic grade book, create a symbol or system that will allow you to recognize which students need direct instruction on which standards. You can choose some kind of entry notation that will let you know which items have been checked on each student's learning contract.

In the center section of the Learning Contract, list two or three extension activities you want to make available. Include a place for student choice ("Your Idea") so students can suggest other activities they would like to use as extension activities with teacher approval. All extension activities should be self-correcting by using prepared answer keys, because grades for them will not be entered as a formal score. This is justified because the only content you are obligated to grade is that which is connected to the required standards. On subsequent contracts, keep the extensions you've already used and add one new option for each contract. In this way, students who join the Learning Contract method later in the process can learn how to use earlier extension activities from other students who have already used them.

Each day a student has worked on extension activities and has followed the expected working conditions, enter the grade the student earned *on the preassessment for the direct instruction material taught that day.* Enter the grade at the same time you do so for other classmates working on the day's direct instruction content. Students on contract understand that anytime they fail to follow the expected working conditions, they must return to the direct instruction mode for the remainder of the chapter. Since you have not recorded their mastery grades for each page ahead of time, they know it will be easy for you to reassign them into the larger group for the balance of the chapter. All students in the class will take the posttest together at the end of the chapter.

For students whose posttest score is not adequate, inform them they will not receive a contract for the next chapter or unit so you can work with them to help them with any problems they are having. Use language that creates growth mindsets, such as "You have not mastered this concept yet, but you will get there soon." You might also make the extension activities available for students who are not on a contract, as the situations allow.

For primary students, follow all the same procedures, but do not give students a hard copy of the contract. Instead, when your recording system indicates that certain students do not have to be in the direct instruction group for the day, allow them to work on extension activities for the class period. Be sure to make time to visit their group to encourage them in their efforts to work on challenging tasks. If you don't have enough space in your room to create an area for groups to work on extension activities, instruct the students to select an activity and return to their desks or tables to work on it.

You can facilitate this process by meeting with these students for a few minutes, before you begin the direct instruction, to show them where the activities are located and to be sure they know how to begin their extension work. Encourage students to work in pairs or triads on the extension activities so they can help one another.

Using the Learning Contract Day by Day

Day one: Have students examine upcoming content and take the chapter pretest while other students are enjoying an engaging activity that reviews previously learned concepts. Correct the pretests and prepare contracts and indicators in your grade book for students who achieve the necessary level of competence.

Day two: Prepare work groups for this chapter. Place all students on contract in pairs or triads with one another. Place all other students in mixed-ability groups. Meet briefly with the students on contract to familiarize them with the extension activities. Ask students to work on the activities until you return to their group within fifteen minutes. Teach the day's concept for no more than fifteen minutes to the students who need direct instruction. Give these students time to start the practice work for the day's lesson. As groups start their work, go to the students on contract, answer their questions about the extension activities, show them how to keep records of their work, and encourage them to persevere with difficult activities. Your goal with this group is to help the students learn that really smart people stay with difficult tasks until they figure them out. Reassure students that no one will doubt their intelligence if they have to work hard.

All other days: For each instructional period, check your records to be sure that contract students who should be attending direct instruction are doing so and that students who are supposed to be working on extension or differentiated activities are doing just that.

Begin each lesson with direct instruction. At the first practice period for the lesson, offer Most Difficult First to all students who wish to try it. As the groups of students get started on their practice work, work first with students on contract so they don't perceive they will lose touch with you because they are working more independently. During this time, encourage them to take pride in pursuing challenging work to develop an appreciation of working hard to learn something new; also check their record keeping.

Students on contract need to pay attention to direct instruction only when you are presenting material they have not mastered. When you are teaching content they have already mastered, or when they have demonstrated through Most Difficult First that they do not need direct instruction for part of the class period, they are working on extension activities. Every day that the standards lend themselves to compacting, offer Most Difficult First at the end of the first fifteen minutes of instruction when it is time for students to begin practicing what you have just taught. In this way, you make extensions accessible for more students, because students who can demonstrate their mastery of the day's content can join the students working on extensions.

Suggestions:

- Use a plastic crate that holds hanging file folders for students to store their contracts and the extension activities they are working on. Be sure all students in the class have a folder in the crate. Also be sure to provide time when all students can work on extension activities, even if it's just for fifteen minutes of an instructional period.
- Give each group a token, such as a poker chip, at the beginning of each period. Call it the Question Chip. Explain that the students in each group want your full attention when you are with them and that all groups have students who can help other students. Encourage group members to ask one another for answers to their questions. Explain that each group will be allowed to ask you only one question each period during group practice time. Reassure them that, during instruction, they can ask as many questions as they want. While working in their groups, if they are certain that no one in their group can answer the question, they can send someone to find you and bring the chip and the question with them. When you answer their question, you will take the chip. If students need a reward for

collecting their chips and not spending them, suggest that each time a group collects five chips, they earn a homework pass, chat time, or another equally desirable perk. Once students experience their perk, collect the tokens from students in that particular group. Then begin the collection process again.

Communicating with Parents About Learning Contracts and Extension Activities

You will notice that the Learning Contract asks only for signatures of the student and the teacher. Parents do not sign the contract, since this is an agreement between the teacher and the student. To inform parents that their child is using the Learning Contract method, and to help them understand that they are not responsible for the outcomes of the contract, send home a letter explaining the contract and the extension work their child will be doing. A sample letter follows, and you'll find a reproducible version of this letter on page 129.

Keeping Records of Student Work

The Daily Log of Extension Activities

The Daily Log of Extension Activities is useful to keep records of gifted students' differentiation experiences. Using the Daily Log is particularly helpful for students who have trouble beginning and completing long-term assignments. Breaking those down into daily goal-setting experiences can lead to better self-confidence and better student tracking of the entire project. It also helps kids who worry about being perfect learn that long-term success depends on one's ability to set and accomplish realistic short-term goals.

On the Daily Log, students record details about their progress with their extension activities. Show students how to use one horizontal row for each day they are working on differentiated activities. At the beginning of a work period, students write the date in the left column and describe in the center column the portion of

FIGURE 5-3 Sample Letter to Parents Explaining Learning Contracts and Extension Activities

Dear Parent/Caregiver:

Your child, Emma, has demonstrated outstanding ability in mathematics in our class. She has already mastered much of the grade-level material and is able to extend her learning to other topics in math. Emma will be using a Learning Contract during the present chapter on decimals. This means she will be attending direct instruction lessons with her classmates when I am teaching topics she *has not* already mastered. When I am teaching concepts she has already mastered, she will be working on extension activities. I will be closely monitoring Emma's math work and will be helping her learn to be comfortable with the more challenging work found in the extension activities. Sometimes, students will be working together on extension activities to provide encouragement and assistance to one another.

There is nothing you need to do at home to facilitate this Learning Contract process. If any problems occur in school while Emma is working with a Learning Contract, I will be in touch with you. If you have any questions, please contact me.

Sincerely,

Mr. Schumacher

Mr. Schumacher

FIGURE 5-4 Sample Entries from a Student's Daily Log of Extension Activities

Student's name: Jamal

Project topic: Babylonian math system

Today's Date	My Plan for This Period	What I Completed Today
March 2	Understand the symbols in the Babylonian math system	Understand half the symbols
	Finish learning all the symbols in this math system	

work they plan to complete that day. A few minutes before the end of the work period, prompt students to complete the right column, labeled "What I Completed Today." When students discover they planned more than they could complete, they make a note in the center column of the *next* horizontal row, which reminds them where to start when they return to their extension work. They should not fill in the next date until you tell them that a particular date may be used for their extension work. In this way, students will not get too far ahead of the group with their extension work. See the example in **figure 5-4**.

Completed Daily Logs help you provide an accurate record for parents that clearly documents how much class time students spent on differentiated activities during a unit of work. For the Daily Log to be highly effective, it should never leave the classroom. You can keep logs in folders, color-coded by class period. You can store hanging folders neatly for easy access in the plastic crates along with Learning Contracts and extension activities.

The Compactor Record Sheet

The Compactor Record Sheet (see reproducible form on page 131) is a form to use with students who experience compacting and differentiation opportunities on a regular basis. Use one sheet per student until it is filled up; then begin another. Keep all completed forms in a compacting folder you maintain for each student. Alternate activities are usually drawn from the same subject area in which the student has demonstrated mastery. However, in the case of a student working on an ongoing independent study, there are times when the independent work will be related to the individualized topic the student is studying. The information does not have to be specifically related to individual standards. For instance, the right column of the Compactor Record Sheet might say "Created an imaginary country" as the extension activity.

- In the left column, record the area of the curriculum in which the student is experiencing compacting.
- In the center column, describe how previous mastery was determined, such as from a pretest or work sample.
- In the right column, describe the type of activity the student is working on *instead of* continuing with the grade-level work.

See **figure 5-5** on page 118 for an example of sample entries on a Compactor Record Sheet.

The Extension Activities Feedback Form

Even when you are doing a great job compacting and differentiating for your advanced learners, they probably aren't communicating much about that to their parents or other caregivers. Most kids are unresponsive when parents ask, "What did

FIGURE 5-5 Sample Entries from a Student's Compactor Record Sheet

Student's name: Anali

Teacher's name: Ms. McMann

Grade in school: 5

Area of Learning Strength	How Mastery Was Documented	Extension Activities
Math	Chapter Review as pretest with 82% mastery	Learning Contract and extensions

The Compactor Record Sheet is adapted from *The Compactor* developed by Joseph Renzulli and Linda Smith.

you do in school today that was different from what other students in the class were doing?" The usual answer is "Nothing." Teachers must be proactive in giving parents the information they need to feel reassured that the cluster grouping model is indeed creating challenging learning opportunities for their kids.

At the end of any unit in which students have spent time working on extensions, send home a packet of the work, the Daily Log of Extension Activities, and the Extension Activities Feedback Form (see reproducible on page 132). Ask parents and students to discuss the packet's contents, then sign and return the feedback form only. The work can stay at home. The form is short, so you'll find two reproducible forms on a single page. You can send forms home for two subject areas at once.

Grading Extension Work

The only standards for which you are required to assign grades on report cards are the grade-level standards. In the case of accelerated curriculum, you can assess the advanced standards in any way that you perceive is fair, but the actual report card always describes competency on grade-level standards. Extension work, when it replaces work that has been mastered, should be evaluated and credited, but not graded. If the work is graded and the possibility exists that the student will end up with a lower grade than what she would have earned had she just remained with the class doing grade-level work, she is likely to opt out of the extension work. Older students, on the other hand, may refuse to work on extensions if no grade is attached. In this situation, we recommend that students earn the same grade for the extension activities as the average grade they are carrying in the grade-level work. This applies every day they successfully follow the expected working conditions—the Five Essential Rules (see reproducible on page 124). Other grading options are discussed in chapters 6 and 8.

All learning activities should have preassessment opportunities available for students who volunteer to demonstrate prior knowledge and mastery of concepts, ideas, and skills. Whatever method is planned for assessing student progress during or at the end of a particular unit of study is the same method that you can use for the preassessment.

Whether the preassessment takes the form of a written test, a measurement of student response as the class brainstorms all they know about an upcoming topic, or performance on a designated task, any student who chooses to participate in the preassessment is allowed to do so. When the preassessment is open to all who think they can demonstrate the required degree of mastery, there should be little resentment from students who are unable to do so, particularly if the regular activities are interesting and challenging.

Let's reconsider the two conditions that must be present to entice gifted students to work on extension activities: they should not have to do more work than their classmates, and their extension work should not lead to lower recorded grades than those they would most likely have earned by limiting their work to grade-level standards. Clearly, students are not being required to do more work than other students are, since their *extension work replaces the additional practice* other students are completing. However, the grading implications deserve attention.

When you are using Most Difficult First, four examples out of five correct equals 80 percent—and 80 percent is not an A. However, if you record any grade lower than what the student is accustomed to receiving, it is highly likely that the student will choose *not* to participate in compacting the next day. With this in mind, be prepared to add a bonus to the actual score. Mastery of four of the five most difficult problems is clearly mastery. The letter grade for mastery is A. We recommend that you allow students to earn the same average they had from the previous chapter or unit in this subject area, since it can be assumed that they would continue to earn grades at that level. For example, if Roberto had a 96 percent average in the previous chapter, you would add 16 percentage points to his score of 80 percent, so the grade you formally enter for him would be not just an A, but an A in the numeric range he is expecting. Similarly, if Kim's previous average was 94 percent, her bonus added to a score of 80 percent would be 14 percentage points.

What About Homework?

The purpose of homework is to provide time for students to practice new skills in order to master new content. If that content has already been mastered, students must be excused from the homework related to that content. If the student is being taught at an advanced level, his homework would come from that content. If a parent insists that a child have some homework in a particular subject area, send home a short list of websites that contain appropriate extension-type activities. If you do a search for websites that provide math enrichment, word study information, or whatever you are looking for, the list will be easy to assemble. If families do not have internet access, prepare a packet of extension activities students can take home at the beginning of a chapter and use each time they are not required to do the regular homework. Send home a copy of the Daily Log of Extension Activities for students to keep track of their work each evening. Collect those logs weekly or at the end of each chapter.

Homework should be assigned to all students as a time-period expectation, rather than as an arbitrary chunk of work. Your school board policy probably describes it this way. Since homework is used to keep content fresh in students' minds, students should receive full credit for their homework if they return what they have completed. Gifted students tend to spend way too much time on homework, and this policy would relieve them of the anxiety that their homework has to be the best example when compared with that of other students in the class.

Modifications of Compacting and Differentiation Techniques for the Whole Class

Following are suggestions for ways in which you can sometimes make the compacting and differentiation opportunities often experienced by the gifted-cluster students available to all students in the class.

Most Difficult First for the Whole Class

- From time to time, allow all students to choose a smaller number of the entire practice set as their goal.
- Let students choose odd or even problems or examples.

- All students can stop practicing as soon as they have correctly completed five designated problems or examples. You might provide multiple checkers or answer keys at several checking stations. Provide only one color marker at a given station each time you do this, and instruct the students to use only the marker that is at the station for their corrections. You can also place a basket there where students can deposit their completed papers.
- At least once a week, allow all students to spend twenty to thirty minutes working on extension activities of their choice.

Pretest for the Whole Class

- Since very few students ever do miraculously better on review units for skill work than they have done on the previous units in a particular set of lessons, skip all review units for the entire class. Instead, during that week, invite all students to choose from the same extension options made available weekly to students who pass Monday's pretest.
- Allow students who never pass a pretest to set their own goal each week about how many words they will focus on for testing purposes. It is very important that the goal come from the student and not from you. On test day, students write the items they have studied in another color, or at the end of the test, they go back and check off the words they want you to use for grading purposes. Once a student has reached her goal one week, do not insist the goal be raised immediately. Doing so actually creates a fear of success in students who are unaccustomed to it. You may gently encourage the student into considering a higher goal after a few weeks of success. Keep in mind that students are improving right along and that reaching grade-level expectations is a goal that can be achieved over time.

Learning Contracts for the Whole Class

On a regular basis, give everyone in the class time to select and work on an extension activity of their choice, either alone or with a partner. Extension activities usually build on previously mastered standards, so this time will not be wasted, and the bonus to students' self-esteem is significant. Since all students have a folder in the folder crate, this will give everyone a chance to add extension activities to the collections in their folder. All students can have a Daily Log of Extension Activities (explained on pages 116–117) in their folder; keeping track of their own extension activities on the log is a positive experience that helps students understand that everyone has opportunities to work on extension activities from time to time.

Building a Unified Learning Community

To build a unified learning community, you will want to provide many opportunities for all students in your class to work together. This section describes some activities that provide whole-class interaction. The Name Card Method described in chapter 6 serves the same purpose.

Designated Partner Talk

Once a month, have each student fold a piece of 8½" x 11" paper into four sections. Label the sections A, B, C, and D. Then tell students to find partners by saying, "First, find one other student to be your '*A*partner.' *A* partners should write their names in the A section of each other's paper. Do the same to find a *B* partner, a *C* partner, and a *D* partner, writing your names in the B, C, and D sections of the papers. At least two of your four partners must be students you don't usually spend time with in or out of class."

You may want to keep a record of the partner information for students who will inevitably lose their papers. During the month, use the partner papers as an opportunity for movement, interaction, and variety. For example, when you say, "Find your *B* partner and discuss whether Pluto should continue to be considered a planet," partners meet and talk about the assigned topic for three to five minutes. These small chats help create ideas to use during an upcoming discussion. Topics can range from subject-area information to procedures to be used in and out of the classroom.

Classroom Academic Baseball

This is an enjoyable method for reviewing previously mastered content for upcoming assessments. Create designated areas of the classroom that will serve as home plate, first base, second base, third base, left field, center field, and right field. Form two teams and play a game of academic baseball (description follows) to review the content discussed. If there are too many students for two teams, form four teams and trade off having teams play and observe.

Steps for playing classroom academic baseball:

1. Assign students to heterogeneous teams of six to eight students.
2. Create questions, based on previously learned content from any subject, on four levels of difficulty, with level 4 being the most challenging. Creating these questions at all levels could be an extension activity some students might enjoy.
3. Provide material you have taught for the teams to review.
4. Point out the locations in the room that will serve as home plate, first base, second base, and third base.
5. One team at a time comes up to bat. Each player asks for a question from a level that is comfortable for that person. A student who correctly answers a level 1 question walks to first base; students who correctly answer level 2 or 3 questions walk to second base or third base; and students correctly answering a level 4 question get a home run.
6. The team continues to answer questions until they have three outs.
7. Have the second team come up to bat and answer questions until it has three outs.
8. If four teams are playing, switch and let the second two teams have a turn or start the game with the other two teams the next time the class plays baseball.

SUMMARY

This chapter has provided information about how to compact and differentiate the curriculum when students have previously mastered the content. Since much of grade-level content is redundant for gifted students, they will be immensely grateful that you have provided these compacting and differentiation opportunities for them.

Following these steps for compacting and differentiating content that some students have previously mastered helps ensure that compacting and differentiation will be successful:

- Identify the essential learning standards.
- Document which students have already mastered those standards.
- Compact the part of the curriculum that has previously been mastered.
- Make extension activities available for students who will spend some class time working on them.
- Manage a classroom in which students are simultaneously working on differentiated learning tasks.

Most Difficult First

Directions for Students

- Pay close attention to the lesson your teacher presents.
- If you think you fully understand the concepts, use the first fifteen minutes of the practice time to try the work your teacher has designated as Most Difficult First.
- You must work alone, without help from the teacher or any other student. You must finish those examples in the time period set by your teacher. Your work must be readable by the checker, and you may have no more than one error.
- If you are done before the teacher has announced who the checker will be for today, take your paper to the teacher for correction. If you are the first to demonstrate you have no more than one wrong, you may serve as the checker for the rest of the lesson time today. You may be the checker only once every week. On other days, you may work on extension activities for the rest of the period.
- If a checker has been named today, raise your hand when you are ready for him or her to check your work. You have only one chance to show that you already understand the material being taught. If you have more than one item wrong, that means *you need more practice* and you should start at the beginning of the practice set or homework assignment.
- At the end of each class period, be sure to enter information about your extension activities in your Daily Log of Extension Activities for that subject area.

How to Be a Checker

- You may be a checker once each week. On other days, you are to work on extension activities if you have met the requirements for Most Difficult First.
- As the checker, you may not provide any help to students whose papers you are checking. You may not return to any student more than once.
- If the student's paper has one or none wrong, take the paper with you. If the student's paper has more than one wrong, say, "You have more than one wrong, so you need more practice. Please start at the beginning of the practice assignment."
- Never discuss any information about students' correct or incorrect answers with any other students. You must keep that information confidential.
- Give all papers you have collected to your teacher. Place your own paper on top of the stack and write "Checker" and the date on your paper.

Five Essential Rules for Working Independently

Rule #1
Do not bother anyone else while you're working. If you need help, ask the teacher. If the teacher is helping someone else, ask another student who is also working on extensions.

Rule #2
Do not call attention to yourself or to the fact that you are working on extension activities.

Rule #3
Work on the task(s) you have selected until the end of the period.

Rule #4
Keep accurate records of your extension activities on the Daily Log of Extension Activities according to your teacher's directions.

Rule #5
You may work alone on a self-selected extension task, or you may work with another student. You must keep your own records each day in your Daily Log of Extension Activities.

For every day that you follow these rules, you may work on extensions. If you cannot follow the rules, you will rejoin the class for direct instruction.

Note: All students do not have to work on the same extension activities. It is okay for you to help other students work on their activities, as long as you also work on your own. It is also okay for students to work together on the same activities.

Suggested Extension Activities for Primary Students

1. Using graph paper, rearrange our classroom to make it work better.
2. Design the perfect playground.
3. Create healthy eating menus for school lunches.
4. Write a letter to a teacher, principal, mayor, president, or prime minister telling what you believe the person should do to make things better.
5. Interview someone you think is wonderful. Prepare the questions ahead of the interview.
6. Record your favorite story for other students to listen to.
7. Create a play and show other students how to present it to the class with you.
8. Write a letter to someone that starts: "I don't think it's fair that ____________________________________."
   Suggest ways to improve the problem. Then send the letter.
9. Write story problems in math that use the concepts the class is learning.
10. Monitor the daily weather for a week or month. Give daily weather reports and your own forecasts for tomorrow's weather to the class.
11. Create graphs or other types of charts that show your classmates' preferences for meals, desserts, movies, music, books, vacations, or other topics.
12. Create mazes for other kids to try.
13. Create a code and ask other kids to figure it out.
14. Ask your teacher for logic puzzles and do them. Then, try to teach someone else to do them. Also try geoboards, attribute or pattern blocks, or tangrams.
15. Study programming languages online. Show someone else how it works.
16. Learn to tell riddles you have read, then make up some of your own.
17. Learn to use the calculator. Then try problems that involve adding, subtracting, multiplying, or dividing numbers, big and small.
18. Draw cartoons to tell a story about characters you make up.
19. Translate this week's vocabulary words into another language. Use as many of the words in as few sentences as possible.
20. Make up an acronym to use as a memory clue for any list of things the class is trying to learn.
21. Use the internet to find ten wonderful facts about something that interests you.
22. Create your own star constellation by pricking pinholes in dark paper. Then make up a myth that explains the groups of stars in your constellation.
23. Create a trivia book of questions (and answers) we could use for a class game.
24. Create and publish a class or school newspaper.
25. Learn to use VersaTiles. Teach other kids to use them.
26. READ, READ, READ!
27. WRITE, WRITE, WRITE!
28. Interview the oldest person you know. Find out how the person's life as a child was different from yours.
29. Draw or cut out pictures from magazines to describe:
    Things you can do alone
    Things you need help with
    Favorite toys, real or imaginary
    Favorite animals, real or imaginary
    The perfect birthday party
    Your jobs at home or school
    Things that make you feel proud
    Things you want to learn more about
    Your favorite things
    Special clothes for special occasions
    Things you really need
    Things you really want
    Favorite celebrities
    YOUR OWN IDEA
30. Make up your own idea to work on and discuss it with your teacher.

Suggested Extension Activities for Students in the Upper Grades

1. Using graph paper, rearrange our classroom to make it work better. Use a different size scale than that which is illustrated on the paper.
2. Design the perfect playground for our school. Include information about its safety features.
3. Create healthy eating menus for our school lunches that follow the recommendations for healthy eating at www.choosemyplate.gov.
4. Write a letter to the editor of your local paper explaining your reaction to an article in the paper or to a current event.
5. Interview a family member who remembers information about the first person in your family to immigrate to this country OR find another interesting story about any major family transition or change that was experienced and report on it. Prepare your questions ahead of the interview.
6. Create word problems for other students using concepts the class is currently studying in math.
7. Find out how a local weather forecaster creates weather forecasts. Present information about the forecast for the upcoming storm season in your area.
8. Ask your teacher for Mind Benders or other logic puzzles. Do them and then teach other kids how to do them.
9. Create a story in some manner that appeals to you and share it with a group of students.
10. Follow a story in the newspaper for several days or weeks. Find a way to share with other students what you have learned about the story and why you think the story is important.
11. Visit approved websites to find ten fascinating facts about a topic that interests you. Find a way to share your findings.
12. Create and publish a digital newsletter for our class.
13. Interview the oldest person you know. Find out how the person's childhood was different from the way yours is now.
14. Explore tourist attractions in your community and create a brochure about them to entice tourists to visit.
15. Attend a theater production or a concert of music or dance. Find a way to share your impressions of the event with other students.
16. Investigate the similarities and differences between your school system and the school system of a child your age in another country.
17. Create or describe an invention you think might help some person live a more satisfying life.
18. READ, READ, READ!
19. WRITE, WRITE, WRITE!
20. Create your own idea for an activity. Share it with your teacher before you start to work on it.

Teaching Skills to Students in Mixed-Ability Classes for Already-Mastered Content

Introduce topics to the whole class:

- Allow students to briefly examine upcoming content.
- Invite students who want to demonstrate prior mastery to take a pretest.

Provide a voluntary pretest:

- The test is conducted in one class period, corrected by the teacher.
- Students not taking the test work on enjoyable activities.
- Students who demonstrate previous mastery work on differentiated activities throughout the chapter or unit, returning for direct instruction only when standards not yet mastered are being taught.

Daily routine:

- Teach standards in chunks of time that do not exceed fifteen minutes.
- Provide any needed guided practice.
- Attend to different sensory learning modalities.
- Check frequently for understanding.
- Offer Most Difficult First for every lesson at the end of the first direct instruction time.
- Have students who successfully complete Most Difficult First move on to extension activities for the balance of the instructional period.
- Spend some time daily with students who work on extension activities.

Regroup for review or extensions as needed.

Teach students to do their own record keeping.

Allow students to share their extension work with one another.

Allow all students to work on extension activities regularly.

Learning Contract

For: ______________________________

Student's name: ______________________________

	Page/Concept		**Page/Concept**		**Page/Concept**
___	___________	___	___________	___	___________
___	___________	___	___________	___	___________
___	___________	___	___________	___	___________
___	___________	___	___________	___	___________

Extension options: (Record your extension activities on the lines below.)

____

____

____

Your idea:

____

- -

Working conditions:

1. ______________________________

2. ______________________________

3. ______________________________

4. ______________________________

5. ______________________________

Teacher's signature: ______________________________

Student's signature: ______________________________

Dear Parent/Caregiver:

Your child, ____, has demonstrated outstanding ability in ______________________________ in our class. S/he has already mastered much of the grade-level material and is able to extend her/his learning to other topics in ______________________________________.

______________________________________ will be using a Learning Contract during the present chapter on ______________________________________. This means s/he will be attending direct instruction lessons with classmates when I am teaching topics s/he has not already mastered. When I am teaching concepts s/he has already mastered, s/he will be working on extension activities. I will be closely monitoring ______________________________________'s ______________________________________ work and will be helping her/him learn to be comfortable with more challenging work represented by the extension activities. Sometimes, students will be working together on extension activities to provide encouragement and assistance to one another.

There is nothing you need to do at home to facilitate this Learning Contract process. If any problems occur in school while ______________________________________ is working with a Learning Contract, I will be in touch with you. If you have any questions, please contact me.

Sincerely,

____

Daily Log of Extension Activities

Student's name: ______________________________

Project topic: ______________________________

Today's Date	My Plan for This Period	What I Completed Today

The Compactor Record Sheet

Student's name: ______________________________

Teacher's name: ______________________________

Grade in school: ______________________________

Area of Learning Strength	How Mastery Was Documented	Extension Activities

Adapted with permission from *The Compactor* by Joseph Renzulli and Linda Smith.

Extension Activities Feedback Form

Student's name ______________________ Teacher's name ______________________

Subject area represented ______________ Time period covered ______________ Today's date ______________

Dear Parent/Caregiver:

Attached are some of the activities your child has experienced to extend the regular curriculum and pacing in our classroom. Please discuss the activities with your child and place a checkmark on the lines below if you agree with the statements. Return to me ONLY the signed form.

_________ Yes, my child showed me the extension packet and explained some of the activities.

_________ Yes, I understand that this work represents the differentiated activities for my child in his/her classroom.

Comments: ______________________________

Signature of parent or guardian: ______________________________

Extension Activities Feedback Form

Student's name ______________________ Teacher's name ______________________

Subject area represented ______________ Time period covered ______________ Today's date ______________

Dear Parent/Caregiver:

Attached are some of the activities your child has experienced to extend the regular curriculum and pacing in our classroom. Please discuss the activities with your child and place a checkmark on the lines below if you agree with the statements. Return to me ONLY the signed form.

_________ Yes, my child showed me the extension packet and explained some of the activities.

_________ Yes, I understand that this work represents the differentiated activities for my child in his/her classroom.

Comments: ______________________________

Signature of parent or guardian: ______________________________

From *The Cluster Grouping Handbook: A Schoolwide Model* by Dina Brulles, Ph.D., and Susan Winebrenner, M.S., copyright © 2019. This page may be reproduced for individual, classroom, or small group work only. For all other uses, contact Free Spirit Publishing Inc. at freespirit.com/permissions.

6

Compacting and Differentiating Curriculum When the Content Is New to Students

GUIDING QUESTIONS

- How can teachers compact and differentiate the curriculum for gifted learners when the content is new for them?
- What can a teacher do to increase access to extension activities for gifted English language learners (ELL students) and culturally and linguistically diverse (CLD) students?
- Where can effective extension activities be found?
- How can teachers create their own extension activities?
- What are effective ways to facilitate independent study for students who need it?
- What methods can be used to support and sustain a unified learning community in the classroom?

You may have noticed that some of the strategies from chapter 5 are not applicable to subject areas in which the content is new to the student. In the case of new content, teachers must compact the amount of *time* highly capable students need to document mastery of required standards, rather than compacting the actual content. Mastering the standards is nonnegotiable. Being allowed to master them in less time than is needed by classmates is definitely possible.

You probably have taught many students who were not as productive as you wanted them to be in terms of completing the required work but who were able to ace the assessments. This creates a dilemma for everyone concerned. If you give these students full credit for the entire unit based solely on their performance on the assessments, you might wonder how fair it is to students who need the required practice to learn the material. On the other hand, you might also be concerned about whether it's fair to average zeroes or Fs from missing work into the grades of students who can reach the goal of learning the grade-level standards without actually completing all the required assignments.

You'll need methods to give advanced learners full credit for their ability to learn without completing required activities, to allow these students to do meaningful work during a unit of study, and to accommodate their abilities to explore topics beyond the parameters of required standards. This chapter demonstrates ways to accomplish these goals while still teaching the necessary content to all students. It describes how to compact new content for gifted learners by providing options for faster pacing. It explains how to find or create appropriate extension activities and how to use them effectively with advanced learners. The chapter also describes ways to make these options available for all students, as well as ways all class members can work together on exciting activities. On page 160, you will find a reproducible form titled "Teaching New Content to Students in Mixed-Ability Classes." This document summarizes the specific steps involved in this process.

Preparing to Work with Gifted Students in the Content Areas

As you prepare to compact and differentiate in curriculum content areas, it is important to keep in mind the needs of all identified gifted students, including those who lack fluency in the English language or who are challenged by learning differences. You will also want to plan for flexible grouping and learning centers that allow you to adjust students' work according to subject areas, learning modalities, interests, and content levels.

Empowering Twice-Exceptional Students to Access Advanced Curriculum

Some students assigned to the gifted cluster will have special learning challenges. Although their gifted ability has been documented, these students might also have a learning disability, a physical challenge such as a hearing problem, difficulty paying attention, or in the case of ELL and CLD students, language or cultural differences. Some students who have been identified as gifted by a nonverbal test may not be proficient enough in English to understand the advanced learning tasks you have made available. Indeed, they may not even possess the language skills needed to understand grade-level material that is presented predominantly through oral or written language.

The recommendations that follow describe ways in which you can teach the same concepts and topics with twice-exceptional students as you do with other gifted students. All of the suggestions are effective with students who have any type of learning challenge along with their gifted ability. Be aware that sometimes the extension activities themselves may lead to more rapid understanding of the required standards, because they represent more active learning experiences. Information about the resources recommended here can be found in the references and resources for chapter 6 beginning on page 241:

- Some resources effective with twice-exceptional students include digital media, such as interactive websites, webinars, and videos.
- Assume that students with learning challenges, including ELL students, will respond more successfully to visual and kinesthetic teaching strategies. Always provide visual-kinesthetic ways for students to demonstrate what they have learned.
- When teaching reading, use graphic organizers that have consistent formats for charting story elements, character traits, and

vocabulary. Teach only three to five words per story to mastery level and choose words that are related to each other in some way. Mastering a smaller number of words for each story will have longer-lasting effects than learning too many words less well.

- Use visual or graphic organizers to teach content in other subject areas as well. Graphic organizers help students by presenting the content in a highly motivating visual format that allows kids to manipulate the information until it makes more sense to them. Visual learners are better able to understand and remember information they have learned through these types of assistive learning tools. Two of the best resources are Thinking Maps and Inspiration/Kidspiration software. These materials help visual learners become more effective writers through a process that capitalizes on their visual strengths.
- When using vocabulary flash cards, have students draw a picture on the back of each card to help them remember the meaning of the word.
- Check out Learning Ally as a source for digitally recorded textbooks and literature. A student can listen to a recorded book at a slower speed, or can listen several times to the same section, without slowing down other students.
- Use digital media applications that move back and forth between visual representations and written and spoken language. Content-rich materials that rely heavily on pictures, graphs, charts, data, and video clips allow CLD and ELL students to learn at the same level of difficulty as other students for whom culture and language are not a barrier.
- Use programs that enable ELL students to hear phrases spoken in correct English and that also record students as they speak.
- When using partner activities (such as the Name Card Method, described beginning on page 154), pair gifted ELL and CLD students with other gifted students who have nurturing personalities. Gifted students emerging into English will make faster progress when interacting with advanced content and advanced thinkers.
- Whenever possible, connect the content being learned to students' personal experiences. During discussions, supplement talking by having students act out what is being said.
- Use interactive journals and respond in writing to what students have recorded. The journals can also be used as reading logs where students write or draw incidents from the story or novel they are reading.
- Encourage group interaction so that students can plan projects together, create learning goals, assign roles, and identify topics to be researched.
- Teach the research process using students' strongest learning modality.

Facilitating the use of these interventions increases the likelihood that twice-exceptional students will achieve at higher levels, thus positively impacting *schoolwide* achievement levels.

Using Flexible Grouping in SCGM Classrooms

In gifted-cluster classes, the grouping is flexible and changes regularly. The groups change as learning tasks change. Sometimes the teacher creates the groups, and at other times the students themselves form groups. Teachers may form groups for direct instruction or reteaching based on the results of ongoing assessments.

When designated students come together to receive instruction on a particular topic, a flexible group has been formed that might remain together for a few minutes or for several lessons. When strategies presented in this chapter (including study guides, extension menus, learning centers, and tiered lessons) are used, flexible groups are based upon activities chosen by the teacher or the students, and students in those groups may remain together for longer periods of time. The strategies described in this chapter allow you to group and regroup students who need more complex activities in any area of learning.

Using Learning Centers or Stations

Learning centers provide an ideal way to adjust students' work according to subject areas, learning modalities, special interests, or levels of content. Students generally move through centers according to a schedule you explain and post. Centers may be available for a short time or may be permanent. Tasks in a center are continually changing. Students need direct instruction in how to keep records of the specific tasks they work on while they are there.

An effective learning center should contain:

- clearly stated directions about the number of students allowed to use the center at one time, how to use it, how to choose tasks, and where to work on the activities
- descriptions of the standards being addressed
- activities, resources, and materials that use various learning modalities
- examples of what completed tasks should look like
- answer keys, if needed
- rubrics or other guidelines for students to use so they know when their work has reached acceptable standards
- suggestions for how to get help
- guidelines for expected behavior
- directions for what to do before leaving the center
- procedures for students to store their work between visits, turn in completed work, and keep records of their visits (the Daily Log of Extension Activities discussed on pages 116–117 is useful here, as is the Choice Activities Log, described on pages 142–143)

Some teachers use one designated extension center for all subjects or units. Gifted students might be allowed to omit certain activities in order to spend more time on the extension activities. Color-coded folders may be useful to identify activities for all the different subjects. Tasks from Curriculum Planning Charts, Tiered Lesson Planning Charts, Extension Menus, and the ThinkTrix Model—all described in detail in this chapter—or those from other methods of differentiating instruction may be used in learning centers.

Using the Curriculum Planning Chart

The Curriculum Planning Chart offers a user-friendly way to plan differentiated learning activities for all your students simultaneously. You will find an example of a completed chart on page 137 and a reproducible chart for your own use on page 161. The left column describes the required standards. You may list these vertically, all at once. After you have described the standards, work each row horizontally, one standard at a time. In this way, you get the experience of planning several ways to teach the same standard.

In the second column, labeled "Regular Learning Activity," describe the way you usually teach the standard. In the third column, labeled "Alternate Learning Activity," describe an activity that uses a different learning modality. For example, if the task in the "Regular" column appeals to students who love to read and write, the task in the "Alternate" column should appeal to students who prefer visual or tactile-kinesthetic learning. The column to the far right, labeled "Extension Activity," describes an activity that stretches the parameters of the required standard but is still linked to it. Use any critical or creative thinking model to formulate extension activities, including the Taxonomy of Thinking verbs on page 163.

Each time you create an activity for the chart, stop and ask yourself the following question: "If a student did *only* this activity, and no other activity on this same horizontal line, would she learn the required standard?" Be sure the answer is yes. When students use the activities, they should be allowed to choose any activity described for that particular standard—regular, alternate, or extension—and know that by doing that activity they will be learning the designated standard.

For ease in record keeping, each task or space on the chart could have a label. For example, the tasks on the first horizontal row might be 1a, 1b, and 1c, and tasks in the second horizontal row might be 2a, 2b, and 2c. You can make photocopies of the entire chart and invite students to choose their activities from it. You may choose to hide the top horizontal line for the student copies so the category labels do not influence students in their task selection.

After you have completed the chart, you can display the regular, alternate, and extension activities in other ways. For example, you may want to replicate them on large index cards color-coded by column label and place these task cards in a learning center. If you do not use learning centers, you can place the task cards in containers on bookshelves or tables or insert them into plastic sleeves in a notebook or on a hanging display.

FIGURE 6-1 **Sample Curriculum Planning Chart**

UNIT: SOLAR POWER AND ENERGY

Required Standard	Regular Learning Activity	Alternate Learning Activity	Extension Activity
1. Understand that solar power comes from the sun.	**1a.** Read about how solar energy travels from the sun to the earth and tell about what you learned.	**1b.** Draw a picture to show how solar energy moves from the sun to the earth.	**1c.** Research and describe the relationship between solar energy and the earth's atmosphere.
2. Describe several ways that solar power is used in homes.	**2a.** Describe at least four ways in which solar power can be used in the home.	**2b.** Create a chart showing at least four ways in which solar power can be used in the home.	**2c.** Compare and contrast the advantages and disadvantages of using solar power in your home.
3. Explain why solar power causes less pollution than other power sources.	**3a.** After listening to a talk about pollution and solar power, prepare a short talk to present at home to convince your family of the benefits of solar power related to pollution.	**3b.** Watch a program about pollution related to solar power. Create a visual that compares pollution from solar power and pollution from fossil-fuel power.	**3c.** Research ways in which reduced pollution from solar power can impact your home and community over the next five years. Present the information to an appropriate audience.
4. Analyze short- and long-term comparisons of the costs of solar power to the costs of other sources of power for the home.	**4a.** Gather data about the cost of heating and cooling your home with various energy sources over a twelve-month period. Share what you learned.	**4b.** Create a chart to demonstrate the difference in home heating and cooling costs from various energy sources over a twelve-month period.	**4c.** Efficient technology can allow solar energy to be infinitely renewable. Find a way to describe the short- and long-term benefits as they relate to costs for your family.

Each day teach a short lesson (no longer than fifteen minutes) related to a required standard. Be aware that some students may not need to *watch* you to hear you! If other students ask why it is okay for some students not to watch you, explain that these students have demonstrated that they can perform acceptably on related assessments, and any other student who can show that ability will be allowed the same consideration. Then have students work for a designated time on activities related to the designated standards. You may repeat the process several times during an instructional period, even though students might continue to work on the same activity during each segment in which they are working more independently. Teach students to use the Choice Activities Log (see reproducible on page 167) so they can keep track of the tasks they are working on.

Planning Tiered Lessons

The Curriculum Planning Chart describes one way to create differentiated learning tasks that accommodate different learning modalities. Tiered lessons allow you to differentiate by creating several alternate learning tasks at varying degrees of difficulty, so although all students are learning the same standard, they are learning it at a level that is personally challenging. You can develop tiered lessons for specific skills as well as for standards from content areas or entire units.

Using Bloom's Revised Taxonomy to Create Tiered Lessons

One effective way to plan tiered lessons is based on Bloom's Revised Taxonomy of Educational Objectives, which describes six levels of thinking: Remembering, Understanding, Applying, Analyzing, Evaluating, and Creating.* **Figures 6-2** and **6-3** represent two different ways in which you can use that taxonomy of thinking.

FIGURE 6-2 **Taxonomy Triangle for Typical Learners**

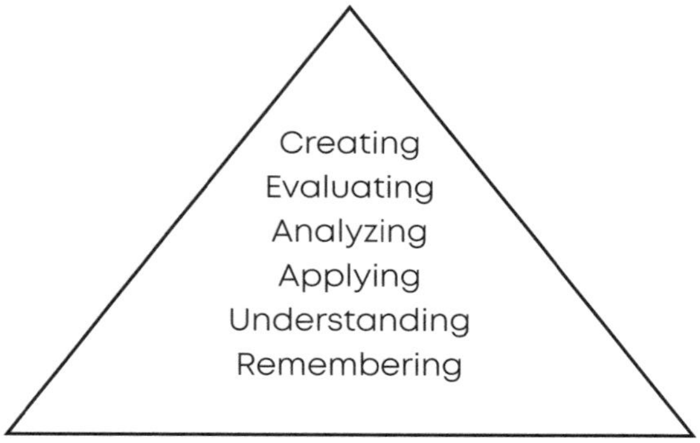

FIGURE 6-3 **Taxonomy Triangle for Gifted Learners**

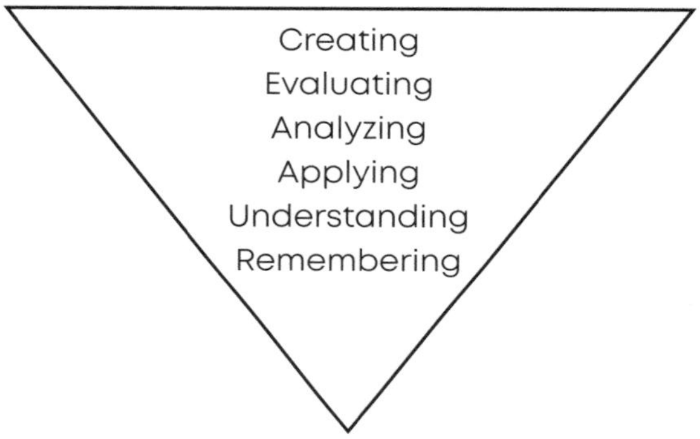

The top triangle illustrates that students who need to learn grade-level standards spend more of their learning time at the Remembering and Understanding levels before they can move on to the advanced levels of thinking. The bottom triangle illustrates that gifted students spend more of their learning time at the higher levels of Analyzing, Evaluating, and Creating, while spending less at the information intake levels of Remembering and Understanding. The goal is to move all students into the higher levels of thinking sometime during the learning process. Tiered lessons allow this to occur.

With tiered lessons, you use direct instruction for ten to fifteen minutes to introduce and explain a standard, after which you direct students

*Anderson, Krathwohl, Airasian, Cruikshank, Mayer, Pintrich, Raths, Wittrock. *A Taxonomy for Learning, Teaching, and Assessing: A Revision of Bloom's Taxonomy of Educational Objectives, Abridged Edition, 1st Ed., © 2001*. Reprinted by permission of Pearson Education, Inc., New York, New York.

to work on a task at a level appropriate for them. You can plan the leveled tasks on a Tiered Lesson Planning Chart (see **figure 6-4**), and students can work in groups formed on the basis of readiness, learning modality, or interest. Following direct instruction, students either choose or are directed to one of the tasks for the standard being taught. Students might work on the task for more than one class period, especially if it is an advanced task. If students are still working on a task when you are ready to move to another concept, that should be okay. They will be required to be attentive during the direct instruction segment of all concepts, but they can still return to a complex task as long as they are mastering the grade-level standards.

You can create your own chart on blank chart paper or use the reproducible Tiered Lesson Planning Chart on page 162, making an enlarged copy on 11" x 17" paper. If you want other teachers to work with you, invite them to help you brainstorm ideas. This is also an ideal task for a meeting of gifted-cluster teachers. (See "Schoolwide Gifted-Cluster Teacher Meetings," page 193.) Select as many standards as you have room for on the chart. Design learning activities at three levels: entry, advanced, and most challenging.

The verbs from the Taxonomy of Thinking reproducible on page 163 can help you in designing tasks. Trigger words that support Remembering and Understanding would be entry level, words that lead to Applying and Analyzing would be advanced, and those that call for Evaluating and Creating would be most challenging.

One additional resource for creating learning tasks is the ThinkTrix Model, described in the reproducible on pages 164–165. The categories in the ThinkTrix Model are flexible, and each category describes a range of thinking activities.

The products for tiered lessons are interchangeable among categories. You can have students use the Choice Activities Log (see reproducible on page 167) to keep track of their tasks.

FIGURE 6-4 Samples of Tiered Lessons in Several Subject Areas

Required Standard	Entry-Level Activities	Advanced Activities	Most Challenging Activities
The number of objects can be represented by a numeral.	Count items from 1 to 10 and write corresponding numerals.	Count items in pictures from 1 to 1,000 and write corresponding numerals.	Translate base 10 numbers into other number bases such as base 5 and base 7.
Sedimentary rocks are formed from layers of sand and earth.	Draw pictures of sedimentary rocks.	Select sedimentary rocks from photos or collections of rocks and explain how you know they are sedimentary.	Discover methods used by geologists to tell the difference between sedimentary and other types of rocks.
Tall tales are found in many cultures.	Read the story and retell it in your own words.	Describe an event in nature or history that the tall tale might explain.	Write an original story that contains all the elements necessary to make it a tall tale.
The causes of the Civil War were social, political, and economic.	Name and describe one social, one political, and one economic cause of the Civil War.	Explain how one social, one political, and one economic cause of the Civil War led to the actual conflict.	Compare social, political, and economic causes of the Civil War to those same influences in the last war fought by US soldiers.

Incorporating Depth, Complexity, and Novelty into Curriculum Differentiation Planning

Two other methods from the field of gifted education can assist teachers seeking ways to provide appropriate extension activities for gifted students. One method is based on the work of Sandra Kaplan.* She teaches how to utilize the concepts of depth, complexity, and novelty when designing rigorous curriculum activities.

Depth refers to students' abilities to understand the "big ideas," including theories, generalizations, and principles that govern the study of a discipline. Depth also attends to the specific language used in different disciplines and to the ability to recognize patterns, be aware of trends, and understand the myriad details related to the study of a discipline. *Complexity* describes students' abilities to make connections and understand interactions over time and to study a situation from several perspectives. Attention to *novelty* recognizes the enthusiasm of gifted learners for learning about topics that are unusual and provocative. Please use the resources developed by Dr. Kaplan to learn more about this model and how it can have a positive impact on instructional strategies for students.

In recent years another method for developing depth and complexity has emerged through the use of Depth of Knowledge (DOK) as described next.

Developing Depth of Knowledge (DOK)

Depth of Knowledge is a process that inherently differentiates instruction by categorizing learning tasks according to the complexity of thinking required for task completion. Similar to Bloom's Revised Taxonomy, learning using DOK levels begins with students being able to demonstrate basic knowledge and understanding through recall (DOK 1), then progresses to a skill and conceptual level of understanding (DOK 2). From DOK 2, learning activities progress into more complex levels that involve strategic thinking (DOK 3) and finally extended thinking (DOK 4). By connecting DOK levels to specific types of learning activities, teachers can direct students to appropriate levels of learning complexity. The higher levels of DOK activities naturally subsume understanding of the lower level skills and content.

DOK offers a clear and concise framework for designing content-based learning tasks that challenge students and place them in productive struggle. This struggle increases their complexity of thinking and establishes a rigorous learning environment. Educators seeking to enhance the complexity of thinking within their classrooms support the process by developing DOK level 3 and level 4 activities (see **figure 6-5**). These tasks require the student to engage in complex learning situations. The DOK structure can expand student understanding within a unit of study or as a follow-up to a unit of study. Through the development of the extension lesson, you can address the varied learning modalities of your students.

DOK Levels of Cognitive Rigor

The Depth of Knowledge model categorizes tasks according to the cognitive rigor and complexity of thinking required to successfully complete them. The questions listed for each level are designed to support the teacher in developing tasks at different levels of complexity. When teachers are designing tasks using verbs, it is important to remember that *the focus is on the complexity of the task that follows the verb rather than the verb used to describe the activity.*

*Information on Dr. Kaplan's model for incorporating depth, complexity, and novelty into curriculum planning is adapted from Kaplan, Sandra, Ed.D., *Theory and Practice: Curriculum Instruction for Educators* (Los Angeles: University of Southern California, 2000–2006). Used with permission.

FIGURE 6-5 **Webb's Depth of Knowledge: Context Ceilings***

DOK Level 1

Recall & Reproduction

- Who?
- What?
- Where?
- When?

DOK Level 2

Basic Application of Skills & Concepts

- How did it happen?
- Why did it happen?
- How does it work?
- Why does it work that way?

DOK Level 3

Strategic Thinking

- How can you use it?
- Why can you use it?
- What is the cause?
- What is the effect?
- What is the reason?
- What is the result?

DOK Level 4

Extended Thinking

- What is the impact?
- What is the influence?
- What is the relationship?
- What if?
- What would happen?
- What could happen?
- What do you think, feel, believe?

*Adapted from work by Erik M. Francis, Maverik Education (maverikeducation.com), copyright © 2014.

DOK LEVEL 1: RECALL AND REPRODUCTION

Tasks at this level require recall of facts or rote application of simple procedures. The tasks do not require any cognitive effort beyond remembering the right response or formula. Copying, computing, defining, and recognizing are typical level 1 tasks.

DOK LEVEL 2: SKILLS AND CONCEPTS

At this level, students must do something with the content. They must make some decisions about their approach. Tasks with more than one mental step, such as comparing, organizing, summarizing, predicting, and estimating, are usually level 2.

DOK LEVEL 3: STRATEGIC THINKING

At this level of complexity, students use at least three resources. Students must use planning and evidence, and thinking is more abstract. A task with multiple valid responses, in which students must justify their choices, would be a level 3 task. Examples include solving a nonroutine problem, designing an experiment, or analyzing characteristics of a genre. Designing an experiment requires level 3 strategic thinking; however, if a student were to design, conduct, and analyze the experimental outcomes, the student would be functioning at the highest level of complexity, level 4.

DOK LEVEL 4: EXTENDED THINKING

Level 4 tasks require the most complex cognitive effort and use at least four resources. Students synthesize information from multiple sources, often over an extended period of time, or transfer knowledge from one or two domains to solve problems in another. You may notice that the words *design* and *analyze* are frequently used in level 4 tasks. Designing a survey and interpreting the results, analyzing multiple texts to extract themes, or writing an original myth in an ancient style would all be examples of level 4 tasks.

The following example uses the verb *describe* differently in each activity. In this structure, what follows the verb determines the level of complexity of the activity. The levels of complexity are vastly different in the three activities.

- **Describe** three characteristics of metamorphic rock. (recall task: DOK level 1)
- **Describe** the difference between metamorphic and igneous rock. (requires distinguishing between rock types: DOK level 2)

- **Describe** a model that you might use to represent the relationships that exist within the rock cycle. (requires strategic understanding of the rock cycle and a determination of how to best represent it: DOK level 3)

When lesson planning, remember that DOK levels are not sequential, nor are they developmental. Giving students tasks at levels 3 and 4 can provide the context and motivation needed to engage learners better than tasks at the more routine learning levels 1 and 2. Even the youngest learners are capable of strategic and extended thinking. All students need the opportunity to engage in complex thinking.

As a teacher, you are likely often locked into instructing at levels 1 and 2. The tasks you present to students are probably geared to these two levels. However, generalizable learning occurs when students are working in level 3 (strategic thinking). "Teach at 3" is a concept that encourages teachers to instruct learners at the strategic thinking level. This kind of instruction requires students to do more than just use the content; they must justify their choices and determine the most viable solution; they must remember what they need to know. Teaching at the strategic level provides students with "need to know" learning opportunities. Student engagement increases when learners participate in seeking the information needed. When you teach at DOK level 3, you can scaffold the instructional methods and activities using varied levels of complexity to adjust for student readiness.

Figure 6-6 shows sample activities for the four DOK levels.

See page 166 for a reproducible lesson template to use when creating extension lessons using the DOK format.

Record Keeping with the Choice Activities Log

All students in the class may use the Choice Activities Log to keep records of the activities they choose from learning centers, the Curriculum Planning Chart, the tiered lesson options, or project work. Keeping personal logs of individual progress helps students feel more in charge

FIGURE 6-6 **Sample Activities at All DOK Levels**

DOK Level 1	Given a diagram of the heart, *label* the parts listed and show the flow of blood. *Sequence* the directions for making the paper airplane from the story.
DOK Level 2	A customer is looking for a rectangular ottoman. He wants one with the most storage space possible but needs a height between 14 and 16 inches. What are the options available in a rectangular design? Identify the *cause-effect* relationships in the short story.
DOK Level 3	*Evaluate* how the different backgrounds and cultures of the characters in the story influenced the events and outcome of the story. *Develop* a model to represent the relationship between lift and drag.
DOK Level 4	*Connect* two of the common themes discussed in class across texts in different cultures. *Create* representations of the three data sources that would lead the audience to come to different conclusions regarding the data.

of their own learning and also communicates your confidence in their ability to take personal responsibility for this. The Choice Activities Log helps you support and sustain a unified learning community in the classroom, where more students than just those formally identified as gifted can learn how to become more independent workers.

A reproducible Choice Activities Log is included on page 167. It is designed for students to keep track of their self-selected extension activities you make available to them, and it can easily be used to record short-term extension experiences. (This is different from the Daily Log of Extension Activities, described in chapter 5, which is used by students to monitor ongoing independent study.) Explain how you expect students to use the Choice Activities Log. At the beginning of an independent work class period, students write today's date in the left column. In the center column, they briefly describe the task they are working on today. Near the end of the class period, in the right column, students describe two things they learned from working on their chosen task. See **figure 6-7** for an example.

Keep all logs in a crate that holds hanging file folders so students can easily locate them and have ongoing records of the work they do. The folders hold their work in progress, and the Choice Activities Log helps them keep track of which tasks they are currently working on.

Gifted students might be using the Daily Log of Extension Activities on page 130 instead of the Choice Activities Log to keep track of the extensions they are working on from various sources. If you prefer to have all students in the class using the same type of log, use the Choice Activities Log for everyone.

Using Study Guides and Extension Menus to Compact and Extend Learning

The use of Study Guides enables you to compact in literature, science, social studies, problem-based learning, and thematic, integrated units by reducing the amount of time gifted students must spend on designated content. Study Guides are designed for students who can demonstrate mastery on assessments without actually doing the regularly assigned activities.

Students who are effective independent learners use the information on the Study Guides to ensure they will learn the required standards and be ready for each assessment at the same

FIGURE 6-7 **Sample Choice Activities Log**

Student's name: Hannah

Project topic: Female Antarctic Explorers

Today's Date	My Chosen Activity	Two Things I Learned
March 2	Read about Fiona Thornwell	1st British woman to reach South Pole in 2002 Led several expeditions to both poles
March 3	Read about Liv Arnesen	From Norway Sailed and skied across Antarctica with Ann Bancroft

time all students take it. They are excused from the regular requirements for daily work as long as they continue to demonstrate they are mastering the required standards and achieving at or above a level of 85 percent on all formal assessments. Each day they work on alternate activities that are related to the designated unit content but extend the parameters of that material.

There is no pretest with this method, since the material is new. If a student feels he is extremely familiar with the content and asks for a pretest, you can consider making the pretest available for the first day of the unit only. The Study Guide is developed from the standards all students are required to master. Those are the same standards that will be assessed for all students at the end of the unit.

Once your standards have been designated, create a Study Guide that describes all the standards that will be formally assessed in the order you will teach them. Build in three or four assessment dates (checkpoints) when all students must demonstrate their competence with the standards taught to that point. The idea is that *some students can learn the required standards without actually doing the assigned work*. Rather than insist that they do all that work anyway, use the Study Guide method. It allows you to get the proof you need that students have mastered the required standards, and they can use the opportunity to extend their learning into related areas for equal credit. Students and their parents will be pleased to know you recognize that advanced learners need this essential accommodation to remain motivated and productive in school. Providing this Study Guide option changes the emphasis for gifted students from "you are required to do all the grade-level work" to "you must master all the required standards." This is a fair accommodation and sends a clear message that their teacher understands that being gifted means students are operating on a higher grade level than their age peers. If the issue of fairness comes up, you might find this quote from special needs educator Rick Lavoie helpful: "Fairness has little to do with treating people in an identical manner. The true definition of fairness is: 'Fairness means that everyone gets what he or she needs'" (Lavoie, accessed 2019).

Figure 6-8 is an example of a Study Guide.

Explain to all students that you are offering a more independent path through the unit for students who are presently exhibiting the following learning characteristics:

- can read successfully independently and remember most of what has been read
- desire a faster pace of learning
- enjoy learning about topics that extend the parameters of a particular unit of study
- presently maintain an average of B or higher in this particular subject

Explain that the method would not be a good choice for students who are not demonstrating those characteristics, because it requires a good deal of independent reading and work.

Please notice that "turn in all homework" is not listed as necessary criteria. If you stipulate that students who want to experience differentiation must have turned in all their homework for the present unit, you will automatically eliminate many students who would greatly benefit from these methods, which were actually designed primarily to entice nonproductive gifted students into being more productive in class. Explain that all students will be experiencing the same assessments together, so if students choose the Study Guide option, they will be responsible for learning the required standards more independently.

If you explain this option very matter-of-factly, without making it sound like an opportunity that no one will want to miss, students will very likely take their cue from your attitude and make appropriate judgments about whether the option is right for them. Since there is no pretest, it could happen that a student who is not a good candidate for this option chooses it anyway. You can remedy a problem this may create by scheduling the first checkpoint on the Study Guide for no more than three days after the unit begins. Students who are not able to demonstrate mastery of the concepts being assessed rejoin the direct

FIGURE 6-8 **Study Guide Example: Mythology**

1. Be able to name at least six gods or goddesses from the culture we are studying and know what powers, abilities, and challenges each one had.
2. Understand the elements of a myth so you can identify and describe them in a myth you read.
Checkpoint: ______________________: Assessment for 1–2
3. Describe the dwelling places of the gods and goddesses as well as other locations where the myths took place.
4. Be able to share one myth with your classmates that includes the telling of the story, pictures of the characters and events, and an explanation of the forces of nature or human characteristics it explains.
5. Myths belong to many categories, including Ritual, Origin, Prestige, Social, and Trickster. Investigate myths from several cultures related to two of these categories and create a visual representation of what you learn.
Checkpoint: ______________________: Assessment for 1–5
6. There are heroic characters in the stories from every religion. Compare and contrast three heroes from one religion with the stories from the mythologies being studied.
7. Many stories from literature and film, such as *Star Wars, The Lion King, The Hobbit,* and *Lord of the Rings,* share components of mythology. Locate and describe information about at least three of those similarities.
8. Compare and contrast the elements of myths to the elements of two of the following: folktales, fairy tales, fables, or legends.
9. Based upon an event in history during the last fifty years, create a myth about that event, including all the elements contained in myths.
10. Investigate the heroic stories of a great writer from the same culture being studied. Determine the elements from myths that you find in the stories.
Checkpoint: ______________________: Final Assessment for 1–10

instruction group at that time for the remainder of the unit. Some teachers allow all students in the class to spend two or three days at the end of the unit working on one extension activity. At that time, a student who had begun work on an extension activity but needed to return to direct instruction for the balance of the standards could return to his chosen activity.

Explain this Study Guide method briefly to the whole class and invite volunteers to attend a meeting to learn all about it so they can make an informed decision on whether they want to try it out. At the meeting, hand out copies of your prepared Study Guides to students who want to see them. Reassure students that the only standards that will be formally assessed are those listed on the Study Guide. Students who want to learn at a faster pace might worry that they'll miss out on important standards if they don't stay with the teacher-directed lessons every day. Your reassurance that there will be no surprises on formal assessments will be welcome. You might also reassure them that while working independently they will be hearing the direct instruction all the time, whether they are actually watching the lesson or not.

You may have some students who declare, after looking at the Study Guide, that they already know most of the required standards. In that case, you may decide to let them take the summative (end-of-unit) assessment at that point. Resist requests to allow students to take this assessment anytime they feel ready for it. Either they take it the first day of the unit, or they use the Study Guide method for that unit. Otherwise, you will get bogged down with too much record keeping.

The idea of exempting some students from regularly assigned work may make you uncomfortable. You may worry that they will learn poor work habits or that other students will resent what they perceive to be special privileges. Consider why you create assignments in the first place—to help students learn the material. With the Study Guide method, you will have documentation that all students have learned the required material, and they are held accountable for demonstrating that mastery on your timetable. It is the alternate work they do that has a more flexible format, and it is the faster pacing that makes them (and their parents) happy.

When advanced students are not working on required assignments, they work instead on a related topic of interest, which they are encouraged to share in some way with the entire class, thus enriching everyone's experience with the content. These options are described in the following section. What you are differentiating is simply the amount of regularly assigned work that advanced students have to do to prepare for the assessments. Because all students experience the required assessments together, you never lose control over the necessity of having all students master the required standards.

Two Ways to Use the Study Guide

THE STUDY GUIDE ON ITS OWN

The first way to use the Study Guide is on its own. The Study Guide itself is the differentiation tool; students use it to study another example of what the whole class is learning.

With this option, you create a "generic" Study Guide. This allows a student to connect her independent study to the same general standards being learned by other students. For example, if the class is studying a unit on the mythology of ancient Greece and Rome, the Study Guide can be on the generic topic of mythology rather than on Greek and Roman mythology. Your direct instruction is about Greek and Roman myths. Students who already know a good deal about Greek and Roman mythology can use the Study Guide to learn about the mythologies of other civilizations. The Study Guide provides structure to their independent study, because it clearly describes the elements they should consider in learning about all mythologies. This is preferable to simply telling students to study other topics without giving any guidelines for that study. The formal assessments for *all* students will be about Greek and Roman myths.

THE STUDY GUIDE WITH AN EXTENSION MENU

With the second option, the Study Guide is used in combination with an Extension Menu or other extension opportunities. This option invites students to focus intensively on a topic related to what the whole class is learning. They choose a topic from the Extension Menu (or come up with one on their own), pursue it in depth, and later share some of what they learned with the class or another appropriate audience. This expands the unit and makes it more interesting and enjoyable for everyone. Using Extension Menus also allows you to reintegrate interesting content and activities you have previously enjoyed using that you may have given up because they weren't directly tied to the required standards. These activities can now be explored by some of your students who then share them with the rest of the class.

In all cases, students are expected to master the same required standards as the rest of the class, and they are held accountable for regular assessments along with other class members. They are excused from actually completing the required activities as long as they work on an extension topic instead and meet all the expectations described on page 144. With Study Guides and Extension Menus, gifted students are allowed to learn at a faster pace and spend the balance of their time in school on activities that are more challenging and rewarding for them.

Using Extension Menus

Extension Menus provide eight suggested activities from which students can choose to do an in-depth study. The goal is to learn about one topic in great detail—not to work on several topics. If a student wants to choose his own idea, he can do that with the approval of the teacher. Students may work on one extension activity over time, keeping track of their work on the Daily Log of Extension Activities (see reproducible on page 130). **Figure 6-9** is an example of an Extension Menu. Other Study Guides and Extension Menus on more than one hundred topics are available in the book *Differentiated Lessons for Every Learner* by Dina Brulles, Karen L. Brown, and Susan Winebrenner.

FIGURE 6-9 **Extension Menu Example: Mythology**

Discover how myths are invented to explain events that people experience. Create a myth of the same type as ancient myths to explain a contemporary event. Hypothesize reasons why ancient myths have remained popular over many centuries.	Find characters from books from other religions that share characteristics with mythological heroes or heroines. Compare and contrast their powers, behaviors, and daily lives.	Choose a superhero from modern times and compare and contrast his or her characteristics with a character from an ancient mythology.
Compare and contrast the myths of cultures native to certain continents (North American Indians, Aboriginal people of Australia, and so on) with those written about ancient civilizations.	**STUDENT CHOICE**	Assume the role of a storyteller from any culture for which you have read some mythology. Present a story to an appropriate audience in much the same way a storyteller from that culture would have done it.
Compare and contrast religions in which multiple deities are honored to those that believe there is only one deity. Describe the pros and cons of each approach from the viewpoint of an ordinary citizen, a holy person, and a government official.	Investigate words, expressions, and ideas from mythology that have become part of our daily language usage. Decide how the meanings of those words have either remained the same or changed over time.	Visit an art museum and observe how works of art have been influenced by mythology. Create a report of your findings.

Adapted from *Differentiating Content for Gifted Learners in Grades 6–12* by Susan Winebrenner (Minneapolis: Free Spirit Publishing, 2005).

Using the Daily Log of Extension Activities with the Study Guide Method

The Daily Log of Extension Activities (explanation on page 116, reproducible form on page 130) is essential to the success of students using the Study Guide method. Teachers who try compacting and differentiating often ask how they will be able to monitor students who are working more independently. The answer is to use the Daily Log of Extension Activities. It is amazingly successful in supporting students who need to keep track of their differentiated work, so they never get lost in managing their more independent working time. Every time a student is working more independently on extension activities, the student should start a new entry in the Daily Log of Extension Activities. Students who experience compacting and differentiation in several subjects should maintain separate Daily Logs for each subject.

A Word About Independent Study

Gifted students are generally inquisitive and love discovering information about topics near and dear to their hearts. Therefore, one of the best approaches to their extension activities is to facilitate their engagement in an ongoing independent study on a topic of their choice, especially if you are not currently offering the Study Guide method. When students can return over time to learn more about a topic that excites them, their teacher does not have to provide so many separate extension activities for each unit the class is studying. Keeping up with the Study Guide and the assessment checkpoints for the grade-level unit is all that is required for documenting mastery. Several of the forms in this chapter and chapter 5 can be utilized in an independent study, especially the Daily Log of Extension Activities (page 130) and the Independent Study Agreement (page 169).

You may notice that on the Independent Study Agreement, there is no room for a parent's signature. Information about this agreement should be shared with parents, but if they sign, they may feel obligated to ensure their child is complying with the required conditions. Since almost all of this independent work will be done at school, it is best if the formal agreement is between the teacher and student only.

If parents *want* to help with the project, that's fine. Have the family choose one portion of the project to be designated as the home portion; the construction or experiment aspects might be good choices here. Students may include their home portion when they describe their findings to an appropriate audience, but that portion should not be graded, since the degree and type of parent involvement may impact the quality of the home-based work. **Figure 6-10** shows a sample letter communicating information to parents about the Study Guide and independent work.

Students working on Extension Menu projects are not required to complete an entire project by the end of the unit. This is the reason their reports are called "progress reports." In real life, researchers may spend a lifetime on one project. The more often you bring the students back for whole-class activities, the less time they have to work on their project. Furthermore, gifted learners have a unique capacity for wanting to learn all there is to know about a topic of interest. If they think their learning will be limited by a timeline, they might not volunteer for the Study Guide option again. Besides, you really don't want them to finish their project, since that would mean you have to help them find and plan another. The best thing that could happen is for a student to become so engrossed in a project that he wants to work on it for many weeks or months—even into subsequent units. As long as the learning and working conditions are being met, and the student continues to demonstrate mastery of the required standards, there is no reason to insist that a student stop working on a project that clearly interests him.

FIGURE 6-10 Sample Letter to Parents Explaining the Study Guide and Independent Activities

Dear Parent/Caregiver:

Your son Henry has demonstrated outstanding ability in social studies. He is able to learn much of the basic material independently and enjoys working on activities that extend the required standards. During the present unit on mythology, Henry has agreed to work with a method that allows him to use a Study Guide to master the required standards. I will be checking often to make sure he is learning those standards successfully.

During some of his time in class, Henry will be working on an independent study project. He has chosen a topic related to the larger unit we are studying and will do research on that topic. He is not required to complete the project until he feels he is done learning about the topic, but there are certain working conditions and expectations he has agreed to follow. He will be presenting a progress report at regular intervals to share what he is learning with others.

Henry may choose to work on one part of the project at home, and that work might replace other homework he does not have to do. Some students prefer to do all their work related to the project in school and that is also acceptable.

This independent study method will provide excellent experience for Henry in guiding his own learning experiences. I will be providing ongoing coaching for him as it is needed, and he might spend some time working with other students who are doing similar work.

There is nothing you need to do at home to facilitate Henry's independent study. If any problems occur in school while Henry is working with a Study Guide, I will be in touch with you. In the meantime, if you have any questions, please contact me.

Sincerely,

Mrs. Ozolins

Mrs. Ozolins

It is also okay if students want to switch to a different topic after a progress report has been completed. Remember, they are being held totally accountable for the required standards and for the same long-term projects required for all your students. They will be given a new Study Guide for the next unit, and they will also be held accountable for learning the standards associated with the new unit of study during the same time frame.

Grading Independent Study Projects

When students are old enough to use the Study Guides and Extension Menus, they have probably developed an attitude of not wanting to do the work if there are no grades attached. In chapter 5, we explained that when differentiating content students have previously mastered, there is a good case for not grading extension activities related to skill work, since the pretest provides proof of mastery. However, when using the Study Guide and Extension Menu method, the only formal grades you will have for students working independently are those from the checkpoint assessments. These students or their parents may wish to have a grade for the students' extension work connected to new content. If all interested parties are okay with the idea of no grade for the project work, that's fine too. It might indicate a positive attitude toward being intrinsically motivated to learn something simply for the sake of learning it.

The reproducible Evaluation Contract on page 171 may be used to help students plan the grade they will earn for their independent study work. As it illustrates, the grade earned by students using the Study Guide and Extension Menu approach should reflect the complexity and sophistication of content and thought processes rather than the appearance of the product or the amount of work. It should be based on substance rather than form. Rubrics work well for this purpose and are generally well received by students on independent study. Use rubrics you already have or can find on the internet. (Two good sources are The Curriculum Project and Professional Associates Publishing, see page 242.) Rubrics might be constructed by the students themselves, either by modifying existing rubrics or by creating their own. See an example of a Rubric Planning Form on page 172.

Using Primary Sources in Internet Study*

A primary source is one that can be accessed in its original form rather than being learned about through reporting on the topic by someone else. The use of primary sources in independent study brings a sense of real discovery and high relevance to students' research efforts. Primary sources include original documents, diaries, letters, news reporting sources, speeches, first-person accounts of events, original artifacts, photographs, movies and television shows from other time periods, and other similar materials.

For truly rigorous independent study, the use of primary sources is essential. These sources stimulate students to develop a deep understanding of content, and they create learning excitement that comes from going way beyond a simple understanding of facts and information. When gifted students do independent study, the use of primary sources greatly facilitate access to appropriately advanced content.

Primary sources provide opportunities for students to engage in active investigations that enable them to learn concepts, apply information, and represent what they have learned in interesting ways. Primary sources facilitate collaboration among students, teachers, and others in the community to share and enjoy firsthand knowledge about ideas, objects, and events. Examination of primary sources and the investigations related to them take a significantly longer time period and may be more exciting for students than doing more traditional research.

Following are examples of suggested primary sources and ways in which students might use them. All of the suggestions can be supplemented with the students' own ideas. Many of these sources are freely available online.

Objects or artifacts. These include documents, objects people used, items from important events, and other actual objects. Students carefully examine the objects, making notes of their observations. Students notice a given object's specific traits, determine how those traits give evidence of the way the object might have been used, and make hypotheses about how the object was made. Students might tell a story from the perspective of the object, paying attention to how the object may have impacted people and events. Students might compare several objects, noticing similarities and differences, and do research to discover all they can about that particular object as well as other similar objects. Students might discover what types of articles are used in present times for similar purposes.

Visual sources. Visual sources include art, photographs, advertising material, and digital resources such as documentaries, films, and other viewable material. Students create an annotated display of

*The section on using primary sources is adapted from the work of Margaret Wilks of the Paris School District in Paris, Arkansas, and Gwen Morgan of Arkansas Tech University, Russellville, Arkansas. Used with permission.

similar items or compare similar items from several different time periods. Students survey several sources that reported on the same event and compare and contrast the findings. Students study advertisements over time for similar items—such as clothing, cars, or household goods—and determine themes or trends. Students create a visual representation of how a category of things might appear twenty-five or fifty years into the future.

Verbal sources. Letters, speeches, articles, stories from news sources, diaries, logs, emails, interviews, and written or recorded first-person accounts are among the many possible examples of verbal sources. Students report the content of the documents and hypothesize the feelings and opinions of the people who wrote them. Students study the time period involved to determine events that led to the documents. Students examine several types of documents from the same time period and analyze why similar documents expressed similar or different ideas. Students examine reports of similar events over time and compare historical documents with similar artifacts written more recently. Students investigate the life of the writers and hypothesize how the documents came to be written. Students draw pictures or create digital or electronic presentations about the documents. Students impersonate the person who created the document or article and present information about that person in a "You Are There" presentation.

Preparing Your Own Study Guides and Extension Menus

You may work on your own or with other teachers to develop topics and prepare Study Guides and Extension Menus, but the following documents are essential for this effort to become a successful experience. Start with the Topic Development Sheet (page 173). Then create the Study Guide from the topics listed on the left column of that sheet and the Extension Menu (page 168) from the topics on the right column of that sheet.

Finding Extension Activities

There are many sources available to teachers that provide the actual extension activities for students. Two of our favorites for challenging gifted learners include Renzulli Learning and Khan Academy. Renzulli Learning (www.renzullilearning.com) is a website that provides a service to help gifted students identify topics that interest them for independent study. Once the student has selected a topic, the site provides links to numerous places where the information they are seeking may be found. Khan Academy (www.khanacademy.org) offers free, expert-created online tools for learning math, science, engineering, humanities, language arts, the arts, economics, and so on. The learning activities are presented in an attractive and engaging game-style format through video instruction.

Many other resources are available just by searching the internet for challenging activities for gifted students in a designated subject area. Parents of gifted students are usually aware of topics that interest or excite their children. Some parents are even willing to spend time in their children's classrooms assisting any student who needs help in locating materials and resources to use in independent study.

If your gifted students attend a content-replacement or resource class, *the work from those classes should replace the grade-level work they do not have to do.* In content replacement, students are regrouped by learning level and may leave your classroom to learn with another teacher every day, usually for reading or math. If they have work to do between those classes, those activities could be used as extension activities in your class. Likewise, if students are working on projects they began in a pull-out class, that work serves as extension activities.

1. Using the Topic Development Sheet, list eight to ten required standards you want all students to master by the end of the unit.
2. In the right column, list topics related to the unit theme but not included in the "Required Content Standards" list. These may be topics you would want to include if you had unlimited time for this unit or topics you think would appeal to students with interests that extend beyond the unit parameters.
3. Create a Study Guide that includes only the required standards in the order you will teach them. Build in the first checkpoint to occur no more than three days after the unit begins. This way, it will be easy to notice if some students have made inappropriate choices and have not been able to keep up with learning the required content.
4. Use or create an Extension Menu with a nine-square grid that includes eight related topics. Leave the center space free for Student Choice. Use a creative or critical thinking model that you are confident will provide activities that will expand students' learning experiences. The extensions should be connected to the general unit of study but are purposefully not limited to the exact standards being taught and assessed. This is why they are called "extensions" instead of "enrichments" or another term.

Describe the topics, but *not* the specific ways students should present the information they find. They can choose their own products from the reproducible Product Choices Chart on page 174. In this way, students will not reject an extension idea simply because they do not like the product you have suggested. You might offer six to nine products that are appealing to auditory, visual, and kinesthetic learners. Include products for which you already have rubrics, or for which rubrics are easily available, if you want to guarantee that the extension work will be of high quality.

Helpful Information When Using Study Guides and Extension Menus

Gifted students who work independently should have access to their teacher on a regular, planned basis. You have worked hard to offer more challenging options so they can work at their challenge level. They need to know that it is perfectly all right to need assistance from you, even though they are smart kids.

Insist that students keep all documents related to the Study Guide method at school at all times. Provide special folders for that purpose and keep them easily accessible for students. The Daily Log of Extension Activities (or the Choice Activities Log), especially, isn't to be taken out of the room or mixed in with the student's other materials, since the information on it contributes to the student's success for the entire unit's work.

Some students might try to convince you that they should be allowed to work on homework from another class and not do the alternate work you have offered. Or they might suggest that their entire grade should come from the formal assessments only and not the alternate work for the unit. Since you know that your content is broader than what the required standards describe, tell the students that these are not available options. They must understand that you are offering only two options: staying with the class and doing all the work they do or working on an alternate learning activity related to the unit you are teaching.

At the end of each unit in which gifted students have experienced differentiation, it's a good idea to send home an Extension Activities Feedback Form to give parents concrete evidence that their children have been challenged in your class. You will find the form in chapter 5 on page 132.

Project-Based Learning for All Students

All students can benefit from working on projects, even though the level of difficulty of the projects will vary according to the students. If you use projects, simulations, or other types of realistic learning strategies, be sure all your students are participating.

The most powerful motivation tool you possess is *choice*! Being able to have some choice in what they will learn inspires students, including those who struggle to learn, and brings excitement and energy to learning tasks. Struggling students can be enticed to learn required standards when they are taught through their preferred learning modalities and when those standards are somehow linked to things kids are interested in.

If you have access to multiple computers, consider WebQuests as a vehicle for independent projects. A WebQuest is an inquiry-based activity for which students gather information from the internet. Many websites offer free information and WebQuest samples. To find these, type the term *WebQuests* into your search engine or consult the recommended sources on pages 242–243.

Another good resource for project-based learning involving internet research is the I-Search Process, which links effective teaching, learning (content knowledge and research processes), and assessment. An I-Search unit has four phases of instruction:*

In Phase I, teachers immerse students in the unit's theme (a socially relevant topic that naturally links science, social studies, language arts, and mathematics). Students engage in a variety of activities, not only to discover what they already know about this theme, but also to build background knowledge. These activities model a variety of ways for students to gather information. By the end of Phase I, each student poses an I-Search question to guide her personally motivated inquiry.

In Phase II, students develop a search plan that identifies how they will gather information: by reading books, magazines, news sources, reference materials; by watching videos; by interviewing people or conducting surveys; by carrying out experiments, doing simulations, or going on field trips.

In Phase III, students follow their search plans and gather information. They also analyze and synthesize information to reach conclusions or make predictions.

In Phase IV, students draft, revise, edit, and publish an I-Search Report. The I-Search Report includes the following components: My Search Questions, My Search Process, What I Learned, What This Means to Me, and References. The report becomes the foundation for an oral presentation, skit, poster, experiment, or other exhibition of knowledge.

An I-Search Unit is an excellent context for alternate assessment, the inclusion of students with diverse learning abilities, and technology integration.

For independent project-based learning that extends the curriculum, students can plan their research using a planning tool similar to the reproducible Project Planners on pages 175–177. (Copy the second page of the upper grade planner on the back of the first page.) Have students break down their main topic into subtopics. For each subtopic, they should come up with specific questions to research. Older students can have six subtopics with three questions for each; primary students can have four subtopics with two questions each. The example in **figure 6-11** on page 154 shows a subtopic and questions related to the study of life on the American frontier.

Each of the subtopics and questions can be transferred to 5" x 7" index cards. Students may then record appropriate information on each card, which helps them organize the information they gather. Color-coded cards are especially helpful. This is an easy note-taking method, and it works especially well for students with executive functioning challenges. With all the cards available for them each time they do some research, it is very easy to write information on the appropriate card as soon as the information is found.

There are many resources available to you if you want to have your students work on projects. See pages 242–243 for several recommendations.

*Reprinted with permission of Education Development Center, Inc., www.edc.org.

FIGURE 6-11 Examples of Project Subtopics and Questions

Topic: Life on the American Frontier

Subtopic: Wagon Trains

1. Where were the major routes used by wagon trains on their way to the West?
2. What was it like to be a child on a wagon train experience?
3. What dangers did travelers face on wagon trains?

Subtopic: Town Life in the Old West

1. What were some positive aspects of living in a town in the Old West?
2. What were some negative aspects of living in a town in the Old West?
3. How would your life as a child have been different if you had lived in a town in the Old West?

Sustaining a Unified Learning Community

You want to be sure all students in your class are confident that they are equally important to you and to each other. Teachers who differentiate regularly need to make sure students feel that everyone's work is equally valuable and that they all have lots of time for fun. Opportunities to work together as a whole class should be balanced by opportunities for flexible grouping and independent study. Several methods for sustaining a unified learning community are described in chapter 5 (see pages 120–121). This section describes some additional activities that will help the whole class work together on a regular basis.

Structured Partner Discussion

All students are placed in pairs, with one triad possible if the number of students is uneven. The teacher suggests a subject for discussion, such as something from current events, an experiment the class has done in science, or a topic from a book the teacher is reading aloud to the class. First, Partner A listens to Partner B for a designated period of time; then Partner A gets to explain his views on the topic. Next, pairs join pairs to create foursomes. Each person in a foursome introduces his original partner to the other two people and summarizes what that person said when the partners were talking; Partner A describes what Partner B had to say, and Partner B describes what Partner A had to say.

A variation of this method is for students to go through the same steps while trying to solve a specific problem or come up with solutions to a specific scenario. In this option, students should take notes while their partner is talking so it's easier to remember the specifics.

The Name Card Method (Think-Pair-Share)*

The Name Card Method is a magically effective strategy that empowers all students in mixed-ability classes to remain engaged in lessons and discussions and to better understand all the material being taught. Use it first with the one subject area or class for which total participation in discussions has not been attained. Add other subjects or classes as you become comfortable with the method.

*Think-Pair-Share is adapted from the work of Frank T. Lyman Jr., Ph.D., and used with permission of Dr. Lyman.

The Name Card Method:

- ensures nearly total participation in all discussions by all students and makes it impossible for anyone to choose to hide from participation during the entire class period
- minimizes blurting out and other attention-getting, discussion-controlling behaviors sometimes exhibited by gifted students
- eliminates teaching behaviors that may unconsciously or inadvertently communicate ethnic, cultural, socioeconomic, or gender bias
- communicates high expectations for learning success for all students
- encourages students to give thoughtful answers
- improves listening behaviors
- increases participation and student collaboration

GETTING READY TO USE THE NAME CARD METHOD

Write each student's name on a 3" x 5" card. Do not have students create their own cards, and do not use playing cards. Students of all ages appreciate teachers who take the time to know and use their names, rather than call them by some number from a deck of cards. Tell your students that when you use the cards, instead of calling on people who raise their hands, you will call on the person whose name is on the card you've drawn randomly from the stack.

Place students into discussion buddy pairs. (These pairs will remain together for the length of the activity or unit.) First, pair the blurters with each other. They will love this and will blurt out less often because their partners will appreciate their vast knowledge and they will feel that their contributions have been well heard. Students who know a lot about the subject at hand could also be paired together. Pair other gifted students together if they are equally strong in the subject for which you are using name cards. If some of the gifted students are struggling with the content, pair them with average-performing students. Other pairs would consist of average with below average. Never pair struggling students with each other, since there is little chance they could help each other learn the material. Never pair a struggling student with an advanced learner, because most gifted students lack patience and tend to command their partners to say or write something rather than coach them gently. Comments like "Just write this down!" or "I know this is the right answer—use this one" are not going to instill confidence in students who may be insecure about what they know.

USING THE NAME CARD METHOD

Tell your students why you are using name cards. You might explain that this method ensures that all students will take part in the discussion, that it gives kids a chance to develop friendships, that it helps people listen, or other reasons noted previously.

As you explain the method to your students, assure them that you will never use the cards until students have had a chance first to think of the answer themselves and then to confer with their designated partner. Students are highly likely to have some answer to share after they have conferred with a partner.

Start with a discussion that uses open-ended questions (questions that have more than one possible answer), such as a discussion of a book students are reading or of a current event tied to social studies content. Consult the Taxonomy of Thinking reproducible on page 163 to create questions with variety and interest. With the taxonomy, use the verbs to plan questions from all levels.

Use the following format for asking all your questions. Tell students to sit beside their designated partners for all discussion about a particular type of content. Partners may be different for various subject areas or topics but should remain the same for the duration of a learning unit. Ask a question and perhaps also write it in a highly visible place.

Then use Think-Pair-Share by Frank Lyman:

1. Think. Give students thirty seconds to think of their own answer and write it down. This will restrain some blurters who feel the need to inform others of the correct answer.

2. Pair. Demonstrate the signal you will use to indicate when pair time is over. Then give partners approximately thirty seconds to confer with each other during pair time. When you give the prearranged signal, students instantly must stop talking to each other and redirect their attention to you.

You may be concerned that your students will get off task during pair time. If you consistently keep the allotted time to under a minute, they will stay on task. During pair time, walk among the students to monitor that they are using the process correctly.

3. Share. Using the Name Card Method, call on students to share what they have discussed. Don't look at the cards before asking a question. If you do, you'll try to match the question's level of difficulty with your perception of the student's ability. This sends a clear message about the level of your expectations for that student, whether high or low. Since you have paired struggling students with supportive partners, it's okay to ask challenging questions of all students. Do not call a student's name before you ask a question, because then all other students will lose their interest in the question.

Slip the card into the middle of the pack and shuffle the cards continuously during the discussion so students never know when their card is coming up. In this way, students will not be able to disengage by knowing that you are going to call on everyone else before returning to them, and students who have already been called on will not be able to relax. If a student says, "You called on me already," hold up the cards and say, "The cards chose your name—not me."

Do not show the cards to the students. Every now and then, you may want to call on someone other than the person whose name card you pull—such as a student who's getting very impatient to participate. Always call on several students to share before commenting or giving your input.

When students are called on, they may give their own answer or one they heard from their partner. Students are not allowed to repeat answers already given. You as the teacher must avoid repeating students' answers. When we repeat, we make it easy for students to decide not to listen well. No one is allowed to pass when her name is called. When passing is allowed, students are able to choose to disengage.

Wait for approximately ten seconds for a response after calling on a student. Since students have already had more than one minute to consider their answers, more time will not help and will slow down the pace for the class. If a student tries to pass, repeats an answer already given, or cannot answer after being called on, do not ask class members to help and do not ask the student to choose someone to help her. This makes the student's need for help very public. Instead, suggest that the student confer again with her partner for a few minutes. Promise to return to her shortly because you know she will have an answer. *Remember to return to the student for her answer!* In this way, you communicate high expectations for engagement and learning success.

With some students, you might decide to coach them yourself. Provide a clue or hint, offer a choice between two alternatives, or connect the content to something you are certain the student already knows.

4. Receive responses. Receive student responses in a nonjudgmental way. Simply nodding your head or saying "Okay" or "Thank you" is all the response needed at this point. When you show that you'll receive multiple responses to the same question, students won't stop thinking about the question even after someone else has answered it. They know their name card might be next and they'll have to come up with a reasonable response as well. Students soon learn that hand waving, noise making, deep sighs, eye rolling, or other behaviors they use to get your attention will not change your selection of students to participate, since the cards determine who will be called on during this first phase of the method.

When you ask a question, you do not know which student's card will come up, so it's possible a struggling student will be asked to respond to a very challenging question. The student's partner may be the one who actually has an answer, but students may state either their answer or their partner's, and this reduces stress considerably.

After the initial sharing of information and ideas, take time to clear up misconceptions or to correct inaccurate information.

Note: If a student seems very uncomfortable as you begin to use this method, you might stand next to the child and her partner as you ask the question, then squat down to coach the pair toward an answer the nervous student can give. Rehearse it with the student once or twice, then walk away before you call her name.

5. Ask for additions. Before moving on to the next question, and for the benefit of students who enjoy sharing their deep wealth of knowledge, ask, "Does anyone have anything to add *that hasn't already been said*? Raise your hand if you do." Make it very clear that they may only *add*; they may not repeat what has already been said. This encourages students to listen carefully to the contributions of their classmates. If they do repeat, they forfeit their right to add anything more to the rest of this particular discussion. They can continue to participate in the discussion, however, because their name card stays in the stack.

Be sure your class understands that you are the only person allowed to notice a repeat. Apologize in advance in case you inadvertently overlook a repeat but make it clear that you do not want a chorus of reminders. Students who've tended to dominate discussions in the past are now in a very satisfying situation. They get to tell their partners the answers to all the questions, and they always have the opportunity to add to a discussion, so the need for blurting is significantly diminished. If a student does blurt out, ignore it completely. Give absolutely no indication, with gesture or body language, that you heard it. If other students mention it, say you did not hear it.

Note: If you already use a Socratic or Great Books method in which students enter into discussions without being called on, you might use elements of the Name Card Method to improve students' attending and participation behaviors during those discussions.

VARIATIONS ON THE NAME CARD METHOD*

Variations on Think Time

- Partners can write down a few notes before talking to each other.
- Use a question guide such as ThinkTrix (pages 164–165) to be sure your questions give students practice at all levels of thinking.

Variations on Pair Time

Ask students to:

- take turns teaching each other what the teacher just taught
- explain their own thinking to their partner about the concepts being learned
- identify the category of thinking from which questions come
- write about what they learned as a pair
- read aloud certain passages to each other
- review information for upcoming tests

Variations on Share Time

Ask students to:

- read something out loud
- act out a response
- describe ways in which new information is linked to concepts already learned
- use group signaling techniques
- vote for their preferred response with a method suggested by the teacher (such as true or false or a, b, or c)
- use personal whiteboards or tile squares to write their answers and display all answers simultaneously

---

*Adapted from Lyman, Frank, ThinkTrix SmartCard, San Clemente, CA (800-933-2667, www.KaganOnline.com). Copied with permission of Kagan Publishing.

Socratic Seminars

The Socratic Seminar is a time-honored question-and-discussion format that builds and maintains critical thinking as part of discussion. It offers an excellent way to help students move from recall to true understanding, and all students in grades three and up can benefit from it.

The teacher provides students with a reading on a high-interest topic. After students have read it, the teacher begins the discussion by asking a carefully constructed opening question about the assigned reading. Responses to that question lead to other questions, which may be posed by the teacher or by student participants. The teacher may also ask speakers to clarify or find evidence in the reading to support their opinions or statements.

Students in a Socratic Seminar sit in a circle. If there are too many for one circle, students can sit in two concentric circles with those who will actively participate in the seminar seated in the inner circle and those who will mostly observe seated in the "outer circle." Some teachers leave one or two open seats in the inner circle which may be occupied by outer-circle students for the time it takes them to add their contribution to the discussion. During ensuing Socratic Seminars, students rotate between the inner or outer circles.

Participants speak directly to one another, not to or through the teacher. They take turns contributing, listen and respond actively, and observe basic rules that help the discussion stay focused. At the end of the discussion, students in the outer circle provide feedback to those in the inner circle about both the content and format of the seminar, according to observation sheets they have filled out during the discussion.

You may use the seminars for discussions in any content area, including literature or poetry. Plan about thirty minutes for your first Socratic Seminar, then longer time periods as students become comfortable with the process.

Roundtable Discussions

Students are placed in heterogeneous groups and spend time gathering information about a topic they have been assigned. After they have had preparation time, one member from the group will join a roundtable discussion during which that student will serve as an "expert" and share information discovered by his group. Over a period of several days, different experts on the same topics will participate in new roundtable discussions. The benefit is that all students have help with their research, and students can provide good modeling for each other on how to be an effective roundtable participant. The methods used to share may vary, depending on each student's preferred learning style. Each student has a short time period to share his section or part of the topic. Listeners can then ask questions about the topic. The first person to answer the question might be the student who talked about that particular aspect of the topic. Then, other students on the panel can add their ideas regarding the answer to the question.

Walkabout

The teacher hangs as many pieces of chart paper around the room as there are teams that will share information. Each paper has a topic written at the top. As a culminating activity for a lesson or unit, students walk around as a group. At each chart they can use a marker of a designated color to write a one-sentence or single-phrase contribution or draw an illustration or figure. All groups should take a few minutes to read and discuss what is already on a particular chart before adding their own contribution. There is a time limit for each visit, so all groups walk to the next chart when signaled to do so.

When all groups have visited all charts, each group returns to one of the charts and prepares a short presentation, which must involve all students in the group. The presentation is given to the rest of the class and cannot exceed two to three minutes. The teacher might end the activity by making several statements about the studied content. Some statements may be purposely incorrect. Students signal their response all together only at the moment when the teacher says, "Show me." A thumbs-up response indicates a student agrees with the statement, and a thumbs-down response indicates disagreement.

Expert Jigsaw

This cooperative learning method is more effective than having members of one group split up a task and independently research and report back on their portion. With Expert Jigsaw, all students begin in heterogeneous home groups assigned by the teacher. They participate in an introduction to the large topic, presented as a mini-lecture or with the use of audiovisual or multimedia resources. Each person in the group counts off so all students have a number. Students then regroup into expert groups, with all the 1s working together, all the 2s working together, and so forth. With a large number of students, there may be several groups of each designated number.

Home groups then reconvene, perhaps on the next day, to share the information learned by the expert groups. In this way, all home groups are equally strong, and all students receive the same information from their members. Discussions or other activities that follow this sequence of events become strong with great participation, since all students will now have more solid information than they would have had if they had learned the material alone or in a regular cooperative learning group.

Note: There will be times when advanced learners work in their own cooperative learning groups on advanced topics, rather than always working in totally heterogeneous groups. Advanced students can learn the same cooperative learning methods as other class members but through material that is so challenging for them that they need assistance to learn it.

SUMMARY

This chapter has described methods for compacting and differentiating the curriculum in subject areas where the content is new to students. Advanced learners need less time to learn new material and more time to work on extension activities than do students who are learning at or below grade-level standards.

Information has been presented to help teachers:

- teach the required standards while simultaneously motivating gifted students to learn at personally challenging levels
- create activities for learning required standards that challenge students at all levels of performance
- use the Name Card Method and variations to increase the effectiveness of all class discussions
- teach students how to work independently
- incorporate methods that facilitate whole-class participation in certain learning activities

Teaching New Content to Students in Mixed-Ability Classes

- Introduce the entire unit to the class using a survey technique, such as a graphic organizer, that allows students to glimpse an overview of all the content included in the unit.

- Have Study Guides, Extension Menus, and related documents already prepared for students who will need them.

- Each class period, teach for no more than fifteen minutes at a time. Then, allow students to work on self-selected activities that give them practice in what you just taught. You can repeat this pattern several times during a class period. Use the Curriculum Planning Chart, Tiered Lesson Planning Chart, or Extension Menus for the self-selected activities.

- Allow advanced students to learn required standards from the Study Guide and work on extension activities from the Extension Menus or on advanced tasks from the Curriculum Planning Chart or Tiered Lesson Planning Chart. Teachers in grades five through nine may benefit from using the extension lessons from the book, *Differentiated Lessons for Every Learner* by Dina Brulles, Karen L. Brown, and Susan Winebrenner.

- All students experience the same assessments at the same time. Students working independently who are not competent on an assessment rejoin the direct instruction group for the rest of the unit.

- Teach students who are working independently how to keep accurate daily records of their extension work, for which we recommend using the Daily Log of Extension Activities on page 130, with explanation on pages 116–117.

- Make time for students who are working on extension activities to share what they have learned with other class members or another appropriate audience.

- Provide opportunities for all students to work on extension activities now and then.

Curriculum Planning Chart

Unit: ____________________

Required Standard	Regular Learning Activity	Alternate Learning Activity	Extension Activity

Tiered Lesson Planning Chart

Unit: ______________________________

Required Standard	Entry-Level Activities	Advanced Activities	Most Challenging Activities

Taxonomy of Thinking

	Remembering	Understanding	Applying	Analyzing	Evaluating	Creating
Definition	Exhibit memory of previously learned material by recalling facts, terms, basic concepts, and answers.	Demonstrate understanding of facts and ideas by organizing, comparing, translating, interpreting, giving descriptions, and stating main ideas.	Solve problems to new situations by applying acquired knowledge, facts, techniques, and rules in a different way.	Examine and break information into parts by identifying motives or causes. Make inferences and find evidence to support generalizations.	Present and defend opinions by making judgments about information, validity of ideas, or quality of work based on a set of criteria.	Compile information together in a different way by combining elements in a new pattern or proposing alternative solutions.
Verbs	Choose Define Find Label List Match Name Omit Recall Relate Select Show Spell Tell Tell how Tell what Tell when Tell where Tell which Tell who Tell why	Classify Compare Contrast Demonstrate Explain Extend Illustrate Infer Interpret Outline Relate Rephrase Show Summarize Translate	Apply Build Choose Construct Develop Experiment with Identify Interview Make use of Model Organize Plan Select Solve Utilize	Analyze Assume Categorize Classify Compare Conclude Contrast Discover Dissect Distinguish Divide Examine Function Identify motive Identify relationship Identify theme Infer Inspect List Simplify Survey Take part in Test for	Agree Appraise Assess Award Choose Compare Conclude Criticize Decide Deduct Defend Determine Disprove Establish criteria Estimate Evaluate Explain Form opinion Influence Interpret Judge Judge importance Justify Mark Measure Perceive Prioritize Prove Rate Recommend Rule on Select Support Value	Adapt Build Change Choose Combine Compile Compose Construct Create Delete Design Develop Discuss Elaborate Estimate Formulate Happen Imagine Improve Invent Make up Maximize Minimize Modify Originate Plan Predict Propose Solve Suppose Test Theorize

Adapted from *Quick Flip Questions for the Revised Bloom's Taxonomy* by Linda G. Barton (Garden Grove, CA: Teacher Created Resources, 2007), based on *A Taxonomy for Learning, Teaching, and Assessing: A Revision of Bloom's Taxonomy of Educational Objectives* edited by Lorin W. Anderson and David Krathwohl (New York: Pearson, 2001).

ThinkTrix Model

Dr. Frank Lyman

Type of Thinking	Icon for Type of Thinking	Definition	Questions/Discussion Starters (from Simple to Complex)
Evaluation	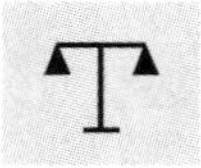	Decide if events or ideas are right or wrong, truthful or not, fair or unjust. Defend your conclusions.	Do you agree or disagree with ________________? Were the people involved right or wrong? Support your opinion. Give reasons for your opinion. Rank the ideas or events from least to most important or significant. Do you like/support ________________? Why or why not?
Example to Idea		Derive and explain a concept, rule, or generalization from examples.	Describe the main idea of ________________. What word best describes ________________? State your hypothesis. ________________ and ________________ are examples of ________________. What type of ________________ is ________________?
Idea to Example		Find data to support ideas or deepen understanding of a concept.	Give some examples of ________________. List several types of ________________. For example, ________________. Give evidence to support your idea or opinion.

CONTINUED > > >

Adapted from Lyman, Frank, ThinkTrix SmartCard, San Clemente, CA (800-933-2667, www.KaganOnline.com). Copied with permission of Kagan Publishing.

ThinkTrix Model, continued

Type of Thinking	Icon for Type of Thinking	Definition	Questions/Discussion Starters (from Simple to Complex)
Cause/Effect	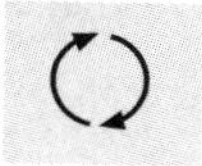	Understand how one action causes another.	What was the cause of ______________________? What was the effect of ______________________? What would happen if ______________________? What influence/impact did ______________________ have? If ______________________ happened, then ______________________ might happen.
Difference	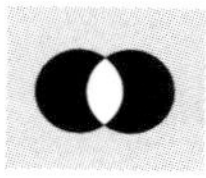	Compare objects, events, or ideas to discover how they are different.	Describe the difference(s) between ______________ and ______________________. What distinguishes ______________________ from ______________________? Contrast ______________________ with ______________________. Why is ______________ not like ______________________?
Similarity	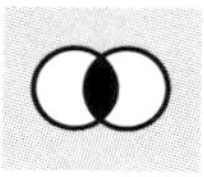	Compare objects, events, or ideas to discover what they have in common.	How are ______________ and ______________ alike? What similarities do ______________________ and ______________________ share? Compare ______________ with ______________. __________ is to __________ as ______________ is to ______________.
Recall	R	Remember what has been learned.	Who? What? When? Where? Why? How?

Adapted from Lyman, Frank, ThinkTrix SmartCard, San Clemente, CA (800-933-2667, www.KaganOnline.com). Copied with permission of Kagan Publishing.

DOK Extension Lesson Template

Directions:

1. Identify the topic that best describes the lesson.
2. Include the content standards prior to creating the learning activities to ensure that the learning activities align with your required standards.
3. Develop two DOK learning activities for each DOK level.

Topic: ______________________________

Content Standards: ______________________________

____

____

____

Learning Activities

DOK Level 1: ______________________________

____

____

____

DOK Level 2: ______________________________

____

____

____

DOK Level 3: ______________________________

____

____

____

DOK Level 4: ______________________________

____

____

____

Choice Activities Log

Student's name: ______________________________

Project topic: ______________________________

Today's Date	My Chosen Activity	Two Things I Learned

Extension Menu

	STUDENT CHOICE	

Independent Study Agreement

Your initial on each line indicates that you understand the condition and are willing to meet it.

Learning Conditions

__________ I will learn independently all the key concepts described on the Study Guide. I will not have to complete the actual assigned activities as long as I am working on an independent project.

__________ I will demonstrate competency with the assessments for the Study Guide content at the same time as the rest of the class.

__________ I will participate in designated whole-class activities as the teacher indicates them—without arguing.

__________ I will record my progress in a Daily Log of Extension Activities.

__________ I will do my work at an A or B level, according to the Evaluation Contract or rubric I use.

__________ I will work on an independent project and provide regular progress reports.

Working Conditions

__________ I will be present in the classroom at the beginning and end of each class period.

__________ I will not bother anyone or call attention to the fact that I am doing different work than others in the class.

__________ I will work on my project for the entire class period on designated days.

__________ I will carry this paper with me to any room in which I am working on my project, and I will return it to my classroom each day.

__________ If I cannot meet these conditions, I understand that my work on my independent study might have to stop.

Student's signature: ____

Teacher's signature: ____

Dear ____:

Your child, ______________________________, has demonstrated outstanding ability in ______________________________. S/he is able to learn much of the basic material independently and enjoys working on activities that extend the required standards. During the present unit on ______________________, ______________________ has agreed to work with a method that allows her/him to use a Study Guide to master the required standards. I will be checking often to make sure s/he is learning those standards successfully.

During some of her/his time in class, ______________________ will be working on an independent study project. S/he has chosen a topic related to the larger unit we are studying and will do research on that topic. S/he is not required to complete the project until s/he feels s/he is done learning about the topic, but there are certain working conditions and expectations s/he has agreed to follow. S/he will be presenting a progress report at regular intervals to share what s/he is learning with others.

______________________ may choose to work on one part of the project at home, and that work might replace other homework s/he does not have to do. Some students prefer to do all their work related to the project in school, and that is also acceptable.

This independent study method will provide excellent experience for ______________ in guiding her/his own learning experiences. I will be providing ongoing coaching for her/him as it is needed, and s/he might spend some time working with other students who are doing similar work.

There is nothing you need to do at home to facilitate ______________'s independent study. If any problems occur in school while ______________ is working with a Study Guide, I will be in touch with you. In the meantime, if you have any questions, please contact me.

Sincerely, ____

Evaluation Contract

I am choosing a grade for my project based on these criteria:

For a grade of B:

1. I will use secondary sources. This means that I will locate what information I can from several existing sources.
2. I will prepare a traditional product. I will present it using a traditional reporting format.
3. I will be learning on the lower levels of the Revised Bloom's Taxonomy: Remembering, Understanding, and Applying. This means that I will find information and be able to describe what I've learned.

For a grade of A:

1. I will use primary sources. This means that I will gather firsthand information myself through surveys, interviews, original documents, and similar methods.
2. I will produce an original type of product. I will present it to an appropriate audience using a unique format.
3. I will be learning on the higher levels of the Revised Bloom's Taxonomy: Analyzing, Evaluating, and Creating.

This is the project I will do: ______________________________

____

____

____

____

____

____

This is the grade I intend to earn: ______________________________

Student's signature: ______________________________

Teacher's signature: ______________________________

Rubric Planning Form

Research Step	Level 1 Below Grade Level	Level 2 At Grade Level	Level 3 Above Grade Level	Level 4 Highly Advanced
Identify research topic				
Locate appropriate resources				
Utilize primary sources				
Organize information				
Create interesting reporting format				
Report to appropriate audience				

Topic Development Sheet

Topics or unit to be learned: ____________________

Required Content Standards	Related Topics

Product Choices Chart

Auditory	Visual	Tactile-Kinesthetic
Audio recording	Advertisement	Acting things out
Debate	Blog	Animated movie
Editorial	Brochure	Composing music
Essay	Comic book or strip	Dance
Fact file	Drawing or painting	Demonstration
Glossary	Flowchart	Diorama
Interview	Graphic organizer	Exhibit
Journal or diary	Illustrations	Experiment
Newscast	Multimedia presentation	Flip book or chart
Oral report	Mural	How-to book
Panel discussion	Newsletter	Learning game
Position paper	Photo essay	Mobile
Rap or rhyme	Playlist	Model
Reader's theater	Political cartoon	Presentation
Reenactment	Poster	Puppet show
Socratic Seminar	Rebus story	Rap or rhyme
Song lyrics	Simulation	Reader's theater
Speech	Textbook page	Reenactment
Story or poem	Video recording	Scale drawing
Teaching a lesson	Webinar	Sculpture
Written report	Website	Skit or play

Project Planner for Primary Grades

Student's name: ______________________ Date project starts: __________

My topic: ______________________

My 4 subtopics and 2 questions for each:

1. ______________________

a. ______________________

b. ______________________

2. ______________________

a. ______________________

b. ______________________

3. ______________________

a. ______________________

b. ______________________

4. ______________________

a. ______________________

b. ______________________

Materials or supplies I need for my project:

What I need:	Where to get it:

How I will keep track of what I am learning: ______________________

How I will share what I have learned: ______________________

Student's signature: ______________________

Teacher's signature: ______________________

Project Planner for Upper Grades

Student's name: ______________________ Date project starts: ____________

My topic: ____

My 6 subtopics and 3 questions for each:

1.	**2.**
a.	a.
b.	b.
c.	c.
3.	**4.**
a.	a.
b.	b.
c.	c.
5.	**6.**
a.	a.
b.	b.
c.	c.

Materials or supplies I need for my project:

What I need:	Where to get it:

CONTINUED > > >

Project Planner for Upper Grades, continued

How I will keep track of what I am learning: ______________________________

____

____

The part of the project I will complete at home (optional): ______________________________

____

____

How I will share what I have learned: ______________________________

____

____

Potential problems:	Possible solutions:

Student's signature: ______________________________

Teacher's signature: ______________________________

PART 3

Sustaining the SCGM

Part 3 addresses the fundamental support system that keeps the Schoolwide Cluster Grouping Model on track: ongoing professional development for teachers and continuous evaluation of the model throughout the school or district.

The focus of chapter 7 is training teachers to work effectively with gifted students while simultaneously ensuring academic progress for all students. While training gifted-cluster teachers is essential, equipping *all* staff with information about giftedness and strategies for compacting and differentiating curriculum will lead to the most effective implementation of the model and to the most broad-based academic success for students at every ability and achievement level. The chapter presents a wealth of workshop and study topics and describes best practices to help you provide professional development within your own time and budget parameters.

Finally, in chapter 8, we share research data on schoolwide cluster grouping, suggest a plan for implementing ongoing evaluation, and provide information that can serve as a guide to help you decide how you will evaluate the effects of the SCGM in your school or district. The information in this chapter offers critical support for establishing a strong evaluative framework from the start of the model's implementation. This includes gathering specific data at the beginning of each school year, recording it throughout the year, and reporting the results at year's end to the board of education and other interested parties.

7

Professional Learning Through Collaboration and Communication

GUIDING QUESTIONS

- How does effective staff development for the SCGM benefit all students, including those working below proficiency levels?
- What professional learning opportunities are essential for teachers in the SCGM?
- What are best practices in providing ongoing professional learning?
- How can teachers be supported to use the strategies they learn?
- How can administrators and cluster teachers build parent communication and support?

For teachers, there are three focus areas essential to the success of schoolwide cluster grouping: an understanding of what the SCGM is and how it works, familiarity with the learning needs of gifted students, and facility in using curriculum compacting and differentiation strategies with gifted students as well as other students who can benefit from them.

Simply using the SCGM structure (as illustrated in the chart on page PNT) will not by itself lead to the desired outcomes of schoolwide cluster grouping. Since most teachers and principals have little training in recognizing and teaching gifted students, workshops devoted to the basic elements of gifted education should be available to all staff. Teachers need to be involved in the model, be ready to teach all students in their classes—including those who are gifted—and be engaged in ongoing professional learning. Learning about gifted students can motivate teachers to volunteer to become gifted-cluster teachers, so do not limit these learning opportunities to gifted-cluster teachers.

Preparing All Teachers for Schoolwide Cluster Grouping

A study conducted at the National Research Center on the Gifted and Talented, University of Connecticut, documents evidence of widespread benefits for all students when all teachers in a school receive professional development on using gifted-education strategies. The study makes the following recommendations (Gubbins et al. 2002):

1. The use of gifted-education methods in the general education classroom provides students with more choices in materials, resources, and products related to their interests and abilities in all content areas.
2. Knowledge and practice of gifted-education strategies helps teachers recognize students' differences in learning styles, expression styles, and abilities.
3. Gifted-education instruction helps all teachers grow both personally and professionally by changing their practice and looking at their instructional methods with renewed eyes.
4. When teachers observe and experience the positive effects of the differentiation strategies they learn, they are likely to continue to use best practices in their classrooms, despite the pressures of daily school schedules, testing, and time constraints.
5. Gifted-education pedagogy encourages teachers to raise their level of expectations for work from all learners, and students respond positively to changes in classroom activities.

Facilitating an understanding of the learning needs of gifted students and the teaching strategies that motivate and challenge them is critical for success in schools that use the SCGM. When all teachers have some involvement in the various aspects of the model, cluster grouping becomes part of the school culture. All staff members need a full orientation in the SCGM to ensure that the teaching and support staff understand the way the model works, how it provides consistent programming for gifted students, and what characteristics of the model lead to a potential rise in achievement for the entire school. Training in specific compacting and differentiation strategies all teachers can use is also essential.

Professional Learning Topics for SCGM Teachers

The following is a list of topics to include in professional learning opportunities for all teachers. The topics will help staff understand the learning needs of gifted students and recognize the value of cluster grouping at their school. These topics can be addressed at the school or district levels or online. With this type of training, teachers are better prepared to provide appropriate differentiation for students who need it and to assume the role of the gifted-cluster teacher.

Topics of Particular Help to Gifted-Cluster Teachers

Information and classroom strategies to address over time can include:

- understanding and implementing the SCGM
- recognizing gifted potential and behaviors, including those found in underrepresented populations
- supporting gifted students' social and emotional needs, including dealing with their fears, worries, and concerns about working with challenging curriculum
- identifying students who need curriculum compacting and differentiation
- providing differentiation and curriculum compacting opportunities in all subject areas
- forming and managing flexible learning groups as needed
- integrating basic skills and higher-order thinking skills into content for all students in order to communicate high learning expectations for everyone
- creating and using learning extensions or acceleration opportunities
- providing open-ended tasks that allow for in-depth learning based on students' interests

- emphasizing creative and productive thinking
- teaching research skills and effective use of the internet
- using appropriate assessment and grading practices with advanced learners
- developing students' abilities to self-direct, keep accurate records of their work, and self-evaluate their independent work
- facilitating whole-class interactions so that gifted-cluster students are sometimes working together but are not separated from their classmates all the time
- building and maintaining effective parent-teacher relationships
- encouraging student collaborative learning

SUPERVISOR SPOTLIGHT

Compacting and differentiation opportunities can motivate and challenge all students toward higher achievement. The learning opportunities needed by gifted students are offered to all students in the class. Professional learning opportunities designed for gifted-cluster teachers should also be available to all interested teachers. However, if space is limited, priority should be given to teachers who are presently teaching gifted clusters. As time passes, more teachers can participate in the learning opportunities.

Topics That Help Teachers Address the Learning Needs of All Students

Staff development meetings can also include information that will be more specific to meeting the needs of the students who are not in the gifted cluster, including the following:

- ways to help all students appreciate everyone's strengths
- teaching strategies that accommodate various learning styles
- strategies for connecting the required standards to students' interests
- teaching routines that allow the classroom to work smoothly as students move in and out of flexible learning groups

Professional development must emerge from the needs of the staff, so the topics addressed, the order in which they are presented, and the depth of training may differ from school to school. Encourage site-based decision making when planning professional learning for gifted-cluster teachers. Factors that influence the targeted topics include the teachers' levels of experience, prior training in gifted education, student diversity, school resources, and school or district initiatives.

Finding Connections to the SCGM in All Staff Development Topics

Nearly all professional learning focused on teaching practices can support gifted-cluster teachers working in the SCGM. This is true even when a particular staff development topic does not specifically address gifted education. Gifted-cluster teachers can still focus on ways to make connections between the in-service topic and the needs of their gifted learners. For example, if a new math series were being introduced, gifted-cluster teachers would be looking for ways they could compact this new program for their advanced students and finding options for acceleration or extensions.

What Are Effective Ways to Provide Ongoing Professional Training?

To accomplish the goals of providing ongoing professional learning opportunities, we recommend using several different engagement formats. This includes workshops during the school year and the summer, gifted-cluster teacher coaching, ongoing study groups during the school year, a gifted resource site, social media, and regularly scheduled gifted-cluster teacher meetings, all of which can provide the necessary support to current and future teachers of gifted students.

Teacher Workshops

In-service workshops provide a useful format for introducing new information to staff. They may be offered as a one-day event, or they may take place over several days, all focused on a designated topic. Workshops can lead to the formation of study groups where teachers can discuss the topics in more detail. Following are some examples of in-service workshop plans.

FULL-DAY WORKSHOPS

Teaching Gifted Students in the Schoolwide Cluster Grouping Model

Description: This in-service will help teachers become knowledgeable about the SCGM and learn teaching strategies for adapting the regular classroom curriculum and activities to meet the learning needs of their most academically capable students. It includes strategies for compacting and differentiating the regular curriculum to provide consistent opportunities for gifted students to be engaged in appropriately challenging learning experiences.

Time: Full day or two to three days over a three-month period

Participants: Gifted-cluster teachers, current or prospective

Gifted Education: Organizing and Managing Your Differentiated Classroom

Description: Learn how to organize and manage your classroom so that differentiation opportunities fit seamlessly into your overall classroom program. Enjoy participating in an exchange of ideas and strategies with colleagues.

Time: Three two-hour after-school meetings

Participants: All district teachers for kindergarten through grade eight

Questioning Strategies for Teachers of Gifted Students

Description: Teachers will explore creative and critical questioning strategies they can use to challenge students and raise the level of complexity in classroom discussions.

Time: Two days, possibly separated by four to six weeks of classroom application sessions

Participants: Gifted-cluster teachers and gifted specialists

AFTER-SCHOOL WORKSHOPS

To encourage participation in after-school workshops, we recommend providing brief ninety-minute or two-hour sessions that relate directly to how students learn and what the students are learning at the time. School districts that employ this method rely on teachers who specialize in various areas and strategies to teach workshops in their classrooms after school. We strongly recommend opening up workshops to all teachers in the district or school, not just the cluster teachers.

Exposing general education teachers to the following topics and strategies encourages them to become aware of gifted students' diverse learning needs and to use differentiated instruction with all students. This exposure also encourages teachers to take on the role of gifted-cluster teacher in future years.

Sample After-School Workshops

- The Schoolwide Cluster Grouping Model: An Introduction
- Teaching in the Cluster Grouping Model
- Understanding Giftedness: How the Identification Relates to Teaching and Learning
- Interactive and Fun: Vocabulary Activities That Engage
- Using Socratic Questioning and Critical Thinking Skills in Language Arts
- Advancing Differentiation: Thinking and Learning in the Twenty-First Century

- Divergent Thinking Through Junior Great Books
- It's Not About More; It's About Different!
- Pop Culture in the Classroom? Absolutely!
- Grammar in Minutes a Day, Taking the Next Step!
- Developing Tiered Assignments and Extension Menus to Increase Challenge Levels Through Depth and Complexity
- Understanding the Twice-Exceptional Student
- Unlock the Strategies to Teaching the Nonverbal Identified Gifted Student
- Let's Talk Assessment: The How and Why of Formative and Summative Assessment in a Differentiated Classroom
- Nonverbal Identification of Giftedness: Using the Test Results to Guide Instruction
- Reaching All Learners: Making Differentiation Work for Gifted Students
- Using Khan Academy to Differentiate Math

State Laws and Mandates for Gifted Education

If your state has a mandate or law for gifted education, full compliance is expected. This strengthens legislation, raises the standards for all schools and districts, and brings favorable attention to the districts that are in compliance. In states that have funding for gifted education, districts are expected to use those funds to improve the quality of education for their gifted students. Most school districts that have access to state funds for gifted education use these funds to provide professional learning opportunities to their staff members, improving teachers' ability to understand and respond to the needs of gifted students. Funds may also be utilized from other title programs, such as special education and language acquisition, to provide for the learning needs of twice-exceptional students and gifted English language learners. Since all targeted teaching strategies have the potential to benefit all students, funds earmarked for general staff development can also support your school's efforts in gifted education.

Gifted-Cluster Coaching

Some midsize and larger school districts have found it helpful to employ a coach to support gifted-cluster teachers. This coach is usually a teacher on assignment (TOA) who has significant experience with differentiated curriculum and instruction. The position can be part-time or full-time.

The responsibilities of the coach will depend on the needs of the cluster teachers. Areas of focus include:

- Meet with individual cluster teachers to provide guidance and lesson plans when needed.
- Model instructional strategies in the gifted-cluster classrooms.
- Help cluster teachers determine how to work with grade-level team members when the teachers may be working on different content levels.
- Attend and model gifted-cluster teacher meetings at the sites. (Schedule directly with the gifted specialists.)
- Attend gifted specialist in-services.
- Provide classroom instructional support for cluster teachers that emphasizes:
  - differentiated instruction in gifted-cluster classes
  - twenty-first-century skills
  - required standards
  - project-based learning
  - coding
  - methods for using data to inform instruction
  - tech integration
  - tools on the gifted resource site
  - STEM

- Provide online professional learning opportunities.
- Provide gifted workshops for gifted-cluster teachers.
- Create newsletters, videos, and so on to support and provide resources for cluster teachers to share with parents.
- Updating the gifted resource site to provide timely resources that support cluster teachers. (See pages 187–189 for more information.)

Study Groups

A study group might be organized around a specific topic, or it can examine a specific book on education. The presence of school-based study groups can create a professional learning community (PLC) in your school and, once in place, provides a format that can be used year after year. The format remains similar, but the specific content being studied may change from year to year. Research on best practices recommends that once a topic is selected, enough time must be devoted to that topic so that educators become highly likely to use what they learn as a regular part of their teaching repertoire. For example, during the first year of training, teachers could learn how to teach gifted students effectively in gifted-cluster classrooms. The following year, teachers might learn how to improve their assessment techniques.

SUPERVISOR SPOTLIGHT

If your state has certification requirements for teachers of gifted students, be sure that all professional learning opportunities in your district use the language and content required by the state for gifted endorsement or certification. Many states require that specific words appear in the course title or description to be accepted for certification credit; the state mandate will clearly denote that language.

Effective study groups follow a pattern. The group identifies a specific strategy, learns the particulars about how to use it in general, and plans its application in their own classrooms. Individual teachers then try the strategy with their students and return to the study group to debrief. Several meetings can be devoted to one strategy until most of the study group members are using it with ease. At that point, another strategy is introduced, and the process is repeated.

FIGURE 7-1 Effective Study Groups

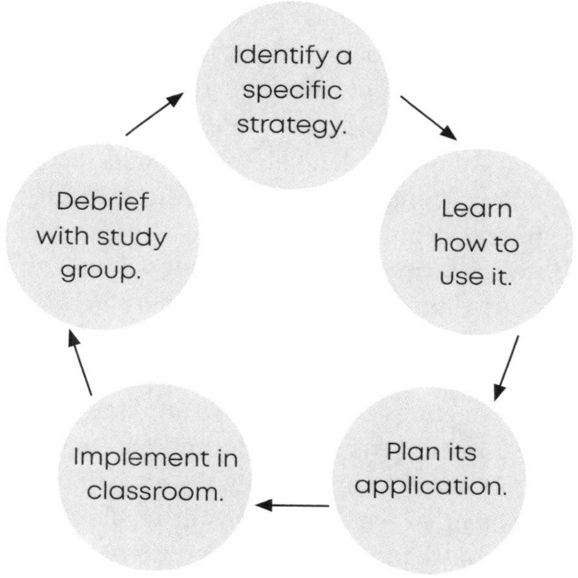

Study groups meet over the course of a semester or school year. Once a topic or book is selected, the gifted mentor or a gifted-cluster teacher assumes leadership for the group. The leader's job is to remind participants of upcoming meetings and communicate information or questions about specific topics or chapters to be discussed at specific meetings. Group members are encouraged to take an active role in topic selection. If the study groups do not provide professional growth credit, teachers may generally join the groups at any time during the year. If credit or a stipend is involved, a start-to-finish commitment is necessary. Teachers who want to study more informally can still attend as they wish, but they won't be eligible for formal credit.

The material used in the study groups can come from gifted-education workshops attended by some teachers or content from more formal training in gifted education, such as courses that certify educators to teach gifted students. Study groups can also focus on other programs being used by the school, with special attention paid to the application of a given program to gifted students.

Book Study Groups

Some schools build their study groups around a specific book. Book study groups represent a less formal approach to ongoing professional learning, yet they can be highly effective in helping teachers understand the nuances of gifted students' learning abilities and in helping teachers learn methods for consistently using effective teaching strategies for gifted students. The principal and staff determine which professional book to study based on the staff's needs and interests. Any person with some training in gifted education can lead the book study meetings.

The meetings can be open to any staff member interested in the topic and may occur weekly, bimonthly, or monthly. Because there should be no expense borne by the teacher for any professional learning opportunity, we recommend purchasing the books for the participating teachers and offering professional growth credit for completing the coursework. School administrators appreciate that their staff members can select the books and topics to reflect specific needs of the school or district. Teachers take ownership of the content when they can see that the topics they are studying have direct relevance to their teaching and to their students and when it is apparent that the district values their participation in these groups.

When teachers work together to learn and implement new teaching techniques—and support one another to achieve a sense of efficacy with those techniques—it is highly likely they will continue to use and build on their new skills. A teacher who is willing to take on the job of study group facilitator may find the following list of tasks helpful:

- Select a book for the group to study, perhaps with the assistance of the building principal, gifted-program coordinator, gifted specialist, or cluster teachers. (Find a way to procure multiple copies.)
- Schedule and advertise the dates, times, and locations of meetings.
- Become familiar with the book in its entirety before the first meeting. Come prepared with a plan for how to consider the content of the book but be open to input from group members about the procedures to be used, the schedules for the meetings, the discussion guidelines for group members, and any other necessary details.
- Invite colleagues to take a leadership role in the discussion for upcoming sections, chapters, or topics included in the designated book.
- Reassure participants that they will be in charge of which strategies to try with their students and of the pace at which those strategies will be implemented.
- Take time at the start of each meeting for participants to discuss the successes and challenges of what they have tried with their students.
- Allow group time during each meeting to plan how content discussed will be implemented by individual teachers or by grade-level teams or department groups.

A list of suggested books for book study groups is provided on pages 243–244. Other books to study can be selected more broadly from the references and resources on pages 235–245.

Online Book Study Groups

Many teachers lament that they have little time available for professional learning opportunities.

Teachers may want to participate in professional learning but be physically tired from spending long hours in the classroom and in planning. One appealing alternative to in-person book study groups is to set them up online. Teachers greatly appreciate the format of online book studies, because they have the ability to access the content at their convenience. They can take time reading and responding to the material and do it whenever it is convenient for them. They can also review past postings when they want to check on a specific strategy discussed during the book study.

Online book studies can be run through the school district's communication system. Ask the instructional technology department for help if necessary. There are also free web-based forums and apps that schools can use to design and run their own online book studies. Moodle or Google Groups (see page 189) are free and easy to use. In most digital communication systems, administrators have a forum where they can set up online book studies for teachers. In this format, administrators will want to post a welcome message along with directions for accessing and responding to questions posed in the book study.

The online book study leader can follow these suggested steps:

1. Select the book that will be studied.
2. Advertise the online book study to the gifted-cluster teachers. Include the study structure, a brief description of the book and activities to be used, and teacher compensation information.
3. Set up the coursework by posting a welcome message and directions for the course participants.
4. Create the questions and activities for each week, and post these to the course site.
5. Send copies of the book to the teachers who have registered for the course.
6. Receive and respond to the teachers' posted entries.
7. Invite participants to share the extension materials they create on the school or district website.
8. Create an online forum through which participants may share their ideas and strategies.

The instructor responds to some of the teachers' postings and teachers respond to one another as desired. All teachers should expect some feedback from the instructor during the time the course takes place. The instructor keeps a record of the teachers who have completed the coursework and sends out certificates of completion.

Developing a Gifted Resource Site*

Teaching in the digital age provides endless opportunities for professional learning. Teachers are now able to access video, scientific research, lesson examples, and so on through electronic devices anytime and anywhere they desire. A district gifted resource site that provides differentiated lesson plans, extension lessons, training tools, standards, classroom management techniques, and more is invaluable for gifted-cluster teachers. One way to build the content for the gifted resource site is to have teachers routinely submit their differentiated lesson plans to the site to share with other cluster teachers in the district. This collaboration can also be part of the gifted workshops and in-service activities provided in the district.

*The "Developing a Gifted Resource Site" section is adapted from Peters, Scott J., and Dina Brulles. 2017. *Designing Gifted Education Programs and Services: From Purpose to Implementation.* Waco, TX: Prufrock Press.

A School District Scenario

In the Paradise Valley Unified School District in Arizona, we created our gifted resource site to support all district teachers, but with an emphasis on those who teach our gifted and talented students. This digital repository provides a wealth of differentiated curriculum, tools to help teachers document achievement for students working at and above grade level, and numerous teacher-training resources.

The site includes:

- web-based training: links to online trainings that support our programs
- differentiated lesson plans: organized by grade level and by content area with a folder for each subject in each grade level
- videos of classroom demonstrations: videos of our own gifted teachers demonstrating strategies we teach in our workshops
- student work products: examples of student-created and -produced, technology-infused schoolwork
- program videos: our district's gifted programming options, so teachers know what options to suggest to parents
- training materials: presentations and lesson planning materials
- achievement documentation: procedures for teachers to use ongoing diagnostic, formative, and summative assessments in their classrooms
- achievement data: from state assessment for gifted students at every school
- program administration: procedures, sample schedules, sample meeting agendas, forms, and so on
- communication tools: forums where teachers within each program communicate to share ideas, lessons, and resources

The resources housed on this gifted resource site support the district's adopted curriculum and initiatives and align with grade-level standards. An important feature of the resource site is its ability to provide ongoing training and resources to teachers who can access the site at their convenience. Broadly speaking, teachers are able to participate in workshops, collaborate, study archived presentations, plan lessons, and learn from others' contributions.

Using free Google tools, the gifted department developed and maintains this effective and cost-efficient system for providing training and access to resources from within and outside the district. The repository incorporates existing district resources and contributions from district teachers to help staff address the diverse learning needs of their gifted, talented, and general education students. The coordinator updates the site constantly, as many new resources become available daily.

GOALS OF THE GIFTED RESOURCE SITE

The following ideas are adapted from *Designing Gifted Education Programs and Services: From Purpose to Implementation* by Scott J. Peters and Dina Brulles:

- Expose teachers to instructional strategies that engage, challenge, and enrich high ability and high achieving students.
- Provide professional development in gifted education based on theory, pedagogy, and current best practices for teachers of gifted students.

- Align teacher support for gifted education with the district's mission of developing and promoting digital-age literacies.
- Provide all district teachers with access to innovative instructional methods, advanced and differentiated curriculum, systems for communication, and collaborative learning and achievement data.
- Encourage collaboration, communication, critical thinking, and creativity throughout the district.
- Motivate all district teachers to incorporate gifted-education instructional objectives and strategies into everyday teaching for all students.
- Finding time to learn and plan new strategies is the most common challenge our teachers face when attempting to differentiate curriculum and instruction. We developed this site to overcome these obstacles.

Using Social Media for Cluster Teachers' Professional Learning

To be effective and successful, gifted-cluster teachers need ongoing support, training, and collaborative learning experiences. The number of teachers who look to social media for professional learning and networking opportunities continues to grow. For those who cannot be present in real time for face-to-face meetings or simply prefer online alternatives, social media offers opportunities to network with and learn alongside local colleagues, national experts, and global thought leaders.

Social media is expanding the opportunities for gifted-cluster teachers to connect, learn, and develop relationships with those who share their interests. Flexibility of the medium gives voice and choice to gifted-cluster teachers to drive their own professional learning, which then drives students' learning. This collaboration can bring cluster teachers together throughout a school or district.

The benefits of using social media to support gifted-cluster teachers not only adds intrigue and novelty but also can help entrench cluster teachers' efforts and build motivation for new professional learning approaches.

USING GOOGLE GROUPS

Much like taking an online course, a big selling point for teachers is the convenience of participating in professional learning anytime that works for *their* schedule, within a given framework. As an example, consider the approach developed by Cathy Mere (@cathymere) and Michelle Nero (@litlearningzone). Mere and Nero launched #cyberpd as a professional learning community that uses Twitter and Google Groups to connect teachers who share the common interest of professional summer reading. At Mere's blog (reflectandrefine.blogspot.com/2018/06/drumroll-please-july-cyberpd.html), she explains the details.

Mere and Nero launched the following idea:

- Take a picture of your stack of professional books for summer reading and post it to Twitter at #cyberpd.
- As facilitators, Mere and Nero select one title that seems to be of common interest and announce the reading schedule to the group.
- A closed Google Group is established for posting reflections about the reading throughout the summer. Mere and Nero establish a timeline and some group norms to maximize the effectiveness of the digital reading forum.

BUILDING A "MARCH BOOK MADNESS" DIGITAL COMMUNITY

Another benefit of networking with like-minded colleagues on social media is the opportunity for connected student learning. Consider the "March Book Madness" digital community as an example with a student-focused audience. Cheryl Gehres, gifted-cluster coach at Paradise Valley Unified School District in Arizona, participated in a March Book Madness group with her middle school gifted students and recruited a cluster teacher to do the same with her elementary-age students. The two teachers were intrigued by the theme "Compelling Characters" and decided to get their students involved. This digital community encourages student voice and choice and is well suited for in-class discussion with Socratic Seminars, a strategy Gehres's school district encourages with cluster teachers.

The March Book Madness community is facilitated by two teachers, Scott Jones (@escott818) and Tony Keefer (@TonyKeefer). Background information and details for participation are available at the March Book Madness website: marchbookmadness.weebly.com. Here are the general guidelines:

- There are three brackets of books, including picture books, middle grade novels, and young adult novels. A selection of sixteen books in each bracket is announced in the fall. This kicks off the reading "season" and is designed to parallel basketball season.
- In mid-February, Tony and Scott announce the brackets by simply drawing cards with the names of the books to determine how the sixteen books will be paired. They create and post a graphic that displays the books in bracket style, which teachers can use to create a bulletin board. A PDF of the brackets is also posted on the website for classroom use. Teachers can play the upbeat video in class, which is posted on Twitter and on the March Book Madness website, to generate excitement in the classroom.
- Once voting begins, a link to a Google form is available on the site for a week. Teachers can conduct a vote in class and then enter their group vote weekly as one vote, or they can share the link with students and allow each student to vote weekly. Each week, the results of the vote narrows the field of contenders to eight, then four, then two, and finally one book is selected to win the competition.
- How-to tips for participating and enhancing the experience for students are listed on the website's tips page: marchbookmadness.weebly.com/tips.html.

TWITTER CHATS FOR PROFESSIONAL LEARNING

Another way social media can support professional learning for cluster teachers is through live Twitter chats. There are excellent forums available to bring together parents, educators, and content experts for one-hour facilitated conversations around topics of common interest. A leader in the gifted field is Global #gtchat (twitter.com/gtchatmod), currently moderated by Lisa Conrad for Texas Association for the Gifted and Talented. Details for participating in this live forum are found at www.txgifted.org/gtchat.

Peer Coaching: Ensuring Long-Term Implementation of Content Learned in Staff Development

A recurring frustration for administrators is that over time, the benefits from professional development often become diluted or disappear from standard classroom practices. A related challenge is bringing new staff up to speed on the methods teachers are expected to use. What are the best ways to provide training for teachers so they get the updated and ongoing support they need to be sure their work with all students consistently reflects best practices?

Figure 7-2 illustrates the research of Bruce Joyce and Beverly Showers showing how dramatically peer support increases the likelihood of ongoing implementation of teaching strategies learned from in-services, workshops, or study group meetings. It illustrates the important differences between just *telling* teachers what to do and providing a collegial peer-coaching model to support the implementation of desired strategies. If collegial peer coaching can lead to such dramatic outcomes, it makes sense to build it into any professional development program.

FIGURE 7-2 Benefits of Peer Coaching to Support Application of New Teaching Techniques

In-Service Component	Knowledge % of teachers who understand the concept	Skill % of teachers who apply the concept	Transfer % of teachers who make the concept part of their teaching repertoire
Study of theory	10%	5%	0%
With demonstrations	30%	20%	0%
With practice	60%	60%	5%
With peer coaching	95%	95%	95%

Adapted from Joyce, Bruce R., and Beverly Showers, "Training Components and Attainment of Outcomes in Terms of Percent of Participants," in *Student Achievement Through Staff Development* (Alexandria, VA: ASCD, 2002). Republished with permission of ASCD (www.ascd.org). Permission conveyed through Copyright Clearance Center, Inc.

Site-based collegial peer coaching can strongly impact the long-term efficacy of the SCGM when teachers work together at a school to support one another's efforts in providing appropriate compacting and differentiation opportunities for students who need them. Facilitating a study group is one highly effective peer-coaching method.

Additional research in staff development confirms the benefits of collegial peer coaching. PLCs incorporate the best elements of collegial peer coaching and validate the Joyce and Showers research. According to Dennis Sparks, longtime director of the National Staff Development Council, high-quality staff development (Sparks 2002):

- focuses on deepening teachers' content knowledge and pedagogical abilities
- includes opportunities for in-house practice, action research, and reflections
- is embedded in educators' work and takes place during the regular school days
- is sustained over time
- is founded on collegiality and collaboration among and between teachers and principals

Sparks's research confirms that when these conditions are present, staff members can provide meaningful and sustained assistance to one another to improve teaching and student learning.

Several researchers have documented the effectiveness of building an internal peer-support system anytime the staff is trying to learn and apply new teaching techniques (Joyce and Showers 2002; Sparks 2002; Kohler, Ezell, and Paluselli 1999). A formal peer-coaching system facilitates the mentoring of novices by highly experienced teachers. By contrast, a collegial peer-coaching system brings together faculty who are all beginning to understand new teaching approaches and sets up a long-term plan by which teachers support one another toward effective implementation. This collegial peer coaching is built upon the premise that teachers are in the best position to identify educational issues that need addressing and that they can help one another become comfortable with new teaching techniques by learning and applying the techniques together.

The following stages of collegial peer coaching are recommended. The partners decide how long to remain at each stage before moving on to the next stage. There is no expected time limit for the stages. All parties agree that they will never discuss anything they see in another teacher's classroom with any other person.

Stage 1: Initial mutual observation. Two teachers meet to decide what each will observe in the other's classroom. They agree that the observer will confine observations and remarks to what was happening to the students during the lesson being observed. They agree in advance on the type of form to be used for record keeping. At this point, the teacher is not the focus of the observation. Rather, the focus is the effect of the lesson on the students. This relieves anxiety for teachers who are not usually comfortable if another educator is in their classroom. For example, the observer uses a classroom seating chart to observe how many students are participating in a discussion. The record-keeping form is left in the room with the teacher who was being observed—it is never carried away by the observer. Discussion after the event happens only at the invitation of the teacher being observed.

SUPERVISOR SPOTLIGHT

Consider having substitute teachers available for the purpose of facilitating classroom visits and meetings between gifted-cluster teachers. If teachers cannot physically visit each other's classes, they can view lessons that have been recorded on video instead.

Stage 2: Observation with follow-up discussion. In the pre-observation meeting, teachers decide what will be observed in each class, select or create a data-gathering form, and also decide when to meet for a follow-up discussion. The teacher being observed decides who the observer should watch: the students or the teacher. All observation tools are left in the classroom of the teacher being observed. After both teachers have watched and been watched once, they hold a post-observational meeting. If asked, observers may offer one concrete suggestion for how the lesson might have been improved.

Stage 3: Collegial peer coaching. Visits between gifted-cluster teacher partners take place as they are needed. There is a free give-and-take of suggestions and advice. At some point, partners can even collaborate with lesson planning or can give feedback regarding each other's lesson plans.

The reproducible Teacher Self-Assessment Checklist on pages 199–201 describes many of the desirable teaching skills and behaviors teachers will want to cultivate. The checklist is designed to be used privately by an individual gifted-cluster teacher. It is not intended for use as an instrument for someone else to evaluate the teacher's performance. (For a more formal approach to evaluating teachers, see the reproducible Administrator Observation Forms on pages 202 and 203.)

Staff Positions in the SCGM

As described in chapter 4, the SCGM uses three key staff positions and one supplemental position:

Gifted-Cluster Teacher (Key)—the teacher assigned to teach the gifted-cluster classroom at each grade level

Gifted Specialist or Gifted Mentor (Key)—a gifted-cluster teacher, content-replacement or resource teacher, or another staff member with training in gifted education, who supports the school's gifted-cluster teachers

Gifted Coordinator (Key)—a district-level administrator who oversees the gifted-education program

Gifted-Cluster Coach (Supplemental)—A TOA who supports cluster teachers in the classroom by modeling differentiation strategies and classroom management techniques

Ongoing Meetings of SCGM Staff

Professional learning opportunities such as workshops, study groups, and peer coaching can occur as part of or in addition to the regularly scheduled monthly meetings of SCGM staff.

Schoolwide Gifted-Cluster Teacher Meetings

Holding regularly scheduled meetings for gifted-cluster teachers builds a system within each school that the teachers come to rely on. These meetings provide opportunities to share teaching strategies and lesson plans and to brainstorm solutions to challenges teachers face. Teachers also find it helpful to incorporate book studies into these meetings. Getting together on a regular basis to share what is working, what is problematic, and other pertinent information is helpful to gifted-cluster teachers' classroom instruction and to maintaining the integrity of the SCGM. Having a scheduled time to plan and learn together also helps prepare new gifted-cluster teachers. They feel more confident knowing there are teachers at their school site with whom they can consult when they are working with their gifted students.

Research on the topic of PLCs by the Southwest Educational Development Laboratory and other organizations highlights the need for professional development that is linked to the work teachers are doing in their classes each day. This research validates that peer coaching is an effective component of PLCs. Partnerships between teachers can be highly effective, provide long-lasting changes in practice, and allow the gifted-education training to benefit more of the teachers in the school. Partnerships help teachers feel positive about teaching in a gifted-cluster classroom (Center for Comprehensive School Reform and Improvement 2007).

Encourage gifted-cluster teachers to become "experts" on specific teaching strategies. Some may be particularly skilled with a specific strategy. Develop and share the knowledge by encouraging informal peer coaching among gifted-cluster teachers or by having the teacher skilled in a strategy lead the discussion on that specific strategy at a gifted-cluster teacher meeting.

ACHIEVEMENT ADVISORY

Gifted-cluster teachers can work in PLCs with cluster teachers at their school to discuss methods for differentiating instruction and implementing interventions based on student data. During PLC meetings, teachers develop SMART* goals, study data, design interventions, share lessons that align with the standards, and so on. Teachers may discuss out-of-level testing and vertical alignment of curriculum. Some schools use the Response to Intervention (RTI) model to plan specific content intervention during PLC meetings. This collaboration time not only supports the teachers but also builds consistent practices throughout the school.

The gifted specialist or gifted mentor is usually the designated leader of the school's gifted-cluster teacher meetings, which ideally occur monthly. The gifted specialist announces the meeting times, sends out reminders, brings necessary materials, and sets the agenda based on the group's needs. If there is no gifted specialist, the building principal or one of the gifted-cluster teachers can lead these meetings. Principals should attend gifted-cluster teacher meetings as often as possible. Attendance at even part of the meetings demonstrates the principal's commitment to the model and shows that she values the time teachers devote to their position as gifted-cluster teachers.

Promote interest in gifted-education professional learning by inviting all teachers to the monthly meetings of the active gifted-cluster teachers. These meetings can develop interests and skills in prospective gifted-cluster teachers. This informal, ongoing training helps build strong gifted-education services in each school as well as a school culture that accepts and supports the SCGM.

*SMART is an acronym that defines goal setting as: S—specific, significant, stretching; M—measurable, meaningful, motivational; A—agreed upon, attainable, achievable; R—realistic, relevant, results-oriented; and T—timely, tangible, trackable.

An informal survey of gifted-cluster teachers can help determine which strategies to address first. Topics may change for each meeting, or one topic may be discussed over several meetings when needed. Teachers report back at the following meeting on how they used these strategies. Use the reproducible Gifted-Cluster Teacher Meeting: Topic Planning Chart provided on pages 204–205 to plan meeting topics and priorities. The reproducible Gifted-Cluster Teacher Meeting: Attendance Chart on page 206 can help you document teachers' attendance in order to give the teachers clock hours in professional learning for participating in the meetings.

SUPERVISOR SPOTLIGHT

Keep careful records of attendance at school and district gifted-cluster teacher meetings to document that teachers are receiving the training they need to be effective in that teaching role.

Gifted-cluster teacher meeting agendas may include:

- discussion of specific strategies from a book study (beginning with this book)
- review of strategies previously discussed and applied
- introduction of new compacting and differentiation strategies
- sharing resources: lessons, materials, websites, learning contracts, extension menus, and so on
- discussion of issues regarding nomination and testing of new students for gifted clusters
- problem-solving regarding specific students, classroom issues, or site concerns
- parent communication tips
- input on the makeup of new gifted-cluster classes for the following school year

Districtwide Meetings of Gifted-Cluster Teachers and Gifted Specialists

When multiple schools in a district are using the SCGM, districtwide meetings of the district's gifted-cluster teachers and gifted specialists can provide a forum for sharing pertinent information that is helpful in all gifted-cluster classes. During these meetings, which ideally take place at least twice a year, gifted-cluster teachers meet and plan curriculum with others teaching the same grade. These meetings can be facilitated by the gifted coordinator or gifted mentors or specialists.

A suggested format for these district-level meetings is to begin with a short presentation by the group leader on a predetermined topic. Following the presentation, the gifted-cluster teachers can meet by grade level to develop and share curriculum or teaching strategies. Teachers working with gifted students find these meetings helpful and productive. They especially enjoy collaborating with others at the same grade level teaching similar curriculum. This collaboration provides a forum to refine and improve the compacting and differentiation skills they are using with their students. Districts that hold regular gifted-cluster teacher meetings at both the school and district level tend to have very successful cluster grouping programs.

Gifted Specialist Meetings

The gifted coordinator, or the person who oversees gifted education for the district, coordinates monthly meetings of the district's gifted specialists or mentors. Scheduling these meetings prior to the start of the school year minimizes possible time conflicts. Meeting schedules should include both administrative information and professional learning components, including topics such as the following:

- scheduling and preparing for testing
- addressing student placement procedures

- preparing and using differentiated education plans (DEPs—see chapter 8, page 211)
- analyzing student achievement
- planning professional learning opportunities
- scheduling and planning gifted-cluster teacher meetings in the schools
- sharing information on extracurricular student opportunities
- planning parent presentations
- dealing with parent concerns

Figure 7-3 on page 196 demonstrates one district's approach to professional learning for gifted-cluster teachers throughout the district. The Cluster Café announcement describes a semester-long monthly meeting schedule by topics. Either the gifted coordinator/specialist or an experienced gifted-cluster teacher presents at the meetings. Gifted-cluster teachers are invited to attend all the biweekly meetings.

Communication for Professional Learning

Communication is critical in building and supporting the SCGM. This section describes three key tools you can use to provide information to gifted-cluster teachers and parents: gifted-cluster teacher email groups, gifted-cluster teacher news briefs, and quarterly newsletters to parents of gifted students.

Gifted-Cluster Teacher Email Groups

Teachers' busy teaching schedules, after-school activities, and staff meetings can leave little time for seeking resources and information. Creating and using a group email for your school and district gifted-cluster teachers ensures that they have access to the information you wish to share, such as parent events, workshops, conference information, instructional ideas, and so on.

The gifted-cluster teacher email group will also encourage teachers to communicate and collaborate with one another, sharing resources, lesson plans, and ideas and information pertinent to teaching gifted students in their classrooms. We also encourage gifted-cluster teachers to create an email group for the parents of their gifted students. This comes in handy for advertising gifted parent night presentations, sharing parent newsletters, and sharing ideas and resources.

Gifted-Cluster Teacher News Briefs

With the goal of intertwining professional learning and communication into a strong foundation that fosters effective teaching in gifted-cluster classrooms, Paradise Valley Unified School District in Arizona publishes biweekly news briefs for its gifted-cluster teachers titled "Gifted-Cluster Teaching in the 602." Gifted-cluster teacher news briefs can provide timely ideas and resources for busy gifted-cluster teachers in response to teachers' needs and school or district initiatives. Feedback from teachers helps drive the content of the news briefs. Topics to date have included:

- Fostering a Growth Mindset
- Teaching and Parenting the Child with Emotional Sensitivities
- Differentiation and Equity in Language Arts
- Depth of Knowledge Levels in Math
- Effective Parent-Teacher Conferences
- Creativity and MakerSpace
- Empowering Girls with Strong Female Role Models
- Reading Lists for Gifted Readers

Gifted Parent Newsletters

Providing quarterly gifted parent newsletters keeps parents informed about your efforts and provides them with specific and timely

FIGURE 7-3 The Cluster Café

Districtwide Gifted-Cluster Teacher Meetings
Fall Semester

The gifted education team will serve up a new gathering this year to meet the diverse needs of gifted-cluster students and teachers: the Cluster Café. Meet twice a month on Thursdays with fellow gifted-cluster teachers and gifted specialists. The first Thursday meeting each month is content-based, including strategies from *The Cluster Grouping Handbook*. The second Thursday each month is a Table Talk* format that includes strategies, technology, resources, and enrichment opportunities. Always bring a charged laptop. Satisfy your appetite for new and engaging professional learning opportunities!

August 31, 4:00–5:30 p.m., Cluster Café Kickoff

Who are gifted students? What are typical traits of gifted children? What characteristics tend to get in the way of gifted identification?

- What does it mean to be identified as gifted?
- What are common myths about gifted children?
- What is your role as a gifted-cluster teacher?
- What are your resources as a gifted-cluster teacher?

September 14, 4:00–5:30 p.m., Table Talks—Differentiated Math Instruction Strategies

- Rubik's Cube for mathematical reasoning
- football math: statistics and predictions
- using Google Classroom
- using Khan Academy for content differentiation and acceleration
- online resources

October 5, 4:00–5:30 p.m., Flexible Grouping and Grading

What can you do with those students who have scored 80 percent or higher on a pretest? Learn strategies such as compacting, learning contracts, and quick and easy differentiation techniques that will challenge students. Learn methods for grading and classroom management when students are flexibly grouped.

October 19, 4:00–5:30 p.m., Table Talks

- Newsela
- ReadWorks
- Khan Academy
- TED Education

November 2, 4:00–5:30 p.m., Depth of Knowledge (DOK)

In this hands-on workshop, you will learn about DOK and how to increase the rigor for your students no matter what grade level you teach. Explore the difference between DOK and higher-order thinking and how to use these frameworks in your lessons. Participants will leave with lessons, ideas for projects, and assessment strategies to use immediately.

November 16, 4:00–5:30 p.m., Table Talks—Math

- coding
- origami
- Khan Academy
- online resources

December 7, 4:00–5:30 p.m., I Learn in Pictures, You Teach in Words: Teaching and Reaching the Nonverbally Identified Gifted Student

If these children are gifted, why are they struggling in my gifted-cluster classroom? Teachers will learn the unique learning characteristics of nonverbally identified gifted students. These students may present unusual learning challenges and require a different approach to learn. Learn the tools and strategies to guide these students to success in their learning environments.

---

*A Table Talk is a method for sharing a specific resource or strategy within twenty minutes. Four topics are decided upon, with a Table Leader prepared to share an example of a strategy or resource she is using in her classroom. Teachers form four groups and rotate among the four Table Talks to learn about ideas to consider using in their classrooms.

information. Topics to consider addressing include upcoming gifted testing, parent night advertisements and recaps, guidance on preparing for teacher conferences, grading methods used for advanced learners, highlighting student accomplishments and gifted-cluster teachers' practices, describing professional learning for gifted-cluster teachers, and the list goes on! Parents truly appreciate a proactive approach to keeping them informed of the school's and district's efforts to support their gifted children and cluster teachers.

Obtaining Gifted Endorsements or Certifications

While it would be ideal for every gifted-cluster teacher to obtain a gifted endorsement or certification, it may be unreasonable to expect this. However, it is essential that all teachers who will teach a gifted cluster have at least one or two in-services or courses in gifted education prior to taking the role of gifted-cluster teacher. Gifted-cluster teachers should attend continuing gifted-education classes, workshops, or courses for as long as they have a gifted-cluster class. In many states, these workshop hours can satisfy part of the requirements of the gifted endorsement.

General college coursework suggested for gifted-cluster teachers includes titles such as:

- The Gifted Child: Theory and Development
- Social and Emotional Needs of Gifted Students
- Creativity in the Gifted Learner
- Advising Gifted Students
- Twice-Exceptional Gifted Learners
- Differentiated Instruction for Gifted Learners
- Advocating for Gifted Learners
- Technology for Gifted Students
- Testing and Measurement in Gifted Education
- Special Populations in Gifted Education

SUPERVISOR SPOTLIGHT

Check to see if your state has a gifted endorsement or gifted-certification requirement. If it does, encourage gifted-cluster teachers to work toward obtaining the endorsement. Encouraging college coursework and offering professional learning opportunities at the school and district level provide teachers the training they need to teach in this model and create interest for other teachers to begin working toward a gifted endorsement.

Monitoring Teachers' Professional Growth

Classroom observations enable administrators to assess how effectively teachers are incorporating key practices for working with gifted students and helps them determine what types of additional professional learning opportunities will be most useful. Since few administrators have had training in how to notice and support effective classroom practices for teaching gifted students, it is helpful when they learn what to look for as they observe classrooms where teachers are differentiating instruction. The two observation guides on pages 202 and 203 may be helpful for this purpose. The first one focuses on observing conditions experienced by the gifted students in the gifted-cluster classrooms. The second one provides a guide to essential conditions for all students in any classroom.

The principal can use or adapt the checklists to support the evolving needs and skills of the teachers they are observing. The point is not to evaluate every item on the list in a single observation session—that has the potential to be somewhat intimidating, especially to teachers who are new to cluster grouping. Rather, the list can serve as a menu in pre-observation meetings so teachers can choose one or two items from the checklist that they are becoming comfortable using. Over time, other items can be observed as well. The first checklist can also be used to describe to potential gifted-cluster teachers the elements they would eventually be expected to incorporate into their own classrooms. Always reassure teachers that the elements on the observation checklists can be addressed one or two at a time until teachers eventually learn how to provide some service in all areas on the checklist. Accept that this process takes time! Additional instructions for using the checklists are on the forms themselves.

The Office's Role

The importance of maintaining accurate records cannot be overstated. Having access to gifted students' records allows you to pull data and run reports for numerous purposes. For example, you may need to pull data on numbers of gifted students at each site who are ELL students or former ELL students, or who receive special education services. You might also have the need to look at the genders or grade levels of gifted students to improve identification practices. The administrator who oversees gifted education in the district may rely on these data for:

- creating and continually updating the gifted-student rosters for the district and each school
- maintaining gifted-cluster teacher rosters for the district
- calculating professional learning hours
- creating and sharing parent information
- state reporting purposes

SUMMARY

This chapter has described ways to provide professional learning opportunities so that gifted-cluster teachers receive the support and encouragement they need to be highly effective in their work with gifted students. We have provided examples, forms, and concrete ideas to make planning and implementation of professional learning in a school or district as effective as possible. We have included information about:

- training staff to become effective teachers in gifted-cluster classes
- facilitating ongoing support for present and future gifted-cluster teachers
- emphasizing how methods that are effective with gifted students are useful with other students as well
- developing systems of communication among parents, teachers, and administrators

Teacher Self-Assessment Checklist

How Well Am I Challenging My Gifted Students?

Note to teachers: You will notice that this checklist describes an ambitious and comprehensive list of teaching behaviors. The checklist serves as a guide and self-evaluation tool. It is not expected that any one teacher will demonstrate all the listed behaviors. You may want to use the checklist several times during the school year to observe your own growth as a gifted-cluster teacher.

Directions: Circle the number at the beginning of each item that indicates the degree to which you are able to incorporate that particular condition into your teaching at that particular time. Each time you use the assessment, use a different color pen to notice the degree to which you have modified your teaching to accommodate the needs of the students in your gifted-cluster classroom. Circling a 1 means you have not yet tried to incorporate that particular condition. A 2 means you are currently trying to provide it. A 3 means you are so comfortable providing that condition that you could coach another teacher to use it too. Remember, this is a private survey! The results are not intended to be shared with anyone, unless you wish to do so.

Survey Code

1 = Not yet tried
2 = Currently trying
3 = Comfortable with this method

Curriculum Content

1 2 3 Do I regularly provide compacting opportunities?

1 2 3 Do I locate or prepare extension activities when I prepare my lesson plans?

1 2 3 Do I provide ample time in class for gifted students to work on extension activities?

1 2 3 If a student is able to learn at advanced levels, do I provide opportunities for acceleration of content?

1 2 3 Do I regularly include critical-thinking questions and strategies for developing creativity?

1 2 3 Do I provide learning experiences that are connected to students' interests?

1 2 3 Do I let students make selections among various activities to learn the same standards?

1 2 3 Do I encourage and assist students in creating their own extension activities?

Learning Processes

1 2 3 Do I use pretests to find out what students already know?

1 2 3 Do I sometimes allow some students to determine the number of tasks they need to learn the content?

1 2 3 Do I provide extension activities to students who complete compacted work?

1 2 3 Do I use posttests to determine when a student has mastered the required standards?

CONTINUED > > >

Teacher Self-Assessment Checklist, continued

Learning Processes, continued

1 2 3 Based on the pretest or posttest results, do I allow students to work on extension activities of various types?

1 2 3 Are the students flexibly grouped according to what they need to learn or by interests?

1 2 3 Do my lesson extensions involve analysis, evaluation, synthesis, depth, complexity, and novelty?

1 2 3 Do students have the tools to evaluate their progress during independent learning times and when doing extension activities?

1 2 3 Do I provide consistent opportunities for students to integrate technology into core content?

Learning Products

1 2 3 Have I provided access to a variety of products from which students may choose to demonstrate what they have learned?

1 2 3 Are there rubrics available for those products to help students produce high-quality work?

1 2 3 Do students have opportunities to create their own rubrics to evaluate their learning?

1 2 3 Have I provided samples of high-quality student products that show appropriate complexity, depth, and breadth?

1 2 3 Do I encourage active participation, experimentation, and constructive and discovery learning?

1 2 3 Have I created ways for students to work in a self-directed manner?

1 2 3 Can my students use effective time-management strategies?

1 2 3 Have I provided students time to share ideas with one another to develop their own plans for products?

Learning Environment

1 2 3 Have I provided opportunities for students to work outside the classroom or on the internet if that will facilitate their project work?

1 2 3 Have I taught students the skills they will need to work independently in a successful manner?

1 2 3 Do I encourage students to collaborate when learning?

1 2 3 Is it convenient for students to locate and use appropriate extension activities?

1 2 3 Do I make appropriate technology available to connect my students to helpful websites, apps, or mentors?

1 2 3 Have I facilitated students' time learning with mentors?

1 2 3 Do I routinely create flexible learning groups based on student readiness and/or interests?

1 2 3 Are materials available for students to access without needing my assistance? Have I taught students how to access and use the materials in a way that does not attract the attention of others?

CONTINUED > > >

Teacher Self-Assessment Checklist, continued

Assessment

1 2 3 Are the required learning standards presented and understood at the beginning of every unit of study?

1 2 3 Are rubrics available to help students understand my expectations?

1 2 3 Am I using appropriate alternative assessment methods to assess students' compacted and differentiated work?

1 2 3 Am I providing clear goals and fair examples to guide student learning?

1 2 3 Am I evaluating progress based on the individual's growth?

1 2 3 Am I using ongoing formative assessments as checkpoints for understanding?

1 2 3 Am I using pre- and post-assessment instruments that are identical?

Administrator Observation Form

For Classrooms with a Gifted Cluster

Note to administrators: The left column describes a specific condition that gifted students need to have available in their classes in order to thrive and learn. When you observe that the element is available to gifted students, use the center column to describe how it was accommodated. If that particular condition is absent, place a check mark in the right column.

In a pre-observation conference, ask the teacher to identify one or two elements he or she is currently providing. Limit your formal observation notes to those elements. In subsequent observations, allow teachers to add components, one at a time, while expecting them to continue to facilitate the conditions they have already provided. In this way, the teacher will be able to build a repertoire of strategies that are extremely user-friendly to gifted students.

Desirable Elements	**Present** (describe evidence)	**Absent** (check box)
Pretests are used whenever possible to document previous mastery of content.		
Students who demonstrate mastery on pretests are engaged in alternate activities while the rest of the class works with teacher.		
Teacher spends time with students who are working on alternate activities.		
Teacher encourages students to take risks and make mistakes as they learn rather than always expecting perfect outcomes.		
Students who need faster pacing with new content are working on independent study projects at the same time other students are working directly with the teacher.		
Students' interests are incorporated into their project work; choices are available.		
Various types of products are encouraged for students to demonstrate their learning.		
Criteria for evaluating projects are mutually developed by student and teacher.		
Gifted students routinely collaborate on appropriately differentiated activities.		
Group grades are not used in collaborative learning.		
Homework is differentiated when daily classwork is differentiated.		
Technology is used as a differentiation tool.		
Students respect individual differences, value diversity, and accept that different students are working on different activities at different times.		

Administrator Observation Form

For All Classrooms

Note to administrators: The left column describes a specific condition that should be present in classrooms where effective differentiation is taking place. When you observe that the element is present, use the center column to describe how it was accommodated. If that particular condition is absent, place a check mark in the right column.

In a pre-observation conference, ask the teacher to identify one or two elements he or she is currently providing. Limit your formal observation notes to those elements. In subsequent observations, allow teachers to add components, one at a time, while expecting them to continue to facilitate the conditions they have already provided. In this way, the teacher will be able to build a repertoire of strategies that provide effective differentiation for students who need it.

Desirable Elements	**Present** (describe evidence)	**Absent** (check box)
Students respect individual differences, value diversity, and accept that different students are working on different activities.		
Opportunities exist for individual and class goal setting.		
Teacher time is divided between whole-group instruction and work with small groups or individual students.		
Attention to various learning modalities is apparent.		
Students are often working on clearly differentiated tasks.		
Pretests and other methods of curriculum compacting are present.		
Challenging extension activities are available for students who need to move beyond the parameters set by required standards.		
High-achieving students experience an appropriate amount of teacher time, rather than always being expected to work independently.		
Students' interests are incorporated into learning experiences.		
Alternate assessment options are available for students who might demonstrate better learning outcomes in atypical ways.		
Gifted students sometimes work with each other, sometimes independently, and sometimes with other students in the class.		
High-achieving students do not serve as peer tutors, except on rare occasions.		
If learning activities are differentiated, homework is also differentiated.		
Technology is used as a differentiation tool.		

Gifted-Cluster Teacher Meeting
Topic Planning Chart

School year: ____________________

School: ____________________

Gifted specialist: ____________________

September	October	November	December	January
Cluster Handbook Ch. 1 Topic(s)	Cluster Handbook Ch. 2 Topic(s)	Cluster Handbook Ch. 3 Topic(s)	Cluster Handbook Ch. 4 Topic(s)	Cluster Handbook Ch. 5 Topic(s)
DI Strategy School Initiative	DI Strategy School Initiative	DI Strategy School Initiative	DI Strategy School Initiative	DI Strategy School Initiative

CONTINUED > > >

Gifted-Cluster Teacher Meeting, continued

February	March	April	May	Other Staff Development
Cluster Handbook Ch. 6 Topic(s)	Cluster Handbook Ch. 7 Topic(s)	Cluster Handbook Ch. 8 Topic(s)	Cluster Handbook Ch. 5, 6 Topic(s)	
DI Strategy School Initiative	DI Strategy School Initiative	DI Strategy School Initiative	DI Strategy School Initiative	

Gifted-Cluster Teacher Meeting

Attendance Chart

School year: ______________________________

School: ______________________________

Gifted specialist: ______________________________

Gifted-Cluster Teacher Name	September	October	November	December	January	February	March	April	May

8

Evaluating the Effectiveness of the SCGM

GUIDING QUESTIONS

- What information is needed to conduct an effective evaluation of the SCGM in a school or district?
- How can teachers tell if they are meeting the needs of their students in the SCGM?
- How can gifted students' short-term and long-term academic progress be monitored and documented?
- What types of assessments can be used to document the outcomes of the SCGM?
- What evidence is available that documents gifted students' academic achievement growth in the SCGM?
- How can academic growth related to the SCGM be monitored for other students?
- How do I know the SCGM is working in my school or district?

Evaluation is critical to the success of the SCGM in a school or district, so we encourage you to refer to this chapter throughout the year. This chapter addresses a range of variables to consider as you begin your work with the model and serves as a guide to help you collect useful data and effectively evaluate the benefits of your own SCGM.

Schools can demonstrate efficacy in the model by ensuring the following:

- All gifted students in your school or district have been placed into gifted-cluster classrooms.
- Gifted students are making continual academic growth with documented yearly achievement gains, and general education students are also experiencing benefits from the model.
- The components and practices of the SCGM (grouping of students, training of teachers, classroom differentiation strategies) are producing the expected and desired results.

ACHIEVEMENT ADVISORY

Begin by setting goals for when and how to evaluate student progress and teacher development over several years. Another critical early step is to establish a gifted database. With the goals and database in place, you can gather the data necessary to assess and evaluate the impact of the SCGM.

This chapter provides information that can guide you through your own evaluation of how well the SCGM is working in your school or district. It includes research data by Drs. Dina Brulles, Scott J. Peters, Sanford Cohn, and Rachel Saunders, as well as results of research from Dr. Marcia Gentry, whose initial research documented achievement gains for all students at grade levels using a cluster grouping model. Data presented in this chapter also serve as a model for the types of data you will want to collect and study at your own site.

Setting Goals for the SCGM

To create and maintain a strong SCGM, school or district staff members should develop specific goals for the first three years. These goals should reflect the needs of the school and district and may be revised as needed. Creating short- and long-term plans demonstrates to the school community that the model does not need to be perfected before it is implemented and that it develops and strengthens over time. These plans also emphasize to staff and parents that the school is committed to the model and is devoting time and energy toward making it work.

Figure 8-1 shows a sample three-year plan for goals for the SCGM.

FIGURE 8-1 **Sample Goals for the SCGM**

Year 1—Planning Year (Preparing to Implement the SCGM)	**Year 2—Implementing Year** (First Year Using SCGM)	**Year 3—Continuing Year** (Second Year Using SCGM)
Provide information to parents, teachers, and administrators.	Update the database of all gifted students by school, grade level, and area(s) of identification.	Identify teachers who will rotate into the position of gifted-cluster teacher.
Provide professional learning opportunities to gifted-cluster teachers.	Attempt to identify gifted students who reflect your student population by grade, gender, and ethnicity.	Expand the grade levels participating in the SCGM.
Administer gifted testing for the grades you will cluster group during the implementing year and create a database of all gifted students by school, grade level, and area(s) of identification.	Compare student achievement in the areas of gifted identification.	Compare student achievement in the areas of gifted identification.
Place all gifted-identified students into gifted-cluster classrooms for upcoming year.	Expand professional development to include all interested teachers in the school or district.	Compare gifted students' growth relative to their areas of identification.

Establishing a Gifted-Student Database

Schools and districts using the SCGM must create and maintain a comprehensive gifted database. The database allows schools to monitor the number of students being tested and served in the SCGM and the academic achievement of gifted students, and it helps ensure that all gifted-identified students are placed correctly into gifted-cluster classrooms. The gifted database should include the names of the students identified as gifted, the dates the students were tested, the name(s) of the test(s) used, the area(s) of identification, and any other information you wish to document. Include all available test scores used in the identification process, including both qualifying and nonqualifying gifted-cluster placement scores, along with the testing dates. Information included in the database will be used over several years to recognize trends, such as which schools have more accurate identification methods.

Keeping ongoing records in the following categories during each year, and from one year to the next, will provide accurate information to help administrators plan and carry out professional development, identification procedures, and staffing:

- percentage of the student population identified and served as gifted, by year
- percentage of the student population identified and served as gifted compared to the state average
- ethnic representation of gifted students in relation to the school or district's ethnic population
- number and names of teachers obtaining a gifted endorsement or certification or participating in professional development offerings in gifted education

In the SCGM, *all* students who are identified as gifted are placed into gifted-cluster classrooms, with special attention to those who may have commonly been underserved in other gifted program models. Since giftedness spans all cultures and ages, the percentages of various student groups in the gifted population should be similar to those represented in the school's total population. This requires that schools examine gifted student data in regard to grade level, gender, ethnicity, and English fluency.

Tracking the identification, placement, and progress for primary, intermediate, and middle school students is an important element of SCGM evaluation. The model should help ensure that primary-age gifted students, who are often not included in traditional gifted-education programs, are identified and served and that gifted middle schoolers—some of whom may stop participating in gifted pull-out programs in response to peer pressure—continue receiving services. Also pay close attention to monitoring effectiveness in identifying and serving gifted students from diverse populations. Check to see if your policies and procedures for gifted identification and programs include tests that identify diverse populations.* If not, focus some staff development on gifted-student identification procedures for the underrepresented populations. Over time, watch for growth in the number of culturally and linguistically diverse (CLD) students who are being identified and served in Group 1 clusters.

Determine from your school's or district's enrollment records the percentage of students in each group. Compare that data to the percentage of identified gifted students from each group. If the percentages are discrepant, seek additional identification methods and procedures that will increase identification and service to the underrepresented populations.

As an example of the kind of information you might collect, **figure 8-2** on page 210 presents data from one school district's experience with

*For recommendations on identifying gifted culturally and linguistically diverse (CLD) students, see chapter 3.

FIGURE 8-2 **Gifted Population Growth Over Six Years**

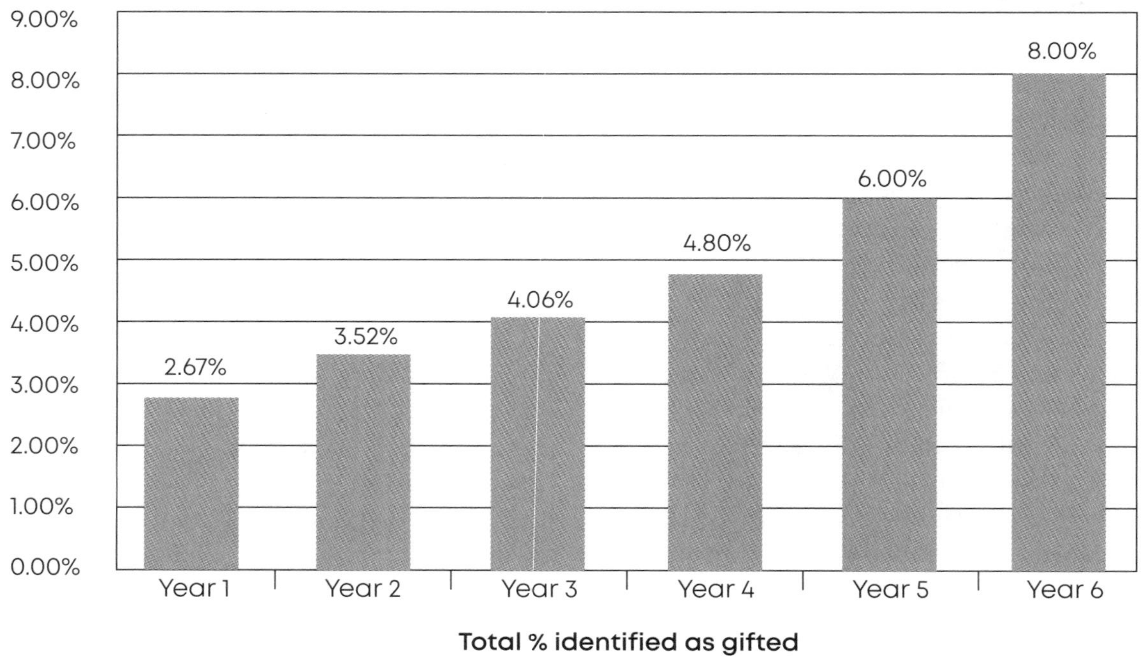

the SCGM. This urban district qualified for Title I funds and had a diverse population. At the time of the study, the district's ethnic representation was approximately 20 percent Caucasian, 68 percent Hispanic, and 12 percent other minority groups. The goal was to identify and serve a percentage of gifted students that more closely met state expectations, since Title I schools tend to under-identify their gifted populations.

The graph shows growth in the district's gifted population over a six-year period during which the SCGM was implemented and maintained. After six years of serving gifted students in the cluster grouping model, including purposefully using a variety of identification instruments to enfranchise traditionally underserved gifted students, the district's identified gifted population increased from less than 3 percent to 8 percent, which was the same as the state average.

Several considerations explain this growth. Primarily, teachers in the SCGM became aware of the characteristics of gifted students and learned to identify gifted students in all populations because of the ongoing training they received. Secondly, the school developed a culture that was accepting of the presence of giftedness in all subpopulations and created an environment that nurtured the learning strengths of all students. Thirdly, professional learning opportunities taught teachers to offer compacting and differentiation opportunities to all students, which led to increases in the numbers of students being recommended by all staff for gifted-testing services.

Examining Student Progress Regarding Classroom Work

As noted earlier, examining student progress in classroom work is one important aspect of assessing and evaluating the SCGM. There are two components to this category: first, monitoring that teachers are receiving adequate and appropriate training to differentiate effectively (described in detail in chapter 7), and second, assessing individual students' academic progress.

Monitoring Teacher Training and Development

The number of teachers receiving a gifted endorsement or a specified number of hours of professional learning in gifted education should increase yearly in the SCGM. Keep track of the number of school and district in-service hours and the topics of gifted-education workshops taken by all staff members and maintain an accurate database to ensure that teachers appointed to teach gifted clusters have adequate training. A record of the professional learning offerings provided to teachers helps ensure that areas of need are addressed through targeted training and that professional growth occurs for teachers at all grade levels (or in all the district's schools if you're incorporating the model districtwide).

Monitoring Individual Student Progress Grade by Grade

A differentiated education plan (DEP) can assist teachers and administrators in monitoring how gifted services are provided in each gifted-cluster classroom and for each identified gifted student. The gifted-cluster teacher completes a separate DEP for each gifted student in the classroom. Gifted-cluster teachers might choose to share information about the plan with parents, but the DEP is an internal document and is not intended to be sent home with students. One copy of the plan will follow the student in the student portfolio or cumulative folder, and one copy is filed at the district office. Teachers and gifted specialists may wish to keep copies to reference in the future when fine-tuning their practices.

The "Social and Emotional Needs Being Targeted" section of the DEP requires teachers' attention to potentially problematic behaviors of gifted students. Students who demonstrate such tendencies can be a challenge for the classroom teacher who is unfamiliar with gifted children. Teachers who are aware of the intensity and perfectionistic, ethical, and creative sensitivities of gifted students can help create a safe and accepting environment in which students can thrive. Students who are twice-exceptional also require special attention to their social and emotional needs, since they are more likely to seek academic challenges when they feel understood and accepted by their peers and by the adults in their lives.

See pages 221–224 for reproducible DEP forms teachers can use in planning differentiation for elementary and middle school students.

Assessments to Use in Documenting Student Achievement Outcomes in the SCGM

Ideally, the types of assessments cluster teachers use are determined at the beginning of the school year, so progress and growth can be documented throughout the year. Assessment can be defined as data that documents student progress in learning. The three general kinds of assessment are preassessment (or diagnostic assessment), formative assessment, and summative assessment. Preassessment allows teachers to identify instructional entry points for students, and it should reflect the summative assessment planned for a given lessen. Preassessment informs the teacher which students have already mastered upcoming standards and determines into which flexible group to place students for a particular lesson, unit, or concept. Specific examples of assessment procedures are described in chapters 5 and 6.

Teachers preassess using both formal and informal measures. Formal preassessment might be by means of a pretest or by giving the end-of-chapter test prior to instruction. Informal preassessment can consist of group responses to teacher statements (such as thumbs-ups, nods, or other simple methods).

Formative assessment occurs during the instructional process. Examples of formative assessment include quizzes, exit slips, informal questioning, self-assessment, reflective writing, interactive notebooks, mapping, and homework.

Formative assessments should not be used for grading purposes. They are used to gauge progress toward a specific and measurable goal. They are intended to inform instruction, and as such, provide information to the teacher and feedback to the students. Student performance rises through effective feedback.

Summative assessments provide information about whether the designated standards have been mastered. They are usually administered at the conclusion of a unit of study. They may be delivered as formal tests or as performance-based assessments that demonstrate students' understanding of required concepts, especially in the case of gifted students who are working on differentiated or accelerated curriculum.

Assessment data can be used to:

- discern strengths and learning levels of all students
- group students for instruction
- determine curriculum levels and instruction methods for advanced learners
- scaffold student learning
- assess the effectiveness of a particular teaching method
- provide an accurate means of sharing student progress with parents
- assist in decision making at the classroom, school, and district level

A Grade-Level Approach to Analyzing Achievement Data

In this model, it is essential that principals take a grade-level approach when analyzing student achievement data. Using aggregate data by grade level to determine student growth (as opposed to comparing individual classes) is fair to all teachers. If one were to look at individual teachers'

FIGURE 8-3 Types of Assessments

Assessment Type	Description	Example
Diagnostic (Preassessments)	Given at beginning of unit or year to quantify what students know about a topic	Pretests Self-assessments Interviews Surveys
Formative	Given along the way to determine how students are progressing Used by both teacher and student to impact future instruction/learning	Observations Homework Reflection journals Exit tickets Conferences Quizzes Questioning
Summative	Given at the end of the unit or year to determine student's mastery of a topic after learning has occurred	Unit exams Final exams Projects Performance-based assessments District/state exams

Adapted from *A Teacher's Guide to Flexible Grouping and Collaborative Learning* by Dina Brulles and Karen L. Brown (Minneapolis: Free Spirit Publishing, 2018). Used with permission.

classes, the gifted-cluster class would likely have the higher test scores. When growth is examined by grade level, teams more readily accept that all or most of the gifted students should be placed into one classroom. Report on percentiles of student growth at each grade level without identifying individual classroom teachers.

Work toward creating a mindset that the school is committed to ensuring that the placements in this model support all learners and all teachers in the school. Build this mentality throughout the school staff, during cluster teacher workshops, and in working with school administrators. This team approach promotes staff buy-in to the SCGM.

ACHIEVEMENTADVISORY

If a gifted student avoids appropriately challenging work despite the teacher's attempts to provide it, a parent-teacher-student conference could help define a plan and structure for working on the differentiated or personalized lessons. The reproducible "Parent-Teacher Planning Guide for Conferences" on page 225 can be helpful in conducting the conference.

Monitoring Gifted Students' Growth on Standardized Assessments

Attending to gifted students' academic growth as demonstrated on standardized tests is another key aspect of evaluating student progress in the SCGM. States require schools to administer standardized achievement tests to monitor student achievement. These tests are either norm-referenced or criterion-referenced. Norm-referenced tests, such as the *Iowa Tests of Basic Skills* or the *Stanford Achievement Tests,* measure knowledge in specific subject areas and can show how a student scores in relation to other students throughout the country. Criterion-referenced tests, such as state-required tests, measure what students have learned according to a set of established standards.

For most students, standardized tests demonstrate whether and to what extent academic growth has occurred. To gauge individual student growth from one year to the next on a norm-referenced test, use the normal curve equivalent (NCE) scores. An increase in the student's NCE scores for consecutive years will show academic growth. Currently, states select their own state assessments, most of which include performance-based assessment criteria. This method can provide more accurate individualized information for students who are working above grade level.

Assessment of gifted students' academic progress has often been the weakest link in gifted education. In order to break free of the "ceiling effect" that occurs when advanced learners are assessed using only grade-level tests, educators need to use assessments in nontraditional ways. This is a critical concern, because grade-level assessments offer very little room to document growth for some gifted students. Since gifted students are capable of learning content that is more rigorous than grade-level standards, it is necessary to assess their learning at that advanced level in order to accurately document progress. This requires out-of-level testing, a practice that allows advanced students to take the achievement tests designed for older students. Such an accommodation is commonly lacking in school practice. Out-of-level testing should be seen as an opportunity for:

- teachers to direct curriculum and instruction at appropriately challenging levels
- students to demonstrate that they are continually learning new material
- schools to provide evidence that the gifted service model is appropriately meeting the academic needs of the students

Some school districts create pre-summative assessments in different content areas for each grade level in order to have evidence of student growth during the school year. Many gifted students *begin* a school year with scores that show they have mastered nearly all of the grade-level content. If you have this information at the beginning of the school year, the students should have access to accelerated curriculum and/or expanded learning opportunities in that specific content area. This type of radical acceleration requires long-range planning among staff and administration about what will occur in that subject area in ensuing years.

If your school or district has pre-summative and post-summative assessments that are aligned to your state standards, consider a process such as the one described here:

1. Administer the pre-summative assessment to the entire class at the beginning of the year.
2. Create a list of students who have exceeded the grade-level standards. These students will need to commence their instruction using the next grade level's standards.
3. Administer the pre-summative assessment for the *next* grade level to the students in the class who exceeded the regular grade-level standards to determine where instruction should begin.
4. Administer a different version of that same advanced test again at the end of the year to observe growth. The data from these tests stays local and is never combined with regular grade-level test results for community information.

Note: Occasionally, an extremely advanced learner will exceed the standards on that next grade level's test. Continue the preassessment until an instructional level is determined. Then meet with parents, future teachers and principals, the district gifted coordinator, and other interested parties to create a multiyear plan for the student's continuous academic program.

High-Stakes Tests: What to Expect from Gifted Students

Achievement tests measure retained knowledge of specific information related to grade-level standards. Students identified as gifted are usually much better at abstract thinking and find recalling concrete details tedious and a waste of time and energy. In their rush to get the big picture of what they are learning, they may miss some of the specific information asked for in the questions or may not feel motivated to engage in the material. Test items designed for grade-level standards are often too simple for gifted learners. They may lose interest in a test because it lacks complexity and does not seem worth the time they will spend on it.

Some gifted students do not take standardized tests seriously. They may be bored by the low level of the content or frustrated that so much valuable learning time is spent taking these tests. Teachers need to let gifted kids know the importance of demonstrating their understanding so an accurate measure of their gifted abilities can be documented. This message should be shared in a low-key, nonthreatening manner. It's important to convey that perfection is *not* expected, but that not taking the tests seriously can keep students from fully demonstrating their advanced learning ability or from being assigned to challenging learning situations. When gifted students have been challenged in their learning experiences throughout the year, they become more accustomed to working diligently and can better understand the importance of these tests.

The entire practice of standardized testing could be improved by using a growth model (described in chapter 2 on page 44) that compares results for all students year by year. This method of reporting test success, combined with the "Student's Self-Evaluation of Academic Progress" (see reproducible on page 226), has the potential to inspire students to set personal achievement goals and to motivate schools to provide out-of-level testing that is more challenging and interesting to advanced learners.

If the state or district specifically forbids the use of out-of-level standardized tests, use other available resources. Some districts use benchmark assessments from higher grade levels. If such benchmarks are not available, gifted-cluster teachers can use whatever tests are being used in the school to assess growth from the advanced grade level at which the student is working. This can include end-of-year textbook assessments and district-created assessments. Allowing students to demonstrate growth in the accelerated content they are learning also provides the district with data showing that gifted students are benefiting from the SCGM.

ACHIEVEMENT ADVISORY

Throughout the book we have emphasized the importance of consistency in implementing the SCGM. **Figure 8-4** demonstrates how academic achievement remained consistent between Title I and Non–Title I schools in a large school district in mathematics and English language arts (ELA) for gifted students who were being served in a cluster model. One explanation for this consistent achievement throughout the district could be that all cluster teachers received similar training opportunities, resources, and support.

Achievement Data: What Information Should Be Tracked?

School administrators can track student achievement in the SCGM using standardized and district test results such as pre-summative and post-summative benchmark assessment data. Track student achievement for gifted students in the following ways:

- by school
- by grade level
- by subject area
- by area(s) of giftedness

Information obtained from this data can guide professional learning and can serve as documentation of progress in the SCGM.

As an example of how to collect and report data, **figure 8-5** on page 216 shows how one elementary school tracked student achievement in math in the fifth year after implementing the SCGM. The assessments used in the school's action research study were Quarter 1 and Quarter 3 of the school's benchmark assessments. Gifted students at the school were *not* given out-of-level tests. This created a ceiling effect, limiting evidence of growth in the gifted populations. A study conducted in 2010 shows significant growth for

FIGURE 8-4 **Passing Rates: Subgroups at Title I versus Non–Title I Schools**

	Grades 3–6 Math	Grades 3–6 ELA
All students	56.2%	55.7%
Gifted students	97.2%	95.9%
Gifted students at non–Title I schools	98%	97.2%
Gifted students at Title I schools	94.3%	90.9%

FIGURE 8-5 **Academic Effects of Cluster Grouping**

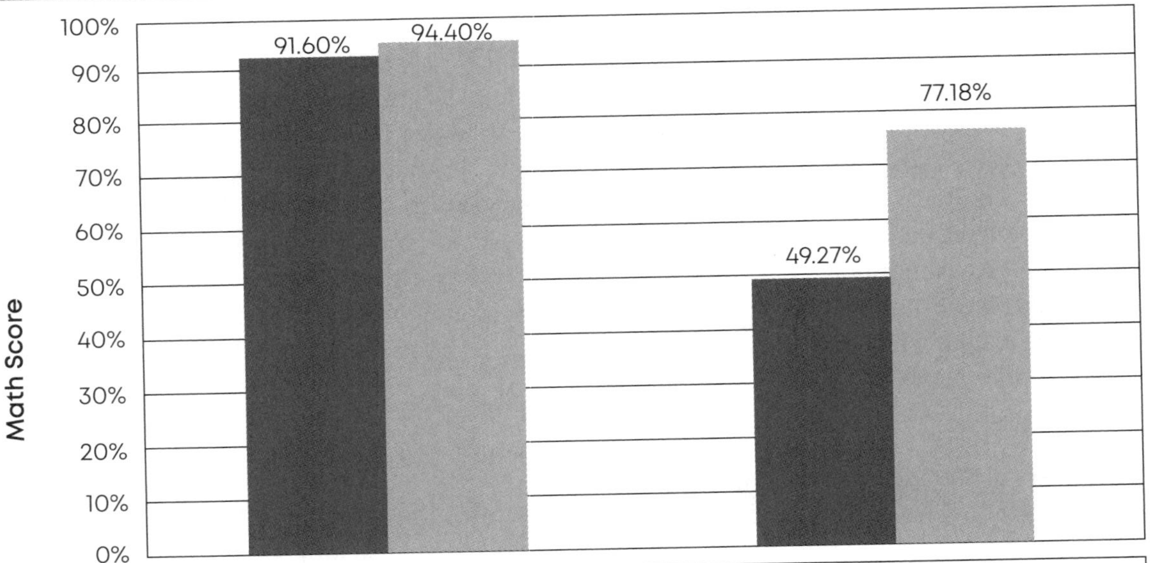

	Gifted Students	All Other Students
Q1	91.60%	49.27%
Q3	94.40%	77.18%

Academic growth in mathematics for students identified as gifted and for all other students

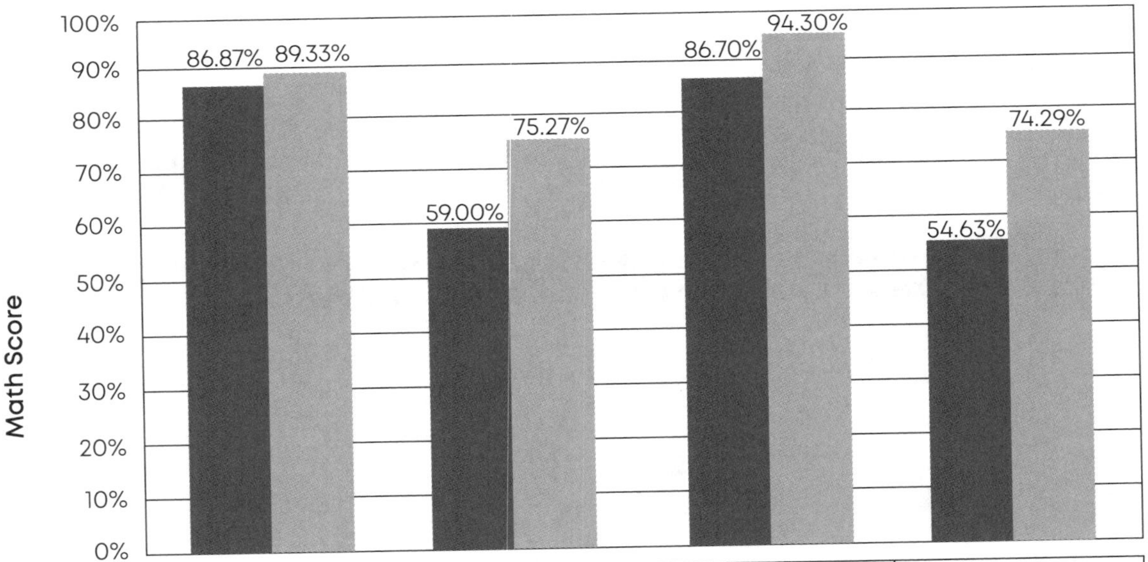

	ELL Gifted Students	All Other ELL Students	Non-ELL Gifted Students	All Other Non-ELL Students
Q1	86.87%	59.00%	86.70%	54.63%
Q3	89.33%	75.27%	94.30%	74.29%

Academic growth in mathematics for ELL students and non-ELL students gifted students placed in a cluster model compared to gifted students in the same district that were placed in regular mixed-ability classes with no clustering (Brulles, Saunders, and Cohn 2010).

The academic achievement charts, along with the identification graph on page 210, show that the SCGM made the identification, service, and academic achievement of gifted students more likely to occur. It also showed that other students in the gifted-cluster classroom made significant achievement gains.

The study on which the "Academic Effects of Cluster Grouping" graphs are based supports the findings of one of the first documented research studies on cluster grouping. In 1999, Marcia Gentry and Steven Owen examined the effects of cluster grouping on all students in a school that used a cluster grouping model. In this longitudinal study, they used standardized achievement scores in math, reading, and the total battery on the *Iowa Tests of Basic Skills*. Findings showed that student achievement increased significantly for students in the grade levels where cluster grouping was used and resulted in higher total achievement than that of the students in the comparison school (Gentry and Owen 1999).

Another study conducted by Drs. Brulles, Peters, and Saunders examined the nongifted students who were placed in a gifted-cluster class versus those who were not in a gifted-cluster class. Results from this study show similar levels of growth for both groups (see **figure 8-6**). This means that the nongifted students were not at a disadvantage when they were not placed in the gifted-cluster classroom (Brulles, Peters, and Saunders 2012).

FIGURE 8-6 **Overall Academic Effects of Cluster Grouping on Nongifted Students**

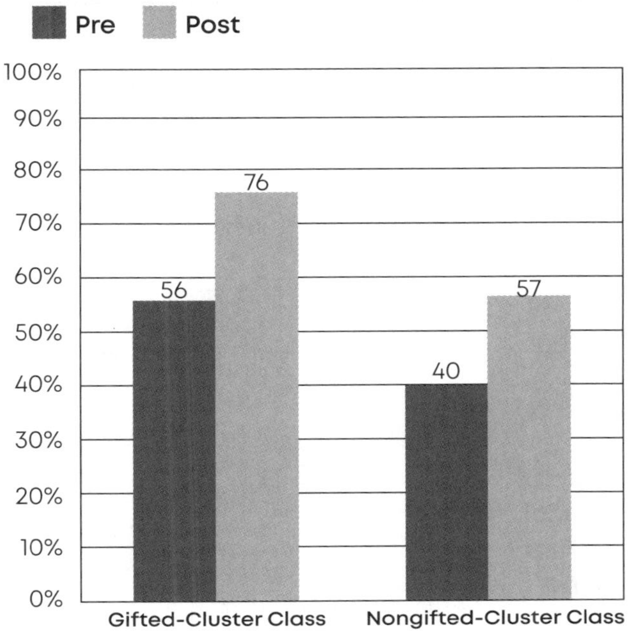

Student Self-Evaluations

All students can use the reproducible form on page 226, "Student's Self-Evaluation of Academic Progress," to track their own academic progress during one school year. The purpose of this form is to help students make long-term progress by learning to set and accomplish realistic, short-term goals. At the beginning of each year, as soon as state or standardized test scores are available, students fill in their own scores, using whatever data make the most sense to them, such as grades, percentiles, or NCE scores.

Explain how students can set goals for their own achievement gains in each subject. Help them set specific goals for each report-card period. When report cards are issued, show students how to record their actual progress in a different color on their chart so they can see whether they reached their goals. Repeat this process between report cards until the end of the school year.

The "Student's Self-Evaluation of Academic Progress" form helps students understand how to get from one goal to another. Because the goals they set are their own, students are likely to be more motivated to move ahead than if they just wait to see what grade the teacher has given them each term. Students make the decisions about which subjects to focus on for each upcoming report-card period. Encourage them to choose no more than two categories at a time, similar to the example in **figure 8-7** on page 218. Students use

FIGURE 8-7 Sample Student's Self-Evaluation of Academic Progress

Student's name: Eric S. Current grade in school: 5

Goals/ Progress	Reading Skills	Reading Compre-hension	Math Skills	Problem-Solving	Writing	Science	Social Studies	
End of Last Year	Attained A	Attained A	Attained B	Attained B-	~~Attained~~	~~Attained~~	~~Attained~~	~~Attained~~
Start of School to First Report Card	Planned A Attained A	Planned A Attained A	~~Planned~~ ~~Attained~~	~~Planned~~ ~~Attained~~	~~Planned~~ ~~Attained~~	~~Planned~~ ~~Attained~~	~~Planned~~ ~~Attained~~	~~Planned~~ ~~Attained~~
First to Second Report Cards	Planned A Attained A	Planned A Attained A	Planned A Attained B+	~~Planned~~ ~~Attained~~	~~Planned~~ ~~Attained~~	~~Planned~~ ~~Attained~~	~~Planned~~ ~~Attained~~	~~Planned~~ ~~Attained~~
Second to Final Report Cards	Planned A Attained A	Planned A Attained A	Planned A Attained A	Planned A Attained B+	~~Planned~~ ~~Attained~~	~~Planned~~ ~~Attained~~	~~Planned~~ ~~Attained~~	~~Planned~~ ~~Attained~~

the same type of data for each marking period, since it wouldn't make sense to notice percentiles in one period and grade equivalents in another. Students can draw a large *X* through the columns for the subjects that are not being targeted. Sharing of this data takes place among students and their teachers and parents.

Evaluating the Effectiveness of the SCGM as a Whole

This section addresses another important aspect of SCGM evaluation. It describes tools your school or district can use to assess the effectiveness of the SCGM in terms of its ability to serve gifted students while having a positive impact on other students in the grade levels using the model. The reproducible forms described here and included at the end of the chapter also are included in the digital content along with all the forms from this book. You may adapt the forms in the digital content to more specifically reflect the unique needs of your own school.

Obtaining Feedback from Teachers, Parents, and Students

The use of surveys can help you monitor the progress students and teachers are experiencing. We recommend using data from surveys as an internal tool for planning and making improvements in the way the model is serving students. Consider making all surveys anonymous to help obtain honest feedback. You may wish to use the three surveys on pages 227–231 to obtain information from teachers, parents, and students about the effectiveness of the SCGM at your school.

Program Evaluation in the SCGM

Gifted programs that are responsive to students' needs rely on information and feedback from teachers, parents, students, and administrators. One way to approach this is to create a rotating schedule of providing surveys to the groups mentioned previously and administering a program evaluation of your cluster model. Here's a suggested rotating schedule:

- Year 1: Survey teachers, parents, students, and administrators in each school that uses the SCGM.
- Year 2: Perform program evaluation for schools that use the SCGM.

Through this schedule, schools will be able to document areas of strength and areas that need attention. The results can inform curriculum development and pacing, professional development, communication efforts, staffing, and student enrichment opportunities. Once completed, consider sharing the results with your district parent groups and cabinet, who may then share with the governing board. Seeking stakeholder approval can greatly advance your efforts in this program model.

What to Include in an End-of-Year Summary Report

The data you gather during the entire school year will allow you to evaluate information about the gifted students being identified and served in the SCGM and about the effect of the model on overall student achievement and teacher effectiveness and development. Consider compiling a year-end report summarizing information the school or district is monitoring, such as the following:

- survey data
- the percentage of students identified and placed in gifted-cluster classrooms
- the degree to which all ethnic and socioeconomic groups are represented in gifted (Group 1) clusters
- the numbers of teachers seeking professional development in gifted education
- a description of the professional development offerings held by the district

- sample curriculum developed for or by gifted-cluster teachers
- analysis of student achievement
- information gained from surveying administrators, teachers, parents, and students
- student success stories
- feedback from all teachers at the grade levels using the SCGM
- areas of concern
- SCGM goals for the coming year

SUMMARY

This chapter has described several methods to use in monitoring progress and evaluating growth in the Schoolwide Cluster Grouping Model. Careful monitoring of the progress in the SCGM in its first few years of implementation can facilitate ongoing success and lay groundwork for an effective and sustainable model in your school or district. When progress is adequately and consistently monitored and evaluated, it can positively impact the achievement of all students in the school. The collection of data will help you:

› verify that gifted students are appropriately placed into gifted-cluster classrooms

› ensure that all classes have a balanced range of student achievement levels

› analyze the achievement of all students in the school or district

› document the effectiveness of professional learning opportunities offered to teachers

Differentiated Education Plan for Gifted Elementary Students

Student: ______________________________ School year: ____________

Grade: ____________ School: ______________________________

Teacher: ______________________ Other information: ______________

Gifted-Identification Areas and Scores
Include all scores even if they are not in the required range for gifted identification.

Name of test: ______________________________

Verbal score: ________ Quantitative score: ________ Nonverbal score: ________

Instructional and Management Strategies Used for Differentiation
Check the strategies you plan to use and indicate the appropriate subject area(s).

Method	Plan to Use	Subject Area(s)
Compacting		
Independent study		
Flexible grouping		
Tiered assignments		
Extension menus		
Interest centers/groups		
Learning centers		
Learning contracts		
Mentorships/ apprenticeships		
Questioning strategies		
Other: ____________		

Description of Implementation

Evaluation of Effectiveness

Social and Emotional Needs Being Targeted

CONTINUED > > >

Differentiated Education Plan for Gifted Elementary Students, continued

DEFINITION OF STRATEGIES

Compacting
Giving students full credit for what they know about an upcoming unit and/or providing advanced students opportunities to learn new material in a shorter time period than needed by classmates

Independent Study
Ongoing in-depth research on a topic of a student's own choosing

Flexible Grouping
Grouping and regrouping students throughout the year according to readiness, interest, learning style, achievement level, activity preference, or special needs

Tiered Assignments
Varying the level of complexity, depth, or novelty of a lesson so students can go beyond basic requirements of an assignment

Extension Menu
A selection of topics from which a student can choose to pursue an independent study that extends the learning beyond already mastered content standards

Interest Centers/Groups
Ways to organize students to work together on learning activities or projects

Learning Center
Location of a collection of students' tasks and activities

Learning Contract
A signed agreement between student and teacher regarding specific tasks to be done by the student

Mentorships/Apprenticeships
Opportunities for students to work with a mentor for guidance in a particular area

Questioning Strategies
Using high-level, open-ended questions meant to challenge thinking and learning

Differentiated Education Plan for Gifted Middle School Students

Student: ______________________________ School year: ______________

Grade: ______________ School: ______________________________

Homeroom: ______________________ Other information: ______________

Gifted-Identification Areas and Scores

Include all scores even if they are not in the required range for gifted identification.

Name of test: ______________________________

Verbal score: ________ Quantitative score: ________ Nonverbal score: ________

Instructional and Management Strategies Used for Differentiation

Check the strategies you plan to use and indicate the appropriate subject area(s).

Subject area:

Teacher:

Method:

- ❑ Compacting
- ❑ Flexible grouping
- ❑ Interest centers/groups
- ❑ Learning centers
- ❑ Independent study
- ❑ Tiered assignments
- ❑ Extension menus
- ❑ Learning contracts
- ❑ Mentorships/apprenticeships
- ❑ Questioning strategies
- ❑ Other ______________

Evidence of Implementation and Effectiveness:

Social and Emotional Needs Being Targeted:

Subject area:

Teacher:

Method:

- ❑ Compacting
- ❑ Flexible grouping
- ❑ Interest centers/groups
- ❑ Learning centers
- ❑ Independent study
- ❑ Tiered assignments
- ❑ Extension menus
- ❑ Learning contracts
- ❑ Mentorships/apprenticeships
- ❑ Questioning strategies
- ❑ Other ______________

Evidence of Implementation and Effectiveness:

Social and Emotional Needs Being Targeted:

Subject area:

Teacher:

Method:

- ❑ Compacting
- ❑ Flexible grouping
- ❑ Interest centers/groups
- ❑ Learning centers
- ❑ Independent study
- ❑ Tiered assignments
- ❑ Extension menus
- ❑ Learning contracts
- ❑ Mentorships/apprenticeships
- ❑ Questioning strategies
- ❑ Other ______________

Evidence of Implementation and Effectiveness:

Social and Emotional Needs Being Targeted:

Subject area:

Teacher:

Method:

- ❑ Compacting
- ❑ Flexible grouping
- ❑ Interest centers/groups
- ❑ Learning centers
- ❑ Independent study
- ❑ Tiered assignments
- ❑ Extension menus
- ❑ Learning contracts
- ❑ Mentorships/apprenticeships
- ❑ Questioning strategies
- ❑ Other ______________

Evidence of Implementation and Effectiveness:

Social and Emotional Needs Being Targeted:

CONTINUED > > >

Differentiated Education Plan for Gifted Middle School Students, continued

DEFINITION OF STRATEGIES

Compacting
Giving students full credit for what they know about an upcoming unit and/or providing advanced students opportunities to learn new material in a shorter time period than needed by classmates

Independent Study
Ongoing in-depth research on a topic of a student's own choosing

Flexible Grouping
Grouping and regrouping students throughout the year according to readiness, interest, learning style, achievement level, activity preference, or special needs

Tiered Assignments
Varying the level of complexity, depth, or novelty of a lesson so students can go beyond basic requirements of an assignment

Extension Menu
A selection of topics from which a student can choose to pursue an independent study that extends the learning beyond already mastered content standards

Interest Centers/Groups
Ways to organize students to work together on learning activities or projects

Learning Center
Location of a collection of students' tasks and activities

Learning Contract
A signed agreement between student and teacher regarding specific tasks to be done by the student

Mentorships/Apprenticeships
Opportunities for students to work with a mentor for guidance in a particular area

Questioning Strategies
Using high-level, open-ended questions meant to challenge thinking and learning

Parent-Teacher Planning Guide for Conferences

Student name: ______________________ School: ______________________

Grade: __________ Teacher: ______________________ Meeting date: __________

Participants: ____

Student's learning strengths and appropriate responses: ______________________

____

____

____

Student's learning challenges and appropriate responses: ______________________

____

____

____

Any other information about the student parent wants to communicate to teacher:

____

____

____

____

Two specific strategies to be tried: ______________________

____

____

____

How progress will be communicated: ______________________

____

____

____

Student's Self-Evaluation of Academic Progress

Student's name: ______________________ Current grade in school: ______

Goals/ Progress	Reading Skills	Reading Compre-hension	Math Skills	Problem-Solving	Writing	Science	Social Studies	
End of Last Year	Attained ______	Attained ______	Attained ______	Attained ______	Attained ______	Attained ______	Attained ______	Attained ______
Start of School to First Report Card	Planned ______ Attained ______	Planned ______ Attained ______	Planned ______ Attained ______	Planned ______ Attained ______	Planned ______ Attained ______	Planned ______ Attained ______	Planned ______ Attained ______	Planned ______ Attained ______
First to Second Report Cards	Planned ______ Attained ______	Planned ______ Attained ______	Planned ______ Attained ______	Planned ______ Attained ______	Planned ______ Attained ______	Planned ______ Attained ______	Planned ______ Attained ______	Planned ______ Attained ______
Second to Final Report Cards	Planned ______ Attained ______	Planned ______ Attained ______	Planned ______ Attained ______	Planned ______ Attained ______	Planned ______ Attained ______	Planned ______ Attained ______	Planned ______ Attained ______	Planned ______ Attained ______

Adapted from *Teaching Kids with Learning Difficulties in Today's Classroom* by Susan Winebrenner (Minneapolis: Free Spirit Publishing, 2014). Used with permission.

Classroom Differentiation Opportunities
Teacher Assessment Survey

Information from this survey will be used to help the school provide training and assistance to enable teachers to provide the best possible differentiation opportunities for students in the Schoolwide Cluster Grouping Model (SCGM). Thank you for taking time to complete the survey.

Please return the form to ______________________________ on or before __________. There is no need to include your name. Please contact the gifted specialist or coordinator if you would like to talk about any issues related to the SCGM.

Please indicate which is true for **this school year**:
______ Yes, I have been teaching a gifted-cluster class this year.
______ No, I have not been teaching a gifted-cluster class this year and have never taught one.
______ I have taught a gifted-cluster class in the past but do not have one this year.

Survey Response Categories
5 = I strongly agree with this statement.
4 = I agree with this statement.
3 = I disagree with this statement.
2 = I strongly disagree with this statement.
1 = I have had no experience with this issue; this item does not apply to me.

Directions: Circle the number that represents your opinion about each statement.

1 2 3 4 5 1. I completely understand and support the Schoolwide Cluster Grouping Model.

1 2 3 4 5 2. I have had adequate training to learn how to compact and differentiate learning tasks for gifted students in the cluster grouping model.

1 2 3 4 5 3. I have a positive attitude about the necessity to compact and differentiate the grade-level standards for highly capable students.

1 2 3 4 5 4. I believe that the time it takes me to prepare differentiation opportunities is worth the advantages such opportunities provide for the students who need them.

1 2 3 4 5 5. I have seen evidence that gifted students willingly tackle difficult tasks in my classroom this year.

1 2 3 4 5 6. I have witnessed advantages for students in my class who have not been identified as gifted because compacting and differentiation opportunities are available for all students.

1 2 3 4 5 7. Other students besides those identified for the gifted cluster have been able to participate in some compacting and differentiation opportunities this year in my classroom.

1 2 3 4 5 8. There is little or no resentment from students in my classroom toward students who are usually eligible for extended learning opportunities.

1 2 3 4 5 9. When gifted students have weaknesses in some areas of learning, I know how to intervene effectively.

1 2 3 4 5 10. I assist other teachers in my grade level in their efforts to differentiate for their gifted students.

CONTINUED > > >

Classroom Differentiation Opportunities, continued

Teacher Comments (Optional)

Please respond to any or all of the following:

1. What do you perceive to be the greatest benefits gifted students have experienced by having differentiated learning opportunities available in your classroom?

2. Describe your greatest frustration in trying to meet the learning needs of your gifted students.

3. Describe resources that could have helped you provide appropriate differentiation opportunities but have not been available.

4. Describe resources you have needed that *have* been available.

5. Describe the reactions from students who were not usually eligible for differentiated tasks.

6. Describe successful methods you used to provide a climate in your classroom in which learning diversity is accepted without resentment from students or parents.

7. Describe any way in which you would like parents to assist you toward meeting the goal of providing challenging learning opportunities for gifted students.

8. Describe ways in which the gifted mentor or gifted specialist could be more helpful to you.

Additional comments:

Classroom Differentiation Opportunities for Gifted Students

Parent/Guardian Assessment Survey

Information from this survey will be used to help the school provide the best possible differentiation opportunities—modifications of curriculum content, pace, process, products, and learning environment—for your child as part of the Schoolwide Cluster Grouping Model (SCGM). If more than one family adult wishes to respond, you may make a copy of the survey and return both at the same time. Thank you for taking the time to complete the survey.

Please return the form to ______________________________ on or before __________. There is no need to include your name, unless you would like a follow-up discussion with the teachers or other gifted-education staff. Please contact the gifted specialist or coordinator if you would like to talk about any issues related to the SCGM.

Survey Response Categories

5 = I strongly agree with this statement.
4 = I agree with this statement.
3 = I disagree with this statement.
2 = I strongly disagree with this statement.
1 = I have had no experience with this issue; this item does not apply to me.

Directions: Circle the number that represents your opinion about each statement.

1 2 3 4 5 — 1. My child has a positive attitude about the available differentiation opportunities in the classroom.

1 2 3 4 5 — 2. My child is willing to take the risks associated with engaging in challenging learning tasks.

1 2 3 4 5 — 3. My child does not perceive that other students resent the differentiated learning opportunities in which he/she has participated.

1 2 3 4 5 — 4. My child's areas of interest have been incorporated into his/her learning opportunities.

1 2 3 4 5 — 5. The teacher has recognized that my child has certain learning weaknesses and has helped my child become more competent in those areas.

1 2 3 4 5 — 6. I have been provided with enough information about how my child's learning program is being differentiated to provide for his/her advanced learning ability.

1 2 3 4 5 — 7. My child feels accepted by the teacher and other students for the type of learner he/she is.

CONTINUED > > >

Classroom Differentiation Opportunities for Gifted Students, continued

Comments (Optional)

Please respond to any or all of the following:

1. Describe what you perceive to be the greatest benefits your child has received by having compacting and differentiation opportunities available in the classroom.

2. Describe your child's favorite differentiated learning opportunity.

3. Describe an opportunity that you would have liked for your child that was not available this year.

4. Please describe any problems your child experienced because he/she was eligible for differentiated learning opportunities.

5. Describe any changes you would like to suggest regarding the classroom or school-based services that are available to provide challenging learning experiences for your child.

6. Describe any way in which you would be willing to assist your child's teachers or school in meeting the goal of providing challenging learning opportunities for your child.

Additional comments:

Classroom Differentiation Opportunities

Student Assessment Survey

Information from this survey will be used to help the school provide the best possible learning opportunities for you. You do not have to sign your name, so please be as truthful as you can.

Please return the form to ______________________________ on or before ____________.

Survey Response Categories

5 = I strongly agree with this statement.
4 = I agree with this statement.
3 = I disagree with this statement.
2 = I strongly disagree with this statement.
1 = I have had no experience with this issue; this statement does not apply to me.

Directions: Circle the number that represents your opinion about each statement.

1 2 3 4 5 — 1. I am aware that I have been allowed to move through grade-level schoolwork at a faster pace.

1 2 3 4 5 — 2. I am aware that I have been able to use school time to work on activities that allow me to explore certain topics in more depth.

1 2 3 4 5 — 3. I am happy that the teacher has made such opportunities available for me.

1 2 3 4 5 — 4. Other students do not seem upset that I have opportunities to do what is described in statements 1 and 2 above.

1 2 3 4 5 — 5. I have had time to work on topics that really interest me this year.

1 2 3 4 5 — 6. I have been able to find and use learning materials for my extension activities.

1 2 3 4 5 — 7. It is okay if people know there are some topics or areas of learning that do not come easily to me.

1 2 3 4 5 — 8. I feel it is safe for me to try to work on difficult tasks even though I have to work hard on them.

1 2 3 4 5 — 9. I realize that all kids have strengths in different areas, and that means that other students may be more capable in certain areas than I am.

Additional comments (optional):

A Note to Parents

This section contains helpful information about how you can use *The Cluster Grouping Handbook* to understand the Schoolwide Cluster Grouping Model (SCGM) and to advocate for your child's learning needs. Although the book speaks directly to educators, reading it can help you become familiar with the model and its potential benefits for all students.

National emphasis on state assessments requires that schools focus on raising achievement scores for all students. Therefore, educators must pay close attention to ensuring that all students meet proficiency levels. With this focus on striving to meet proficiency levels, attention to gifted students' learning needs has been minimized in many schools. The SCGM provides a way for schools to ensure that they are consistently challenging gifted students while also facilitating academic growth for all other students. In the SCGM, gifted-cluster teachers learn how to provide appropriately challenging learning opportunities to *all* students in the class, with an emphasis on their gifted students' distinctive learning needs. This practice allows gifted students to thrive in the model along with many students not formally identified as gifted.

In the SCGM, all gifted students at each grade level are placed together in small groups (clusters) in their home classrooms with students of other ability levels. Other students are purposefully placed in their home classrooms in a way that allows all students to achieve their maximum learning potential, including those students who are presently achieving below required proficiency levels. Classes are carefully balanced to reflect a slightly narrowed range of achievement levels, with high-ability or high-achieving students in each classroom. (See pages 15–26 to understand how students are placed in this model.)

If your school or district is implementing the SCGM, reading this book in whole or in part can familiarize you with how the model can support your child's learning. If the SCGM is not currently in place, reading the book can help you advocate for change. At a minimum, read the introduction and chapter 1 so you can understand how learning outcomes are realized through the model. Chapter 3 describes the learning characteristics of gifted students. Chapters 5 and 6 describe specific classroom intervention strategies teachers can use to challenge all learners. The other chapters explain how the SCGM provides academic benefits for all students and how the model can be implemented and supported most effectively.

Teachers who are trained in using effective instructional approaches for high-ability learners need parental support in their efforts. An important goal for cluster teachers is to teach children to appreciate engaging in rigorous learning opportunities. Students who understand that rigor is a necessary component of achievement are more likely to be highly productive throughout their schooling and lives. For gifted students, the greatest risk to lifetime achievement results from situations in which they consistently receive high grades and significant praise for learning outcomes that took little effort. With some students, this creates a reluctance to attempt any task that does not appear quickly and easily attainable. Many of these students face a rude awakening once they finally encounter truly challenging learning situations, such as when they start attending college. If they arrive at college having developed an appreciation for the benefits of working hard to learn, they are likely to be more successful college students.

Consider the following suggestions for motivating your gifted child to engage in rigorous and challenging learning opportunities:

- Research and understand your school's methods for identifying gifted students. If your child is identified as gifted, support the SCGM, since it is one of the only models that ensures your child will receive daily opportunities to work at her challenge level in school. Even if your child is not identified as gifted, know that the SCGM encourages teachers to offer experiences appropriate for identified gifted students to *all* students in the class.

- If you are the parent of a high-performing student who is very capable but has not been identified as gifted, you may be tempted to request that your child be placed in the same classroom with the cluster of gifted students. If your child is in one of the classes that does not have a cluster of gifted students, he is likely to have a greater opportunity to emerge as an academic leader in the class than he would if he were in the class with the identified gifted cluster, where his potential might be overlooked or where he may be less willing to attempt to step forward as a classroom leader.

- If your child is twice-exceptional (sometimes referred to as 2e)—identified as gifted with an individualized education program (IEP) qualifying her for special education services—be her advocate. Work with her teachers to ensure that they provide learning opportunities that foster her strengths and encourage her to develop interests. This approach also applies to English language learners (ELL students) and those with behavior challenges. All gifted-identified students are entitled to share in the same levels of learning opportunities. Follow these same principles at home: avoid taking away time from areas your child greatly enjoys or in which she excels in order to spend more time on her areas of learning challenge.

- Refrain from telling your child, "Always do your very best work." This may be an impossible task for a perfectionistic gifted child who feels driven to be the first and the best at all times. Instead, focus on the learning process, on the effort being expended, and on the excitement of learning and mastering new material.

- Support the teacher's efforts to provide pretests, learning contracts, lesson extensions, and opportunities for independent study. Don't worry about your child missing the direct instruction on the required grade-level standards. Students work on these alternate learning experiences only after they have demonstrated mastery of required standards. Additionally, students work on the lesson extensions while in the gifted-cluster classroom, where they are also exposed to the direct instruction of others. Insisting that your child always participates in direct instruction denies him the opportunity to learn with appropriately challenging materials.

- If your child's grades are not always perfect, recognize that learning at a challenging level does not immediately result in high grades. Remember that colleges do not ask for grades from the elementary or middle school years, which are the years when a true work ethic must be cultivated. Give your child the time and space she needs to develop that work ethic while pursuing her interests and building on her strengths. This is how real, meaningful learning takes place.

- If your child is working on alternate learning activities in class, he may have different homework than other students have—or he may have no homework at all. If you want your child to do some homework, use internet resources to help him find challenging work in almost any subject area. Visit the Hoagies' Gifted Education Page (www.hoagiesgifted.com) for helpful links to exciting work. This is a better option than simply asking the teacher for more busywork for your child. Children can lose motivation when they discover that the "reward" for finishing their work is more of the same work they have already mastered. Instead, allow children to pursue their interests through research, action, and outside resources. Then encourage teachers to embed the students' supplemental studies into their required school curriculum.

Educating gifted children is a team effort. Parents and teachers each have specific responsibilities in gifted children's education process. As a parent, you are an essential team member who can support your child's experience within the SCGM. We are confident that this model will provide consistently challenging and satisfying learning opportunities that help all children thrive.

Dina Brulles
Susan Winebrenner

References & Resources

Introduction

References

Brulles, Dina. 2005. "An Examination and Critical Analysis of Cluster Grouping Gifted Students in an Elementary School District," Ph.D. diss., Arizona State University.

Brulles, Dina, and Karen L. Brown. 2018. *A Teacher's Guide to Flexible Grouping and Collaborative Learning*. Minneapolis: Free Spirit Publishing.

Brulles, Dina, Scott J. Peters, and Rachel Saunders. 2012. "Schoolwide Mathematics Achievement within the Gifted Cluster Grouping Model." *Journal of Advanced Academics* 23 (3): 200–216.

Brulles, Dina, Rachel Saunders, and Sanford J. Cohn. 2010. "Improving Performance for Gifted Students in a Cluster Grouping Model." *Journal for the Education of the Gifted* 34 (2): 327–350. files.eric.ed.gov/fulltext/EJ910197.pdf.

Brulles, Dina, and Susan Winebrenner. 2011. "The Schoolwide Cluster Grouping Model: Restructuring Gifted Education Services for the 21st Century." *Gifted Child Today* 34 (4): 35–46.

Davidson Institute. "Tips for Teachers: Successful Strategies for Teaching Gifted Learners." Accessed May 13, 2019. www.davidsongifted.org/Search-Database/entry/A10075.

Gentry, Marcia Lynne. 1999. "Promoting Student Achievement and Exemplary Classroom Practices Through Cluster Grouping: A Research-Based Alternative to Heterogeneous Elementary Classrooms." Storrs, CT: National Research Center on the Gifted and Talented. RM99138. files.eric.ed.gov/fulltext/ED429389.pdf.

Gentry, Marcia, Mary G. Rizza, and Steven V. Owen. 2002. "Examining Perceptions of Challenge and Choice in Classrooms: The Relationship Between Teachers and Their Students and Comparisons Between Gifted Students and Other Students." *Gifted Child Quarterly* 46 (2): 145–155.

Kulik, James A., and Chen-Lin C. Kulik. 1990. "Ability Grouping and Gifted Students." In *Handbook of Gifted Education*, edited by Nicholas Colangelo and Gary A. Davis, 178–196. Boston: Allyn & Bacon.

Pierce, Rebecca L., Jerrell C. Cassady, Cheryll M. Adams, Kristie L. Speirs Neumeister, Felicia A. Dixon, and Tracy L. Cross. 2011. "The Effects of Clustering and Curriculum on the Development of Gifted Learners' Math Achievement." *Journal for the Education of the Gifted* 34 (4): 569–594.

Plucker, Jonathan. 2015. "Research to Support Advocacy for High-Achieving Students." *Iowa Talented and Gifted Association News Magazine* 40 (2): 4–8. www.iowatag.org/wp-content/uploads/2013/01/2015SpringSummeritagnews.pdf.

Rogers, Karen B. 2002. *Re-Forming Gifted Education: Matching the Program to the Child.* Scottsdale, AZ: Great Potential Press.

Winebrenner, Susan, and Barbara Devlin. 2001. "Cluster Grouping of Gifted Students: How to Provide Full-Time Services on a Part-Time Budget." ERIC Digest E607, ERIC #451663. files.eric.ed.gov/fulltext/ED451663.pdf.

Chapter 1

References

Brulles, Dina. 2005. "An Examination and Critical Analysis of Cluster Grouping Gifted Students in an Elementary School District," Ph.D. diss., Arizona State University.

Brulles, Dina, and Karen L. Brown. 2018. *A Teacher's Guide to Flexible Grouping and Collaborative Learning.* Minneapolis: Free Spirit Publishing.

Brulles, Dina, Scott J. Peters, and Rachel Saunders. 2012. "Schoolwide Mathematics Achievement within the Gifted Cluster Grouping Model." *Journal of Advanced Academics* 23 (3): 200–216.

Brulles, Dina, Rachel Saunders, and Sanford J. Cohn. 2010. "Improving Performance for Gifted Students in a Cluster Grouping Model." *Journal for the Education of the Gifted* 34 (2): 327–350. files.eric.ed.gov/fulltext/EJ910197.pdf.

Brulles, Dina, and Susan Winebrenner. 2011. "The Schoolwide Cluster Grouping Model: Restructuring Gifted Education Services for the 21st Century." *Gifted Child Today* 34 (4): 35–46.

Feldhusen, John F. 1989. "Synthesis of Research on Gifted Youth." *Educational Leadership* 46 (6): 6–11. www.ascd.org/ASCD/pdf/journals/ed_lead/el_198903_feldhusen.pdf.

Fiedler, Ellen D., Richard E. Lange, and Susan Winebrenner. 2002. "In Search of Reality: Unraveling the Myths About Tracking, Ability Grouping, and the Gifted." *Roeper Review* 24 (3): 108–111.

Gentry, Marcia. 2006. "No Child Left Behind: Neglecting Excellence." *Roeper Review* 29 (1): 24–28.

Gentry, Marcia Lynne. 1999. "Promoting Student Achievement and Exemplary Classroom Practices Through Cluster Grouping: A Research-Based Alternative to Heterogeneous Elementary Classrooms." Storrs, CT: National Research Center on the Gifted and Talented. RM99138. files.eric.ed.gov/fulltext/ED429389.pdf.

Gentry, Marcia, and Jamie MacDougall. 2009. "Total School Cluster Grouping: Model, Research, and Practice." In *Systems and Models for Developing Programs for the Gifted and Talented,* edited by Joseph S. Renzulli, E. Jean Gubbins, Kristin S. McMillen, Rebecca D. Eckert, and Catherine A. Little, 211–234. Waco, TX: Prufrock Press.

Gentry, Marcia, Mary G. Rizza, and Steven V. Owen. 2002. "Examining Perceptions of Challenge and Choice in Classrooms: The Relationship Between Teachers and Their Students and Comparisons Between Gifted Students and Other Students." *Gifted Child Quarterly* 46 (2): 145–155.

Kulik, James A., and Chen-Lin C. Kulik. 1990. "Ability Grouping and Gifted Students." In *Handbook of Gifted Education,* edited by Nicholas Colangelo and Gary A. Davis, 178–196. Boston: Allyn & Bacon.

Rogers, Karen B. 2002. *Re-Forming Gifted Education: Matching the Program to the Child.* Scottsdale, AZ: Great Potential Press.

Saunders, Rachel. 2005. "A Comparison Study of the Academic Effect of Ability Grouping versus Heterogeneous Grouping in Mathematics Instruction," Ph.D. diss., Arizona State University.

Schunk, Dale H. 1987. "Peer Models and Children's Behavioral Change." *Review of Educational Research* 57 (2): 149–174.

Winebrenner, Susan, and Barbara Devlin. 2001. "Cluster Grouping of Gifted Students: How to Provide Full-Time Services on a Part-Time Budget." ERIC Digest E607, ERIC #451663. files.eric.ed.gov/fulltext/ED451663.pdf.

Resources

Assouline, Susan, Nicholas Colangelo, Ann Lupkowski-Shoplik, Jonathan Lipscomb, and Leslie Forstadt. 2009. *Iowa Acceleration Scale Manual: A Guide for Whole-Grade Acceleration K–8.* Scottsdale, AZ: Great Potential Press.

Brulles, Dina, and Karen L. Brown. 2018. *A Teacher's Guide to Flexible Grouping and Collaborative Learning.* Minneapolis: Free Spirit Publishing.

Gentry, Marcia, and Bill Keilty. 2004. "Rural and Suburban Cluster Grouping: Reflections on Staff Development as a Component of Program Success." *Roeper Review* 26 (3): 147–155.

Johnsen, Susan K, ed. 2012. *NAGC Pre-K–Grade 12 Gifted Education Programming Standards: A Guide to Planning and Implementing High-Quality Services.* Waco, TX: Prufrock Press.

Kulik, James A. 2003. "Grouping and Tracking." In *Handbook of Gifted Education,* third edition, edited by Nicholas Colangelo and Gary A. Davis, 268–281. Boston: Allyn & Bacon.

Kulik, James A., and Chen-Lin C. Kulik. 1997. "Ability Grouping." In *Handbook of Gifted Education,* second edition, edited by Nicholas Colangelo and Gary A. Davis, 230–242. Boston: Allyn & Bacon.

National Association for Gifted Children (NAGC). www.nagc.org.

Peters, Scott J., and Dina Brulles. 2017. *Designing Gifted Education Programs and Services: From Purpose to Implementation.* Waco, TX: Prufrock Press.

Peters, Scott J., Michael S. Matthews, Matthew T. McBee, and Betsy McCoach. 2014. *Beyond Gifted Education: Designing and Implementing Advanced Academic Programs.* Waco, TX: Prufrock Press.

Plucker, Jonathan A., and Carolyn M. Callahan, eds. 2014. *Critical Issues and Practices in Gifted Education: What the Research Says.* Waco, TX: Prufrock Press.

Roberts, Julia Link, and Julia Roberts Boggess. 2011. *Teacher's Survival Guide: Gifted Education.* Waco, TX: Prufrock Press.

Rogers, Karen B. 2006. *A Menu of Options for Grouping Gifted Students.* Waco, TX: Prufrock Press.

Ruf, Deborah L. 2005. *Losing Our Minds: Gifted Children Left Behind.* Scottsdale, AZ: Great Potential Press.

Swiatek, Mary Ann. 2001. "Ability Grouping: Answers to Common Questions." *C-MITES News,* Spring. Carnegie Mellon Institute for Talented Elementary and Secondary Students.

Teno, Kevin M. 2000. "Cluster Grouping Elementary Gifted Students in the Regular Classroom: A Teacher's Perspective." *Gifted Child Today* 23 (1): 44–53.

Tieso, Carol L. 2003. "Ability Grouping Is Not Just Tracking Anymore." *Roeper Review* 26 (1): 29–36.

Chapter 2

References

Clark, Barbara. *Growing Up Gifted: Developing the Potential of Children at Home and at School.* Upper Saddle River, NJ: Prentice Hall, 2013.

Resources

Eckert, Rebecca D., and Jennifer H. Robins, eds. 2017. *Designing Services and Programs for High-Ability Learners: A Guidebook for Gifted Education.* Thousand Oaks, CA: Corwin Press.

Gardner, Howard. 2011. "Intelligence, Creativity, Ethics: Reflections on My Evolving Research Interests." *Gifted Child Quarterly* 55 (4): 302–304.

Novak, Angela M., and Christine L. Weber, eds. 2018. *Best Practices in Professional Learning and Teacher Preparation: Methods and Strategies for Gifted Professional Development.* Waco, TX: Prufrock Press.

Peters, Scott J., and Dina Brulles. 2017. *Designing Gifted Education Programs and Services: From Purpose to Implementation.* Waco, Tx: Prufrock Press.

Pfeiffer, Steven I. 2015. *Essentials of Gifted Assessment.* Hoboken, NJ: Wiley Publishing.

Chapter 3

References

Delisle, Jim, and Barbara A. Lewis. 2003. *The Survival Guide for Teachers of Gifted Kids.* Minneapolis: Free Spirit Publishing.

Galbraith, Judy, and Jim Delisle. 2015. *When Gifted Kids Don't Have All the Answers: How to Meet Their Social and Emotional Needs.* Minneapolis: Free Spirit Publishing.

Greenspon, Thomas S. 2012. *Moving Past Perfect: How Perfectionism May Be Holding Back Your Kids (and You!) and What You Can Do About It.* Minneapolis: Free Spirit Publishing.

National Association for Gifted Children (NAGC). "What Is Giftedness?" Accessed May 13, 2019. www.nagc.org/resources-publications/resources/what-giftedness.

Webb, James T., and Diane Latimer. 1993. "ADHD and Children Who Are Gifted." ERIC Digest E522, July, ERIC #358673.

Willard-Holt, Colleen. 1999. "Dual Exceptionalities." ERIC Digest E574, April, ERIC #430344.

Resources for Educators

Bronson, Po. 2007. "How Not to Talk to Your Kids." *New York*, February 17. nymag.com/news/features/27840.

Brown, Scott W., Joseph S. Renzulli, E. Jean Gubbins, Del Siegle, Wanli Zhang, and Ching-Hui Chen. 2005. "Assumptions Underlying the Identification of Gifted and Talented Students." *Gifted Child Quarterly* 49 (1): 68–79.

Castellano, Jaime A., and Andrea Dawn Frazier, eds. 2011. *Special Populations in Gifted Education: Understanding Our Most Able Students from Diverse Backgrounds.* Waco, TX: Prufrock Press.

Clark, Barbara. 2013. *Growing Up Gifted: Developing the Potential of Children at School and at Home.* Upper Saddle River, NJ: Prentice Hall.

Cross, Tracy L., Kristie L. Speirs Neumeister, and Jerrell C. Cassady. 2007. "Psychological Types of Academically Gifted Adolescents." *Gifted Child Quarterly,* 51 (3): 285–294.

Delisle, Jim, and Barbara A. Lewis. 2003. *The Survival Guide for Teachers of Gifted Kids.* Minneapolis: Free Spirit Publishing.

Gardner, Howard. 2011. "Intelligence, Creativity, Ethics: Reflections on My Evolving Research Interests." *Gifted Child Quarterly* 55 (4): 302–304.

Kay, Kiesa, ed. 2000. *Uniquely Gifted: Identifying and Meeting the Needs of the Twice-Exceptional Student.* Gilsum, NH: Avocus Publishing.

Kingore, Bertie. 2007. *Recognizing Gifted Potential: Planned Experiences with the KOI.* Austin, TX: Professional Associates Publishing.

Kingore, Bertie. 2016. *The Kingore Observation Inventory.* Austin, TX: Professional Associates Publishing.

Nielsen, M. Elizabeth, and L. Dennis Higgins. 2005. "The Eye of the Storm: Services and Programs for Twice-Exceptional Learners." *Teaching Exceptional Children* 38 (1): 8–15.

Rimm, Sylvia. 2006. *When Gifted Students Underachieve: What You Can Do About It.* Waco, TX: Prufrock Press.

Sousa, David A. 2017. *How the Brain Learns.* Thousand Oaks, CA: Corwin Press.

Webb, James T., Edward R. Amend, Paul Beljan, Nadia E. Webb, Marianne Kuzujanakis, F. Richard Olenchak, and Jean Goerss. 2016. *Misdiagnosis and Dual Diagnoses of Gifted Children and Adults: ADHD, Bipolar, OCD, Asperger's, Depression, and Other Disorders.* Scottsdale, AZ: Great Potential Press.

Weinfeld, Rich, Linda Barnes-Robinson, Sue Jeweler, and Betty Roffman Shevitz. 2013. *Smart Kids with Learning Difficulties: Overcoming Obstacles and Realizing Potential.* Waco, TX: Prufrock Press.

Resources for Parents

Bronson, Po. 2007. "How Not to Talk to Your Kids." *New York,* February 17. nymag.com/news/features/27840.

Delisle, James R. 2006. *Parenting Gifted Kids: Tips for Raising Happy and Successful Children.* Waco, TX: Prufrock Press.

DeVries, Arlene R., and James T. Webb. 2007. *Gifted Parent Groups: The SENG Model.* Scottsdale, AZ: Great Potential Press.

Galbraith, Judy. 2013. *The Survival Guide for Gifted Kids: For Ages 10 and Under.* Minneapolis: Free Spirit Publishing.

Galbraith, Judy, and Jim Delisle. 2011. *The Gifted Teen Survival Guide: Smart, Sharp, and Ready for (Almost) Anything.* Minneapolis: Free Spirit Publishing.

Greenspon, Thomas S. 2007. *What to Do When Good Enough Isn't Good Enough: The Real Deal on Perfectionism.* Minneapolis: Free Spirit Publishing.

Kerr, Barbara A., and Robin McKay. 2014. *Smart Girls in the 21st Century: Understanding Talented Girls and Women.* Tucson, AZ: Great Potential Press.

National Association for Gifted Children (NAGC). www.nagc.org.

Olszewski-Kubilius, Paula, Lisa Limburg-Weber, and Steven Pfeiffer, eds. 2003. *Early Gifts: Recognizing and Nurturing Children's Talents.* Waco, TX: Prufrock Press.

Rimm, Sylvia B. 2007. *Keys to Parenting the Gifted Child,* Scottsdale, AZ: Great Potential Press.

2e Twice-Exceptional Newsletter. www.2enewsletter.com.

Walker, Sally Yahnke. 2002. *The Survival Guide for Parents of Gifted Kids.* Minneapolis: Free Spirit Publishing.

Tests for Identification

*Cognitive Abilities Test (CogAT) Form 7.*** Grades K–12. Group-administered ability test battery used to assess students' reasoning abilities in three areas: verbal, quantitative, and nonverbal. The test is well suited for helping make placements in gifted programs. No special training is needed by the examiner. Administration time: 30–60 minutes per session, depending on the test level.

*Das-Naglieri Cognitive Assessment System (CAS).** Ages 5–17. Individually administered cognitive-processing measure of ability that is fair to minority children, effective for differential diagnosis, and related to intervention. Measures planning, attention, simultaneous, and successive processes. Administration time: 40 minutes for the Basic Battery, 60 minutes for the Standard Battery.

*Differential Ability Scales-II (DAS-II).** Ages 2–17. Individually administered test battery intended to measure cognitive and achievement levels for children for classification and diagnostic purposes. Measures verbal, quantitative, and nonverbal abilities. Administration time: 45–65 minutes.

Kaufman Test of Educational Achievement, Third Edition (KTEA-3). Ages 4–25. Individually administered test designed to measure school achievement. Can be administered in the Brief or Comprehensive Form. Measures achievement in the areas of reading, mathematics, and spelling. Administration time: 45–90 minutes.

*Naglieri Nonverbal Ability Test (NNAT), Multilevel Form.** ** Grades K–12. A nonverbal group-administered measure of reasoning and problem-solving that is ideal for students with limited English proficiency. The *NNAT* is a culture-fair measure of ability for evaluating students. No special training is needed by the examiner. Administration time: approximately 45 minutes.

*Naglieri Nonverbal Ability Test—Third Edition (NNAT3).** ** Grades K–12. Group-administered test that uses progressive matrices to allow for a culturally neutral evaluation of students' nonverbal reasoning and general problem-solving ability, regardless of the individual student's primary language, education, culture, or socioeconomic background. The *NNAT3* is also available as an online assessment, which allows for automated capture and real-time scoring and reporting. Administration time: 30 minutes.

*Otis-Lennon School Ability Test, 8th Edition (OLSAT 8).** Grades K–12. Group-administered test that assesses students' thinking skills and relative strengths and weaknesses in performing reasoning tasks. Measures verbal and nonverbal abilities. No special training is needed by the examiner. Administration time: 60–75 minutes.

* Indicates tests that are suited to special populations.

** Accommodations are identified for use with students who have disabilities and language differences.

*Stanford-Binet Intelligence Scales, 5th Edition (SB-5).** Ages 2–85+. Individually administered assessment of intelligence and cognitive abilities that measures fluid reasoning, knowledge, quantitative reasoning, spatial processing, and working memory. Used in the diagnosis of learning disabilities and developmental cognitive delays in young children and for placement in academic programs for the intellectually gifted. Administration time: 45–90 minutes.

Universal Nonverbal Intelligence Test—Second Edition (UNIT2). Ages 5–21. A set of individually administered specialized tasks that measure cognitive abilities. Both administration and item response formats are completely nonverbal. Tests measure a broad range of complex reasoning abilities. Because physical manipulation of test materials is required, the *UNIT* may be of limited use for children with fine-motor impairment. Administration time: 45+ minutes.

Wechsler Individual Achievement Test, 3rd Edition (WIAT-III). Ages 4–50. Individually administered test designed to assess individual achievement. A comprehensive yet flexible measurement tool useful for achievement skills assessment, learning disability diagnosis, special education placement, curriculum planning, and clinical appraisal. Administration time: 35–104 minutes.

*Wechsler Intelligence Scale for Children, 5th Edition (WISC-V).** Ages 6–16. Individually administered test that provides subtest and composite scores representing intellectual functioning in general and specific cognitive abilities. The test can be used for identifying the areas of verbal and nonverbal abilities. Administered by a psychologist. Administration time: 60 minutes with most children.

*Woodcock-Johnson IV Tests of Cognitive Abilities (WJ-IV-COG).** Ages 2–90+. Individually administered test that is designed to measure general and specific cognitive functions. The test can be used as a diagnostic tool to help identify specific strengths and weaknesses and can be used to determine verbal, quantitative, and nonverbal abilities. Administration time: 90–120 minutes.

Chapter 4
References and Resources

Gentry, Marcia, Mary G. Rizza, and Steven V. Owen. 2002. "Examining Perceptions of Challenge and Choice in Classrooms: The Relationship Between Teachers and Their Students and Comparisons Between Gifted Students and Other Students." *Gifted Child Quarterly* 46 (2): 145–155.

Gosfield, Margaret Wayne, ed. 2008. *Expert Approaches to Support Gifted Learners: Professional Perspectives, Best Practices, and Positive Solutions.* Minneapolis: Free Spirit Publishing.

Journal for the Education of the Gifted. cectag.com/resources/journal-for-the-education-of-the-gifted.

Schunk, Dale H. 1987. "Peer Models and Children's Behavioral Change." *Review of Educational Research* 57 (2): 149–174.

Teaching for High Potential. www.nagc.org/resources-publications/nagc-publications/teaching-high-potential.

Chapter 5
References and Resources

See also references and resources for chapter 6.

Assouline, Susan G., and Ann Lupkowski-Shoplik. 2011. *Developing Math Talent: A Comprehensive Guide to Math Education for Gifted Students in Elementary and Middle School.* Waco, TX: Prufrock Press.

* Indicates tests that are suited to special populations.

** Accommodations are identified for use with students who have disabilities and language differences.

Assouline, Susan, Nicholas Colangelo, Ann Lupkowski-Shoplik, Jonathan Lipscomb, and Leslie Forstadt. 2009. *Iowa Acceleration Scale Manual: A Guide for Whole-Grade Acceleration K–8.* Scottsdale, AZ: Great Potential Press.

Assouline, Susan G., Nicholas Colangelo, Joyce VanTassel-Baska, and Ann Lupkowski-Shoplik, eds. 2015. *A Nation Empowered: Evidence Trumps the Excuses Holding Back America's Brightest Students.* Iowa City: Belin-Blank Center.

Brulles, Dina, and Karen L. Brown. 2018. *A Teacher's Guide to Flexible Grouping and Collaborative Learning.* Minneapolis: Free Spirit Publishing.

Colangelo, Nicholas, Susan G. Assouline, and Miraca U. M. Gross, eds. 2004. "A Nation Deceived: How Schools Hold Back America's Brightest Students." West Conshohocken, PA: John Templeton Foundation. www.acceleration institute.org/nation_deceived.

Karnes, Frances A., and Suzanne M. Bean, eds. 2015. *Methods and Materials for Teaching the Gifted.* Waco, TX: Prufrock Press.

Reis, Sally M., Joseph S. Renzulli, and Deborah E. Burns. 2016. *Curriculum Compacting: A Guide to Differentiating Curriculum and Instruction Through Enrichment and Acceleration.* Waco, TX: Prufrock Press.

Roberts, Julia L., and Tracy F. Inman. 2015. *Strategies for Differentiating Instruction: Best Practices for the Classroom.* Waco, TX: Prufrock Press.

Robinson, Ann, Bruce Shore, and Donna L. Enersen. 2007. *Best Practices in Gifted Education: An Evidence-Based Guide.* Waco, TX: Prufrock Press.

Rogers, Karen B. 2007. "Lessons Learned About Educating the Gifted and Talented: A Synthesis of the Research on Educational Practice." *Gifted Child Quarterly* 51 (4): 382–396.

Smutny, Joan Franklin, and S. E. von Fremd. 2010. *Differentiating for the Young Child: Teaching Strategies Across the Content Areas, PreK–3.* Thousand Oaks, CA: Corwin Press.

Smutny, Joan Franklin, Sally Y. Walker, and Elizabeth A. Meckstroth. 2007. *Acceleration for Gifted Learners, K–5.* Thousand Oaks, CA: Corwin Press.

Sousa, David A., and Carol Ann Tomlinson. 2011. *Differentiation and the Brain: How Neuroscience Supports the Learner-Friendly Classroom.* Bloomington, IN: Solution Tree Press.

Tomlinson, Carol Ann. 2017. *How to Differentiate Instruction in Academically Diverse Classrooms.* Alexandria, VA: ASCD.

Winebrenner, Susan, with Dina Brulles. 2018. *Teaching Gifted Kids in Today's Classroom.* Minneapolis: Free Spirit Publishing.

Zaccaro, Edward. 2003. *Primary Grade Challenge Math.* Bellevue, IA: Hickory Grove Press.

Zaccaro, Edward. 2005. *Challenge Math for the Elementary and Middle School Student.* Bellevue, IA: Hickory Grove Press.

Chapter 6
References and Resources

See also references and resources for chapter 5.

Burns, Deborah E., Jann Leppien, Stuart Omdal, E. Jean Gubbins, Lisa Muller, and Siamak Vahidi. 2006. *Teachers' Guide for the Explicit Teaching of Thinking Skills.* Storrs, CT: National Research Center on the Gifted and Talented, RM06218.

Cannaday, Jessica. 2018. *Curriculum Development for Gifted Education Programs.* Hershey, PA: IGI Global.

Fisher, Douglas, and Nancy Frey. 2014. *Checking for Understanding: Formative Assessment Techniques for Your Classroom.* Alexandria, VA: ASCD.

Heacox, Diane. 2012. *Differentiating Instruction in the Regular Classroom: How to Reach and Teach All Learners.* Minneapolis: Free Spirit Publishing.

Kingore, Bertie. 2007. *Reaching All Learners: Making Differentiation Work*. Austin, TX: Professional Associates Publishing.

Lavoie, Richard D. "Fairness: To Each According to His Needs." Accessed May 13, 2019. www.rick lavoie.com/fairnessart.html.

Lyman, Frank. 2005 and 2003. "ThinkTrix SmartCard" and "Think-Pair-Share SmartCard." www.kaganonline.com.

MacFarlane, Bronwyn, ed. 2016. *STEM Education for High-Ability Learners: Designing and Implementing Programming*. Waco, TX: Prufrock Press.

Marzano, Robert J. 2000. *Transforming Classroom Grading*. Alexandria, VA: ASCD.

Renzulli Learning. www.renzullilearning.com.

Smutny, Joan Franklin, Sally Yahnke Walker, and Ellen I. Honeck. 2016. *Teaching Gifted Children in Today's Preschool and Primary Classrooms.* Minneapolis: Free Spirit Publishing.

Tallent-Runnels, Mary K., and Ann C. Candler-Lotven. 2008. *Academic Competitions for Gifted Students: A Resource Book for Teachers and Parents*. Thousand Oaks, CA: Corwin Press.

VanTassel-Baska, Joyce, and Tamra Stambaugh. 2006. *Comprehensive Curriculum for Gifted Learners*. Upper Saddle River, NJ: Allyn & Bacon.

Winebrenner, Susan, with Lisa Kiss. 2014. *Teaching Kids with Learning Difficulties in Today's Classroom*. Minneapolis: Free Spirit Publishing.

Wormeli, Rick. 2018. *Fair Isn't Always Equal: Assessment and Grading in the Differentiated Classroom*. Portland, ME: Stenhouse Publishers.

Catalogs and Online Resources

Center for Creative Learning. www.creative learning.com.

The Curriculum Project. www.curriculumproject .com. 800-867-9067.

Engine-uity. www.engine-uity.com.

Free Spirit Publishing. freespirit.com. 800-735-7323.

Greenhaven Publishing. greenhavenpublishing .com. 844-317-7404.

Hoagies' Gifted Education Page. www.hoagies gifted.com.

Magination Press. www.apa.org/pubs/magination. 800-374-2721.

McGraw-Hill Education. www.mheducation.com. 800-334-7344.

Pieces of Learning. www.piecesoflearning.com. 800-729-5137.

Professional Associates Publishing. www.professionalassociatespublishing.com.

Prufrock Press. www.prufrock.com. 800-998-2208.

Zephyr Press. www.chicagoreviewpress.com /zephyr-press-pages-472.php. 800-888-4741.

Project-Based Learning Resources

Edutopia. www.edutopia.org.

McNair, Andi. 2017. *Genius Hour: Passion Projects that Ignite Innovation and Student Inquiry*. Waco, TX: Prufrock Press.

McREL International. www.mcrel.org.

Project Based Learning. pblchecklist.4teachers.org.

Teacher Planet: Rubrics for Teachers. www.teacher planet.com/rubrics-for-teachers.

Resources for Critical and Creative Thinking

The Critical Thinking Co. www.criticalthinking .com. 800-458-4849.

Discovery Education. www.discoveryeducation.com.

The Stock Market Game (SMG). www.smgww.org.

Thinking Maps, Inc. www.thinkingmaps.com.

Torrance Center for Creativity and Talent Development. coe.uga.edu/directory/units /torrance-center.

Programs for Student Teams

Future Problem Solving Program International (FPSPI). www.fpspi.org.

Odyssey of the Mind. www.odysseyofthemind.com.

Chapter 7

References

Center for Comprehensive School Reform and Improvement. 2007. "Maximizing the Impact of Teacher Collaboration." *Center for Comprehensive School Reform and Improvement Newsletter*, March. files.eric.ed.gov/fulltext/ED497212.pdf.

Gubbins, E. Jean, Karen L. Westberg, Sally M. Reis, Susan T. Dinnocenti, Carol L. Tieso, Lisa M. Muller, Sunghee Park, Linda J. Emerick, Lori R. Maxfield, and Deborah E. Burns. 2002. "Implementing a Professional Development Model Using Gifted Education Strategies with All Students." Storrs, CT: National Research Center on the Gifted and Talented, RM02172. files.eric.ed.gov/fulltext/ED481293.pdf.

Hargreaves, Andy, and Michael Fullan. 2000. "Mentoring in the New Millennium." *Theory Into Practice* 39 (1): 50–56.

Hord, Shirley M. 1994. "Staff Development and Change Process: Cut from the Same Cloth." *Issues . . . About Change* 4 (3). www.sedl.org/change/issues/issues42.html.

Joyce, Bruce R., and Beverly Showers. 2002. *Student Achievement Through Staff Development.* Alexandria, VA: ASCD.

Kohler, Frank W., Helen K. Ezell, and Maria Paluselli. 1999. "Promoting Changes in Teachers' Conduct of Student Pair Activities: An Examination of Reciprocal Peer Coaching." *Journal of Special Education* 33 (3): 154–165.

Peters, Scott J., and Dina Brulles. 2017. *Designing Gifted Education Programs and Services: From Purpose to Implementation.* Waco, TX: Prufrock Press.

Sparks, Dennis. 2002. *Designing Powerful Professional Development for Teachers and Principals.* Oxford, OH: National Staff Development Council.

Resources

Gentry, Marcia, and Bill Keilty. 2004. "Rural and Suburban Cluster Grouping: Reflections on Staff Development as a Component of Program Success." *Roeper Review* 26 (3): 147–155.

Isaacson, Karen, and Tamara Fisher. 2007. *Intelligent Life in the Classroom: Smart Kids and Their Teachers.* Scottsdale, AZ: Great Potential Press.

Johnson, Nanci W. 2005. "Peer Coaching: A Collegial Support for Bridging the Research to Practice Gap." Ph.D. diss., University of Missouri-Columbia.

Learning Forward. "Standards for Professional Learning." Accessed May 13, 2019. learningforward.org/standards-for-professional-learning.

Novak, Angela M., and Christine L. Weber, eds. 2018. *Best Practices in Professional Learning and Teacher Preparation: Methods and Strategies for Gifted Professional Development.* Waco, TX: Prufrock Press.

Tomlinson, Carol Ann. 2014. *The Differentiated Classroom: Responding to the Needs of All Learners.* Alexandria, VA: ASCD.

Winebrenner, Susan, and Dina Brulles. 2012. *Teaching Gifted Kids in Today's Classroom Professional Development Multimedia Package.* Minneapolis: Free Spirit Publishing.

Books for Book Study Groups

The following resources are suggested for book study group topics regarding understanding and teaching gifted kids, identifying gifted students, and implementing effective differentiation strategies.

Baum, Susan M., Robin M. Schader, and Steven V. Owen. 2017. *To Be Gifted and Learning Disabled: Strength-Based Strategies for Helping Twice-Exceptional Students with LD, ADHD, ASD, and More.* Waco, TX: Prufrock Press.

Brulles, Dina, and Karen L. Brown. 2018. *A Teacher's Guide to Flexible Grouping and Collaborative Learning.* Minneapolis: Free Spirit Publishing.

Castellano, Jaime A., and Andrea Dawn Frazier, eds. 2011. *Special Populations in Gifted Education: Understanding Our Most Able Students from Diverse Backgrounds.* Waco, TX: Prufrock Press.

Coil, Carolyn. 2004. *Becoming an Achiever.* Marion, IL: Pieces of Learning.

Galbraith, Judy, and Jim Delisle. 2015. *When Gifted Kids Don't Have All the Answers: How to Meet Their Social and Emotional Needs.* Minneapolis: Free Spirit Publishing.

Heacox, Diane. 2012. *Differentiating Instruction in the Regular Classroom: How to Reach and Teach All Learners.* Minneapolis: Free Spirit Publishing.

Kingore, Bertie. 2017. *Recognizing Gifted Potential: Planned Experiences with the KOI.* Austin, TX: Professional Associates Publishing.

Rimm, Sylvia. 2006. *When Gifted Students Underachieve: What You Can Do About It.* Waco, TX: Prufrock Press.

Rogers, Karen B. 2002. *Re-Forming Gifted Education: Matching the Program to the Child.* Scottsdale, AZ: Great Potential Press.

Smutny, Joan Franklin, Sally Y. Walker, and Elizabeth A. Meckstroth. 2007. *Acceleration for Gifted Learners, K–5.* Thousand Oaks, CA: Corwin Press.

Smutny, Joan Franklin, Sally Yahnke Walker, and Ellen I. Honeck. 2016. *Teaching Gifted Children in Today's Preschool and Primary Classrooms: Identifying, Nurturing, and Challenging Children Ages 4–9.* Minneapolis: Free Spirit Publishing.

Tomlinson, Carol Ann, and Jay McTighe. 2006. *Integrating Differentiated Instruction and Understanding by Design: Connecting Content and Kids.* Alexandria, VA: ASCD.

Winebrenner, Susan, with Dina Brulles. 2012. *Teaching Gifted Kids in Today's Classroom: Strategies and Techniques Every Teacher Can Use.* Minneapolis: Free Spirit Publishing.

Chapter 8

References

Brulles, Dina. 2005. "An Examination and Critical Analysis of Cluster Grouping Gifted Students in an Elementary School District." Ph.D. diss., Arizona State University.

Brulles, Dina, Scott J. Peters, and Rachel Saunders. 2012. "Schoolwide Mathematics Achievement within the Gifted Cluster Grouping Model," *Journal of Advanced Academics* 23 (3): 200–216.

Brulles, Dina, Rachel Saunders, and Sanford J. Cohn. 2010. "Improving Performance for Gifted Students in a Cluster Grouping Model." *Journal for the Education of the Gifted* 34 (2): 327–350. files.eric.ed.gov/fulltext/EJ910197.pdf.

Gentry, Marcia Lynne. 1999. "Promoting Student Achievement and Exemplary Classroom Practices Through Cluster Grouping: A Research-Based Alternative to Heterogeneous Elementary Classrooms." Storrs, CT: National Research Center on the Gifted and Talented. RM99138. files.eric.ed.gov/fulltext/ED429389.pdf.

Gentry, Marcia, and Jamie MacDougall. 2009. "Total School Cluster Grouping: Model, Research, and Practice." In *Systems and Models for Developing Programs for the Gifted and Talented,* edited by Joseph S. Renzulli, E. Jean Gubbins, Kristin S. McMillen, Rebecca D. Eckert, and Catherine A. Little, 211–234. Waco, TX: Prufrock Press.

Gentry, Marcia L., and Steven V. Owen. 1999. "An Investigation of the Effects of Total School Flexible Cluster Grouping on Identification, Achievement, and Classroom Practices." *Gifted Child Quarterly* 43 (4): 224–243.

Resources

Callahan, Carolyn M., ed. 2004. *Program Evaluation in Gifted Education.* Thousand Oaks, CA: Corwin Press.

Callahan, Carolyn M. 2006. *Assessment in the Classroom: The Key to Good Instruction.* Waco, TX: Prufrock Press.

Hunsaker, Scott L. 2000. "Documenting Gifted Program Results for Key Decision-Makers." *Roeper Review* 23 (2): 80–82.

Kingore, Bertie. 2007. *Assessment: Timesaving Procedures for Busy Teachers.* Austin, TX: Professional Associates Publishing.

Neumeister, Kristie Speirs, and Virginia Hays Burney. 2019. *Gifted Program Evaluation: A Handbook for Administrators and Coordinators.* Waco, TX: Prufrock Press.

NWEA (Northwest Evaluation Association). www.nwea.org.

Glossary

2e (twice-exceptional) student: Student identified as gifted who also has a diagnosis of a learning challenge such as ADHD, autism, or a learning disability.

ability grouping: Grouping together students of similar ability to modify the pace, instruction, and curriculum. Students can be ability grouped for specific subjects, within or between classes, for a lesson, for a unit, for part of the day, or throughout the day.

ability test: Test that measures a student's potential and capability to learn.

acceleration: Moving students forward in a particular subject or topic of study at a rate faster than that of grade-level peers. In some cases, students experience acceleration by moving into a higher grade level for instruction in a particular subject or for full-time placement.

achievement: Student performance; the extent to which students demonstrate they have learned assigned content standards or curriculum.

achievement test: Test that measures what a student has already learned. An achievement test gauges the extent to which students have acquired knowledge of specific information.

action research: Teachers' systematic and careful examination of their own educational practice using research techniques. With action research, teachers conduct a qualitative in-class study of the effectiveness of a specific teaching strategy or learning program. Based on the results, teachers decide whether to continue using the strategy.

assessment: Means of determining what a student knows or has learned. Assessments are usually formal tests but may include performance-based measures.

attention deficit hyperactivity disorder (ADHD): Neurological condition characterized by distractibility, inattentiveness to tasks, inconsistent performance in schoolwork, and/or hyperactivity.

collegial peer coaching: Mutual support among faculty who are all learning to apply new teaching approaches. Successful collegial peer coaching includes a long-term plan through which teachers can cooperatively try out, improve, and reinforce teaching strategies and techniques.

concurrent enrollment: See *dual enrollment.*

content replacement: Method for providing advanced content area curriculum and instruction in a format that replaces the regular grade-level work.

cooperative learning groups: Method of learning in which students work in groups toward a common goal or product. Gifted students should work cooperatively on advanced-level tasks instead of being placed into heterogeneous cooperative learning groups. Working together in this way, gifted students learn the same cooperative learning skills taught to students in mixed-ability cooperative learning groups.

credit by examination: Allowing students to bypass curriculum already mastered by taking a comprehensive test covering a full unit's, semester's, or year's course and receiving full credit for proven mastery. The term also refers to opportunities for students to receive college credit by achieving a certain score on an examination. The best-known agency for this process is the College Board, which offers the College Level Examination Program (CLEP). Information and test preparation support materials are available at www.collegeboard.org.

criterion-referenced test: Test that measures student knowledge against a set body of content, such as a test measuring student performance based upon state standards.

cross-grade grouping: A type of flexible grouping in which students are grouped across grade levels for instruction in a particular content area. Students are assigned to groups based on their appropriate learning level, rather than by the grade level to which that particular content has been assigned.

culturally and linguistically diverse (CLD) students: Students whose culture, ethnic heritage, and/or primary language differs from that of the dominant culture, ethnic heritage, or language in the school environment.

curriculum compacting: Compressing curriculum into a shorter time period by giving students full credit for prior mastery or by allowing them to learn new content standards in a shorter period of time than age peers do. Compacting allows gifted students to spend less time with the curriculum designed for age peers and more time working on curriculum that challenges them.

Depth of Knowledge (DOK): A framework that categorizes tasks according to the complexity of thinking required to successfully complete them.

differentiated education plan (DEP): Document used by teachers and administrators to monitor how gifted services are provided for individual gifted students and within each gifted-cluster classroom.

differentiation: Modifying curriculum content, pace, process, products, and learning environment to meet individual students' needs.

dual enrollment: Usually used with high school students, dual enrollment allows students to be simultaneously enrolled in high school and college classes. College credit is granted by the college or university offering the course, while high school credit depends on the state education guidelines.

English language learners (ELL students): Students whose primary language is not English.

enrichment activities: Activities, usually connected to the grade-level standards, that move students into critical or creative thinking areas. Enrichment activities may take place as part of a pull-out program, during school, or outside school hours.

extension activities: Advanced learning activities that extend the parameters of grade-level standards in order to provide challenging learning opportunities for students who have already mastered the grade-level material.

flexible grouping: Forming temporary student groupings by interest, achievement level, activity preference, or special needs. Flexible grouping ensures that gifted students will have opportunities to work with their intellectual peers based on areas of interest and levels of readiness. Flexible groups can be created within a class, within a grade level, or across grade levels.

formative assessment: Formal or informal test used to gauge progress during the learning process to guide and direct the teacher's instruction.

gifted-cluster classroom: Classroom that contains a cluster of identified gifted students. A typical gifted-cluster class also contains students whose achievement is average and below average, but not high-achieving students or those whose performance is far below average. This configuration allows for a slightly narrowed achievement range within the classroom.

gifted-cluster teacher: The teacher assigned to teach the gifted-cluster classroom at each grade level.

gifted coordinator: District-level administrator who manages the gifted-education program.

gifted specialist (or gifted mentor): A gifted-cluster teacher, content-replacement or resource teacher, or another staff member with training in gifted education who supports the school's gifted-cluster teachers.

high ability: Student capacity to learn at levels higher than what is taught in grade-level content standards. Students with *exceptionally* high ability are referred to as gifted learners.

high-achieving students: Students who demonstrate academic achievement at advanced levels. Not all high-achieving students are gifted, and not all gifted students are high achieving.

inclusion: Practice in which students of varying abilities and conditions are grouped together in a classroom rather than receiving their instruction outside the regular classroom program.

independent study: Ongoing in-depth research on a topic of a student's choosing.

individualized education program (IEP): The individualized education program, also called the IEP, is a document that is developed for each public school child who needs special education.

mixed-ability classroom: Heterogeneous class containing students of various ability levels.

nonproductive gifted students: Gifted students who do not demonstrate high achievement or consistent productivity with grade-level work. They may have high scores on ability tests but low grades in school. Gifted students with this description are sometimes referred to as "underachievers."

norm-referenced test: Test that measures individual student performance against a representative group of students of the same age.

perfectionism: Debilitating need to be perfect at all times and in all situations. Gifted students are particularly prone to perfectionism.

preassessment: Assessment administered before direct instruction to discover students' entry levels into upcoming curriculum. For gifted students, the preassessment documents which content standards students have already mastered before those standards are taught.

professional learning community (PLC): Community of teachers who support one another in professional development efforts and professional growth. PLCs often involve collegial peer coaching and action research.

profoundly gifted: Extreme level of giftedness, typically defined by having an intelligence quotient (IQ) of 180+. By contrast, IQ scores of 130–144 typically categorize students as "gifted," scores of 145–159 categorize them as "highly gifted," and scores of 160–179 as "exceptionally gifted."

project-based learning: Learning strategy in which students learn by working on a self-selected project, either in groups or independently.

pull-out program: Educational service in which students are removed from the classroom at regular intervals during school for content replacement or enrichment.

qualitative research: Process of studying human behavior and the motivation and factors that govern it by gathering information.

quantitative research: Process of studying specific elements in order to construct statistical models to explain what has occurred. Any test data expressed in numerical form represents quantitative data.

self-contained gifted program: School program in which gifted students are assigned full-time to classes that contain only identified gifted students. Self-contained gifted programs have specific entrance criteria and program goals.

standardized testing: Testing students under identical conditions so results can be statistically compared to a standard.

STEM/STEAM: STEM is a curriculum based on the idea of educating students in four specific disciplines—science, technology, engineering, and mathematics—in an interdisciplinary and applied approach. STEAM integrates science, technology, engineering, arts, and mathematics.

student-directed learning: Opportunities for students to guide their own learning experiences based on their abilities and areas of interest.

summative assessment: Assessment used at the end of a unit or chapter to document that students have learned all the unit's material.

telescoped learning: Multiyear plan for profoundly gifted students that moves them through the K–12 sequence in a shorter time period.

tiered lessons: Parallel tasks at varied levels of complexity, depth, and novelty with various degrees of scaffolding, support, or direction. All activities are based on the required standards, and students select or are assigned activities based on their ability level. Tiered assignments accommodate differences in student readiness and performance levels and allow students to work toward individual objectives at levels that are personally challenging.

twice-exceptional (2e) student: Student identified as gifted who also has a diagnosis of a learning challenge such as ADHD, autism, or a learning disability.

Index

A

B

C

D

E

H

I

P

Q

R

U

V

W

Z

About the Authors

Dina Brulles, Ph.D., is a school administrator and the gifted-education director for Arizona's Paradise Valley Unified School District. Recognized for her expertise in creating and supervising schoolwide cluster grouping, she also assists districts throughout the United States in developing gifted-education programs, including those districts serving culturally and linguistically diverse gifted students.

Susan Winebrenner, M.S., is a full-time consultant in staff development. She presents workshops and seminars nationally and internationally, helping educators translate educational research into classroom practice.

Other Great Resources from Free Spirit

Teaching Gifted Kids in Today's Classroom
Strategies and Techniques Every Teacher Can Use
(Updated 4th Edition)
by Susan Winebrenner, M.S., with Dina Brulles, Ph.D.
For teachers and administrators, grades K–12.
256 pp.; PB; 8½" x 11"; includes digital content.

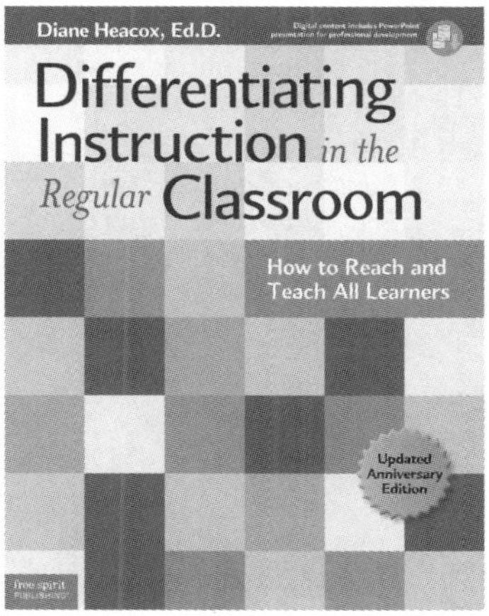

Differentiating Instruction in the Regular Classroom
How to Reach and Teach All Learners
(Updated Anniversary Edition)
by Diane Heacox, Ed.D.
For educators, grades K–12.
176 pp.; PB; 8½" x 11"; includes digital content.

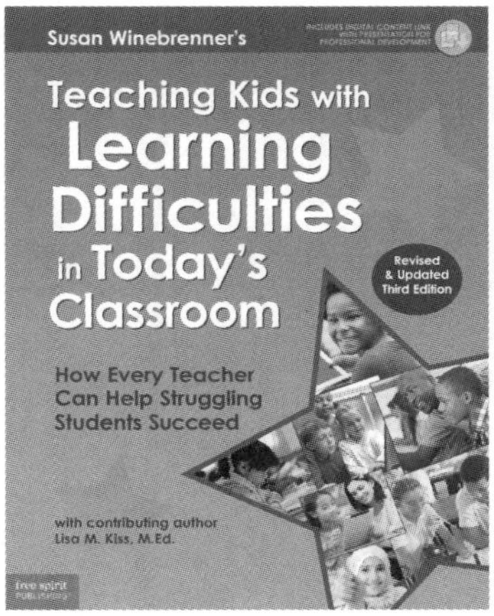

Teaching Kids with Learning Difficulties in Today's Classroom
How Every Teacher Can Help Struggling Students Succeed
(Revised & Updated 3rd Edition)
by Susan Winebrenner, M.S., with Lisa M. Kiss, M.Ed.
For K–12 teachers, administrators, and higher education faculty.
288 pp.; PB; 8½" x 11"; includes digital content.
Free PLC / Book Study Guide freespirit.com / PLC

Making Differentiation a Habit
How to Ensure Success in Academically Diverse Classrooms
(Updated Edition)
by Diane Heacox, Ed.D.
For teachers and administrators, grades K–12.
192 pp.; PB; 8½" x 11"; includes digital content.
Free PLC / Book Study Guide freespirit.com / PLC

A Teacher's Guide to Flexible Grouping and Collaborative Learning
Form, Manage, Assess, and Differentiate in Groups
by Dina Brulles, Ph.D., and Karen L. Brown, M.Ed.
For teachers and administrators, grades K–12.
200 pp.; PB; 8½" x 11"; includes digital content.
Free PLC / Book Study Guide freespirit.com / PLC

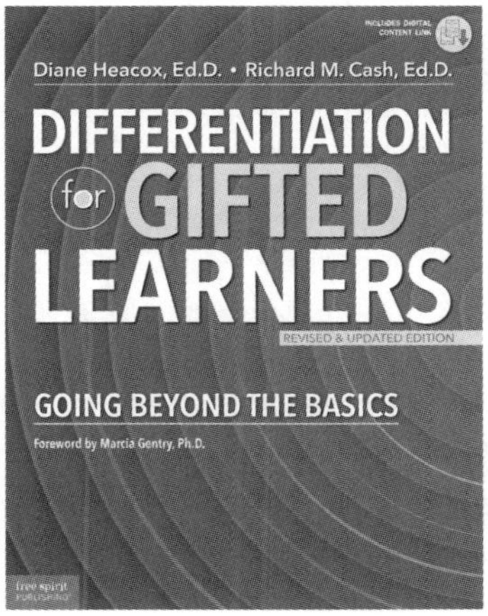

Differentiation for Gifted Learners
Going Beyond the Basics
(Revised & Updated Edition)
by Diane Heacox, Ed.D., and Richard M. Cash, Ed.D.
For K–12 teachers, gifted education teachers, program directors, administrators, instructional coaches, and curriculum developers.
224 pp.; PB; 8½" x 11"; includes digital content.
Free PLC / Book Study Guide freespirit.com / PLC

Self-Regulation in the Classroom
Helping Students Learn How to Learn
by Richard M. Cash, Ed.D.
For eachers, administrators, and counselors, grades K–12.
184 pp.; PB; 8½" x 11"; includes digital content. Free PLC / Book Study Guide freespirit.com / PLC

Visual Learning and Teaching
An Essential Guide for Educators K–8
by Susan Daniels, Ph.D.
For educators, grades K–8.
272 pp.; PB; 8½" x 11"; includes digital content. Free PLC / Book Study Guide freespirit.com / PLC

Advancing Differentiation
Thinking and Learning for the 21st Century
(Revised & Updated Edition)
by Richard M. Cash, Ed.D.
For teachers and administrators, grades K–12.
240 pp.; PB; 8½" x 11"; includes digital content. Free PLC / Book Study Guide freespirit.com / PLC

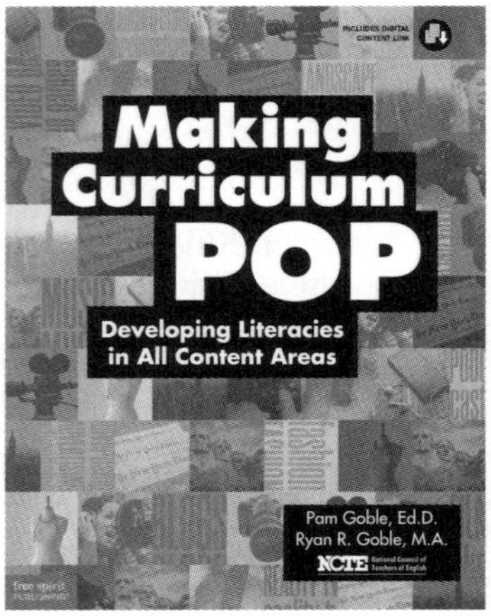

Making Curriculum Pop
Developing Literacies in All Content Areas
by Pam Goble, Ed.D., and Ryan R. Goble, M.A.
Developed in partnership with NCTE
For grades 6–12 teachers, administrators, and curriculum directors.
224 pp.; PB; 8½" x 11"; includes digital content. Free PLC / Book Study Guide freespirit.com / PLC

The Hands-On Guide to School Improvement
Transform Culture, Empower Teachers, and Raise Student Achievement
by Evelyn M. Randle-Robbins, M.A.
For principals, administrators, and school leaders, grades K–12.
208 pp.; PB; 7¼" x 9¼"; includes digital content.

The Principal's Survival Guide
Where Do I Start? How Do I Succeed? When Do I Sleep?
by Susan Stone Kessler, Ed.D., April M. Snodgrass, M.Ed., and Andrew T. Davis, Ed.D.
For principals and administrators, grades K–12.
208 pp.; PB; 7¼" x 9¼".

Interested in purchasing multiple quantities and receiving volume discounts? Contact edsales@freespirit.com or call 1.800.735.7323 and ask for Education Sales.

Many Free Spirit authors are available for speaking engagements, workshops, and keynotes. Contact speakers@freespirit.com or call 1.800.735.7323.

For pricing information, to place an order, or to request a free catalog, contact:

Free Spirit Publishing Inc. • 6325 Sandburg Road, Suite 100 • Minneapolis, MN 55427-3674
toll-free 800.735.7323 • local 612.338.2068 • fax 612.337.5050
help4kids@freespirit.com • www.freespirit.com